W9-CCD-068

Between Worlds

Between Worlds

The Making of an American Life

Bill Richardson

with Michael Ruby

G. P. PUTNAM'S SONS   NEW YORK

G. P. PUTNAM'S SONS
Publishers Since 1838
Published by the Penguin Group
Penguin Group (USA) Inc., 375 Hudson Street, New York, New York 10014, USA •
Penguin Group (Canada), 90 Eglinton Avenue East, Suite 700, Toronto, Ontario M4P 2Y3, Canada
(a division of Pearson Penguin Canada Inc.) • Penguin Books Ltd, 80 Strand, London WC2R 0RL,
England • Penguin Ireland, 25 St Stephen's Green, Dublin 2, Ireland (a division of Penguin Books Ltd) •
Penguin Group (Australia), 250 Camberwell Road, Camberwell, Victoria 3124, Australia (a division of
Pearson Australia Group Pty Ltd) • Penguin Books India Pvt Ltd, 11 Community Centre, Panchsheel
Park, New Delhi–110 017, India • Penguin Group (NZ), Cnr Airborne and Rosedale Roads, Albany,
Auckland 1310, New Zealand (a division of Pearson New Zealand Ltd) • Penguin Books (South
Africa) (Pty) Ltd, 24 Sturdee Avenue, Rosebank, Johannesburg 2196, South Africa

Penguin Books Ltd, Registered Offices:
80 Strand, London WC2R 0RL, England

Library of Congress Cataloging-in-Publication Data

Richardson, Bill, date.
Between worlds : the making of an American life / Bill Richardson with Michael Ruby.
p.   cm.
ISBN 0-399-15324-1
1. Richardson, Bill.   2. Governors—New Mexico—Biography.   3. New Mexico—Politics and
government—1951– .   4. United States—Politics and government—1989– .
I. Ruby, Michael (Michael Handler).   II. Title.
F801.4.R53A3   2005   2005053471
978.9'053'092—dc22
[B]

Printed in the United States of America
1   3   5   7   9   10   8   6   4   2

Book design by Stephanie Huntwork

While the author has made every effort to provide accurate telephone numbers and Internet addresses at the
time of publication, neither the publisher nor the author assumes any responsibility for errors, or for changes
that occur after publication. Further, the publisher does not have any control over and does not assume any
responsibility for author or third-party websites or their content.

To Barbara, my spouse and inseparable partner of thirty-three years, for supporting me and letting me pursue my somewhat unorthodox and diverse career in public service.

To my mother, Luicita, and my sister, Vesta, for always being there with love and support as we all navigated between our two worlds.

ACKNOWLEDGMENTS

In preparation of this book, Mike Ruby, an outstanding journalist—I owe you thanks because you made it all happen with persistence, great research, and beautiful prose.

Special thanks to members of my staff and friends: Dave Contarino, Calvin Humphrey, Isabelle Watkins, Andy Athy, Stu Nagurka, Melanie Kenderdine, Rebecca Gaghen, Butch Maki, Mona Sutphen, Calvin Mitchell, Lalo Valdez, Paul Blanchard, Kip O'Neill, Billy Sparks, Jamie Koch, Gary Falle, Bart Gordon, Mack McClarty, Rich Klein, David Michaels, Dave Gillette, Steve Cary, Amanda Cooper, Brian Condit, and Rick Homans.

The following on my personal staff helped in countless ways: Siri Trang Khalsa, Janis Hartley, Rochelle Thompson, and Lorraine Rotunno.

My thanks to David Highfill, Ivan Held, and Marilyn Ducksworth at Putnam and to my agent, Flip Brophy.

To Ian Jackman, my appreciation for his crucial role in helping as we completed this book.

Between Worlds

Prologue

A T LAST I was going to get my meeting with Saddam Hussein. In the early afternoon of July 16, 1995, along with my aide Calvin Humphrey, a frequent companion on trips like this, I was waiting in a room in one of Saddam's palaces in Baghdad. A huge portrait of the Iraqi dictator hung on the wall and kept us company. It had taken three months to get to this point, and another few minutes weren't going to kill me.

Back in March, two Americans working for defense contractors in Kuwait had taken a wrong turn in the desert and been arrested inside Iraq. The men, William Barloon and David Daliberti, had simply gotten lost looking for some friends manning a United Nations observation station. But they were charged with entering the country illegally. A kangaroo court sentenced the men to eight years, which they were serving at Abu Ghraib Prison.

I'd become involved in April. Through Peter Bourne, who was formerly President Carter's drug czar and was well connected with relief agencies, the Iraqis had reached out to me. Ten meetings with Iraq's UN ambassador established the ground rules, and

I'd traveled to Baghdad to negotiate the two men's release. Dog-tired after a hairy journey through the desert, we'd already met with Foreign Minister Tariq Aziz the night before. Now we waited for Saddam.

We were joined by an interpreter. Five minutes later, our party was escorted to another room, as large as the last, with eight or nine entrances. At first glance, the place was empty, except for a small conference table and a few chairs. But we weren't alone, I realized. Lining the walls were floor-to-ceiling curtains, and beneath them I could see a half-dozen pairs of shoes. From North Korea to Angola, I'd seen a lot of strange and unsettling things, but the sight of these feet sticking out from under a curtain in Saddam Hussein's palace was the most bizarre. We sat in the chairs, ready to wait again.

Very soon, a door opened and eight military officers, all ramrod-straight Republican Guard, each with a sidearm and a carbon-copy Saddam mustache, marched in and lined up along one wall. The show was getting more theatrical by the minute.

Two minutes later, another door opened and Saddam Hussein walked in, trim and broad-shouldered in his uniform. I am a big man, and Saddam, in his shiny black boots, appeared even taller. I thought he seemed relaxed, but he had a twitch on the right side of his face that caused one eye to blink rapidly. As he entered, we stood. He sat and motioned us to do the same. I sat beside him and we stared at each other for a few moments.

I began to speak and Calvin took notes on three-by-five index cards. My hands were sweating. I started by noting all the help provided by Iraq's ambassador to the United Nations and by Tariq Aziz, and I told him how appreciative we were that he had decided to see us to discuss this humanitarian issue. We hoped our differences could be resolved diplomatically and peacefully.

"You spent three hours with Tariq Aziz—which is normal, because Iraq has not received an American in a long period of time," Saddam said. "We are thus required to talk about a great number of issues."

Suddenly, Saddam slammed a hand hard on the table. He stood up and walked out of the room.

"What the hell's going on?" I asked the interpreter.

"You crossed your legs," he said.

"So?"

"You showed the dirty bottom of your shoe," he said. "That's an insult in Arab culture. You must apologize."

Tariq Aziz, who speaks fluent English, came over and repeated what would be required of me.

"He left, Tariq," I said. "What do you want me to do—apologize to an empty chair? Is he coming back?"

Aziz shrugged. Fifteen minutes later, Saddam returned, sat down, and played the staring game again. Now I was really sweating. Should I grovel and apologize or keep on talking as if nothing had happened? If I do, maybe he'll respect me for that, I thought. Option B seemed best. I kept both feet on the floor and plowed ahead.

Saddam and I sparred for nearly an hour. He told me he would release the men to me. At the end of our conversation, Saddam brought in the state-controlled media for a photo op. While they were taking pictures and shooting tape, Saddam told me these images weren't good politics in Iraq, given that they showed him with an American. I responded in kind: I wouldn't be using these pictures in my next reelection campaign either. Saddam briefly smiled. I then told him I would be going to Mass with Tariq Aziz. "I understand Mass is much longer here than in my country," I said.

Saddam smiled slightly again. "That's because you Americans don't confess all your sins. Don't go to confession—you'll be there forever."

"Well, maybe Mass is longer here because you Iraqis have so much more to confess." It was entirely spontaneous. I glanced quickly at Calvin, my aide. His shocked expression signaled what he was thinking: We could die for that smart-ass remark. But Saddam let it pass. He was just warming up. "By the way," he said, "I want you to visit our hospitals so you can see what your sanctions are doing to our people."

"Mr. President," I replied, "I need to get back to Washington. I am missing votes in the Congress." Saddam looked at me as if I were crazy and said we couldn't leave during the day because our cars would overheat. But I wanted to leave as soon as possible before something unexpected happened. I was concerned that someone in the Clinton administration would make a statement that might provoke the Iraqis and kill the deal, since we had no idea how they were spinning the story from Baghdad.

Later that day, Barloon and Daliberti were released into our custody at the Polish Embassy, where we were waiting for them. The two Americans looked scruffy and confused but otherwise reasonably fit. They hadn't been tortured in prison. Both men had been hospitalized in May for heart palpitations. Barloon and Daliberti knew something was going on, because they had been better fed during the past few days, but they didn't know exactly what was happening. It was an emotional moment. They didn't recognize me—there was no reason they should—so I simply held out a hand to each of them and said, "I'm Congressman Bill Richardson from New Mexico and you've been released to me. I'm taking you home." Both men started to cry. Barloon asked me if they were in trouble because they had crossed into Iraq. I smiled and told them no, they were almost heroes, that their wives had organized a brilliant campaign to bring them home, and that everyone in America wanted them back safe and sound.

The two men spent that night at the Sheraton drinking Champagne, eating pizza, and staying up with Calvin to share what he described as a damned good bottle of Scotch. President Clinton called: "Billy, you did it," he said. "Bring them to the Oval Office when you come home." Clinton spoke with both men, who thanked him profusely through their tears. I handled an endless string of press calls and pleas from a half-dozen Iraqis who wanted us to take them with us to Jordan, among them a high-ranking general in Saddam's foreign ministry. I told them I couldn't make such commitments.

That evening, I rushed through an Iraqi hospital with hundreds of media types in tow. Then, about one in the morning on Monday, July 17, what had become a sixteen-car caravan made the Jordan-Iraq run in reverse. At the border, Calvin and I gave U.S. Embassy personnel a ten-minute private briefing on what had happened; then the press was all over us for an hour. We made the embassy in Jordan late that afternoon. Within minutes, President Clinton was on the phone again thanking me for getting Barloon and Daliberti out. A key rule of mine is to share the credit, and I did, properly praising Calvin's good work. "Put him on the phone," Clinton said, and Calvin picked up. Clinton called him Cal and laid it on thick. Then he asked "Cal" to do just one thing: "Call your mom and dad and tell 'em you're okay." Calvin followed his president's orders.

We paid our respects to King Hussein and had a steak dinner before collapsing at the embassy. After a few hours of rest, we cleaned up and dashed for the airport to make an overnight flight to London and a connection that got us to Dulles just before 3 P.M. on Tuesday, July 18. The reporters wanted at us, and we were escorted to a room for a press briefing. Barloon had peeled off in Jordan to catch a flight to Kuwait, where his wife and kids were waiting. But Daliberti flew back with us and was kind and effusive in what he had to say about me.

I stepped forward to the microphone, glancing both left and right. Calvin was nowhere to be seen. He had hung back to make sure our luggage was taken care of. I sent someone to get him. Once again, he more than deserved to share the credit for what we had accomplished.

President Clinton wanted to see me that night, but I needed to stop first and visit my staff on Capitol Hill. In the car, my beeper kept going off, indicating imminent votes on the House floor. I prodded the driver to hit the long pedal. The House floor was packed when I arrived. Ray LaHood, the Illinois Republican, spotted me, asked for recognition, got it, and welcomed me back home. With that, the entire chamber rose as one and applauded. I spoke for a few minutes, asserting that Congress can play an important role in foreign policy if things were done properly.

Foreign policy? I was on top of the world.

THIS VISIT to Saddam Hussein in Iraq on behalf of American hostages was a typical adventure for me in more than thirty years of public service. I have negotiated with many of the most notorious despots and dictators of our times, almost always on their turf and almost always under testing circumstances. Dealing with these often capricious bad guys—whether it is to free captives they are holding or discuss an international dispute or get them to stand down—has become my highly unusual specialty. It evolved by accident over the course of my career, which began as a staffer on Capitol Hill, moved through seven terms in Congress, and has included stints as head of the United States Mission to the United

Nations and the Department of Energy, and continues now as governor of New Mexico and as chairman of the Democratic Governors' Association.

My experience has convinced me there is nothing you can't solve by talking it through. It is always worse not to talk. If two sides in a dispute don't meet and they just restate their positions, it's impossible to resolve anything. I believe in forcing people of different views to come together if necessary. When you bring people together—in negotiations, meetings, task forces, commissions—you can start to build trust. There is a mutual interest in making things work out, and any progress is better than none. Whoever it is, I will always say, "Just talk to them."

Establishing a connection should be the first order of business in any meeting. I knew when I was negotiating with Fidel Castro that we would have a lot in common. I knew he craved respect and that he liked sassiness. We spoke to each other in Spanish and we were both baseball fans. Also I had a Nicaraguan relative who had been a Castro sympathizer, as well as other relations who detested him. I knew if I could get in the room with him, I could convince him to release some prisoners.

None of these despots has intimidated me, nor am I afraid of a crowd. To defuse an issue, you go into the lion's den right away and explain your position respectfully. I'd make an unpopular vote in Congress and then go have a town meeting and talk to people who didn't like my decision. People have shown up at meetings with guns to make a point. I campaigned once for Bob Filner, a candidate who had voted for an immigration bill that many Hispanics didn't like, and there were signs in the crowd that accused me of dishonoring my mother. Even if people don't agree with me, I hope they will concede that I've had the guts to go and explain myself.

Along the way, I have picked up a lot of tips that have helped me in my career as a negotiator, and not just with the thugs. I call them here "Richardson's Rules." Two of the most important rules I've mentioned above. The first I described when I talked up Calvin Humphrey's role in the hostage release to President Clinton; the second has been illustrated by every successful negotiation I describe from here on out.

Richardson's Rules

- Share the credit. Politics and diplomacy are team sports. Acknowledge it.
- Talk about it. It is always better to have a conversation than not to talk.

Negotiating is about finding common ground, bridging gaps that exist between two different worlds. I have spent a great deal of my life in between the Western values and democratic traditions of America and the unpredictable whims of autocrats, between official and unofficial diplomacy, between home and abroad.

Most important, two worlds have come together in me, the child of an American father and a Mexican mother. My dual heritage helps explain why I celebrate difference. Diversity enriches what we do in this country immeasurably, and more and more it is coming to define America. By 2050 or 2060, the United States will be a majority-minority country, meaning the largest single ethnic group will comprise less than half the population. Because of our large Hispanic and Native American populations, New Mexico already is a majority-minority state, along with Hawaii and California (as well as the District of Columbia). New Mexico was the first, and as such, it is something of a template for the America-to-be.

I am representative of that multicultural future. When I first got involved in New Mexico's elective politics, the joke was that I was the perfect political candidate for the state: I have an Anglo surname, I speak fluent Spanish, and I look like an Native American. In New Mexico, we are evolving a style of democratic government we are calling New Progressivism that is a potent mix of opportunity and accountability. The power of each is multiplied many times when they are combined. As we move forward in New Mexico, these are very exciting, and challenging, times for me. I am still absorbing lessons I learned growing up as the son of an American father and a Mexican mother in Mexico City.

One

B Y 1947, my father, a loyal and patriotic American, had been living in Mexico nearly twenty years. When the time came for my mother, who is Mexican born and bred, to be delivered of her firstborn child, my father dispatched her to Pasadena, California, where his sister lived. So it was that I was born on November 15 of that year in Huntington Hospital, safely within the Lower Forty-eight. My father insisted there would be no doubt of his children's citizenship. When my sister Vesta followed eight years later, she too was provided a cast-iron American birthright.

My father, William Blaine Richardson, was posted to Mexico City in 1929 as branch manager for the National City Bank of New York, the institution that became Citibank. Apart from some time in the Army, he spent his whole career with the bank, working in Genoa and Milan in Italy and in Cuba. Mexico City was his last stop, and he retired there after more than twenty-five years of service. My father's determination that I be born in the United States can largely be explained by the fact that he was born on a boat on its way to Nicaragua. His father, also William

Blaine Richarson, was a biologist who collected specimens for several American museums, including the Museum of Natural History in New York, and the family was headed for Central America on a field trip when my father arrived. The fact that he was born outside the country was something my father resented all his life. He had an American upbringing, growing up in Boston and attending Tufts University in nearby Medford.

My grandfather apparently had a roving eye, and the story is that he fathered children by four different women in Mexico and Central America. Occasionally, one of my dad's half-brothers or half-sisters—that's what they were, after all—would show up in Mexico City, and I suspect he did what he regarded as his familial duty by helping them out financially. To this day, I get letters that begin with something like, "My name is Freddy Richardson . . ." from people scattered around the Americas who say that we are related.

My mother, Maria Luisa Lopez-Collada, worked as a secretary at the bank, which was where she met my father. He was older, and her parents were worried about the age gap and the fact that he was American (they called him "the gringo"). My parents were married in 1936, when he was forty-six and she was twenty-two. I came along after they had been married eleven years; Vesta, nineteen.

My father was very proud of his American son, and my mother was very proud of her Mexican son. Their pride was passed down to me, and I grew up honoring both the United States and Mexico and the language and culture of each country. My father would talk to me in English and my mother in Spanish, though she would defer to him when we were all together—at meals, for example. I spent far more time with my mother and we lived in Mexico, so I was more comfortable with Spanish.

Good American that he was, my father made sure his family celebrated Thanksgiving and the Fourth of July, when we would have hamburgers and hot dogs with all the trimmings. My father also developed a deep commitment to Mexico. We would recognize Mexican holidays, especially El Grito ("the cry"), commemorating September 16, 1810, when a priest, Miguel Hidalgo y Costilla, called for rebellion and independence from Spain. My mother and grandmother were proud nationalists; when my mother remembered the Alamo, as she often did during the Davy Crockett craze of the 1950s, she always reminded me, partly tongue in cheek, that it was the army of Antonio López de Santa Anna that won the battle.

It wasn't to keep the peace in his house that my father embraced Mexican history; he genuinely loved the country. He paid Mexican as well as American taxes. The Mexican dues he could have avoided easily, but he didn't, because he thought paying up was the right thing to do. When the Mexican government expropriated foreign oil companies in 1938, he refused to shut down his bank branch as other American banks had done at Washington's behest. He learned Spanish because it was the national language of the country where he lived, and a respect for different languages and cultures was something he drilled into Vesta and me from our earliest days. After my father retired, he stayed on in Mexico City, where he ran a consultancy.

While most American businessmen and their families lived in Lomas, an upscale neighborhood of Mexico City, we lived in a large house in Coyoacán, a neighborhood in the section of the city called Cuadrante de San Francisco. My father didn't feel he had to prove anything to the American colony, and he knew a good real estate bargain when he saw one. Ours wasn't a fancy neighborhood. Coyoacán was populated mainly by less well-off Mexicans, and the Richardson house was something of an island surrounded by *los barrios bajos*, the rougher parts of town.

Today, much of Mexico City feels like a congested armed camp, but in those days there wasn't much crime, or at least that I was aware of. And even though the Mexico City of the mid-1950s was huge—about 5 million people in the city, nearly 10 million in the metropolitan area—it didn't feel crowded to me and my friends.

My dad's career thrived, and we enjoyed a comfortable life. We had a chauffeur, Vicente, who would play catch with me when I took up baseball and wanted to practice my pitching. Our cook, Eloisa, treated me like her own son. My grandmother, Maria Lopez-Collada, also lived with us, so I had a number of strong female influences in my young life: my mother, my grandmother, Eloisa, and after a time, my sister Vesta.

God was very much a part of my young life. My *abuelita*, or grandma, was responsible for my going to catechism school and for my taking my first communion at seven. She'd make sure I went to church on Sunday and that I was well turned out for it. She'd say *baño y peluquería*, or bath and barbershop, meaning I had to wash up and comb my hair. She'd walk me to church and buy me an ice cream cone on the way home. Once I finished that, I was free to go play. The family went to Mass on all the holidays, and when I played baseball, I used to go to church before a game. My *abuelita* also made sure I said my prayers, in Spanish, every night before going to bed.

My parents were a handsome couple. My dad was just shy of six feet tall, a barrel-chested man with curly black hair and spectacles who wore a double-breasted suit every day but Sunday, when he wore his Tufts letter sweater. My mom was probably five-foot-five in those days, a petite and striking woman with a vivacious disposition. She often wore her long blond hair in braids. Vesta is blond like Mom, while I took after my father.

My father became a respected figure in Mexico and understood the larger role in the community that was expected of him. He became president of the bankers' club and served on the boards of a number of Mexican companies. My parents entertained often at home. Guests might be other American businessmen stationed in Mexico or high-ranking figures in Mexican politics and business. One day, it might be the government finance minister or the head of the central bank; the next, the chairman of Pemex, the national oil company. My parents invited people from all walks of life in the city. My father asked members of his large extended Nicaraguan family to dinner, and they would sit and have heated political discussions about Castro.

My father happened to know Dwight David Eisenhower, who was president from 1953 to 1961. As young men, the two of them had had a close encounter on a football field, and they'd stayed in touch over the years. My father was the Tufts University center, and he built a reputation as one of the pioneers of the between-the-legs snap. Everyone played both offense and defense then, and one day on defense he inadvertently injured the knee of the West Point halfback, Eisenhower, ending his promising football career. (This was an honor of sorts that was eventually claimed by some of my dad's teammates as Ike's fame grew over the years.)

My father was a rock-ribbed Republican and idolized Eisenhower. Although I never heard my father make a big deal of it in public, Ike would occasionally call him just to ask how things were going south of the border and to jaw about U.S.-Mexican relations. When Eisenhower called, it made my dad's month.

It's important to remember that my father had his first child at an age when many men are becoming grandfathers. He was well into his sixties when I started elementary school. That could not have been easy, certainly not in the 1940s and 1950s. I admired my father enormously as I grew up, and loved him, too. I only wish I had told him so, just once. Especially now, as I think back to those days and my father's wise guidance, I can still hear him telling me to help those less fortunate, to fight hard and never give up.

Although I believe we had a loving relationship, my father sure had a hard time showing it. He worked very hard to excel and he pushed others to excel, too. Discipline was one of my father's watchwords. He was tough and demanding on everyone, including me. He came home for lunch almost every day, and if I was there, he would turn the meal into a rolling seminar. I'd be quizzed on some reading assignment he had given me in *History's 100 Greatest Events*—a book I vowed, years later, to burn if I ever saw it again. My father had difficulty telling people they had done a good job; he just pushed them to do even better. That's an unfortunate quality I may have developed myself. I put in very long days and I sometimes drive my staff nuts with what I expect of them. "Well done" is not a phrase that comes easily to me.

My mother, who was and remains an elegant and graceful woman, was the softer and gentler parent. She was often a mediator, the counterweight to my father's aggressive nature. She would approach my father on my behalf for a special favor or request and would underscore my accomplishments in conversations with him. She'd also sneak a little extra allowance money to me. My mother was able to move easily between the culture of her native country and the world of her American banker husband. She was often my bridge between the two. As a boy, I was less sure of my place in the world.

I remember thinking, I'm just a kid. It's not fair that I'm a Mexican and an American trapped in one body. I could speak English but I thought and dreamt in Spanish. My schooling, which was unusual for the son of a prominent foreign businessman, may well have contributed to my confusion. Most American kids went to one of the private schools that catered to the expatriate community. But instead of going to the American School or the Crocker School, I spent the first six years of elementary school at the Pan American Workshop, which was made up mostly of

Mexican kids from middle-class families. Classes were conducted alternately in Spanish and English, but given the makeup of the school, English was really taught as a second language. Later, when I went to boarding school in the United States, my bilingual training was not an asset; to the contrary, it set me back academically in an English-speaking environment.

I recall a good example of how I felt uncomfortable in these two worlds as a kid. In September 1954, when I wasn't quite seven years old, my father took me to the North American Bantamweight title fight at Mexico City's Arena Coliseo. Dad was a big boxing fan, something else I got from him. The fight was between Nathan "Nate" Brooks and Raul "Raton" Macias. Brooks was from Cleveland, and he'd won a gold medal as a flyweight at the 1952 Olympics in Helsinki. Local hero Macias was a Mexican champion with ten straight wins behind him. The crowd was wild for Macias. Here I was, an American but also, if not by birth, a Mexican. I knew I couldn't sit on my hands at a championship fight, but whom should I root for, Brooks or Macias? In the end, I cheered for Macias. I felt closer to him, and I'd heard a radio interview with Brooks before the fight in which he'd said he was going to beat this Mexican guy. It sounded like a put-down to me, and I remember being ticked off. Macias won, incidentally, in a twelve-round decision.

I was an average-to-good student at the Pan American, with some problems in math and science. But school was not where my heart was. It couldn't be, not after I discovered baseball. I can't remember exactly when baseball became the ruling passion of my young life. I know my father loved baseball even more than he loved boxing. Perhaps I developed my infatuation when I was a toddler, tossing the ball back and forth to my father.

Dad was a Boston Red Sox fan, of course, and he thought Ted Williams walked on water. When I was about eight years old, we were visiting family in New England and we spotted Williams at the Rib Room, a restaurant in Boston's Somerset Hotel. My dad told me to go get Williams's autograph, despite the protestations of Sidney Wiggin, my dad's best friend and "Uncle Sidney" to me. My father knew Ted Williams liked his privacy, so he wrote a check for $25 for the Jimmy Fund, the charity to help kids with cancer that had long been associated with the team and with Williams. "Go over there and hand him the check, then quickly ask for his autograph," he instructed. I did as I was told, excusing myself to Mr. Williams. Williams frowned slightly, hesitated for a heartbeat that seemed an eternity, and signed his name on the paper I'd given him. "Thanks, Ted," I blurted, then floated on air back to the table. My father, proud of me and a bit puffed-up, said he might just wander over and say hello to Ted himself. Uncle Sidney put his hand on Dad's arm and said, "No, Bill. I think Ted's probably had enough of the Richardsons for one night."

Ted Williams was arguably the best hitter in baseball history, but my idol was Mickey Mantle, who played for Boston's archenemy, the New York Yankees. Because of Mantle, I became a Yankee fan. I was a fan of pitchers like Whitey Ford and Warren Spahn, but Mantle was my guy. In time, baseball consumed me. I started playing and realized that I was good, very good. My father knew it, too, and began to hire former Mexican baseball stars to train me. That was typical of him. At various times, he also hired people to teach me to box and to tutor me in French.

I started playing Little League at age ten. I moved to Pony League at thirteen, and Colt League after that. Baseball was a great leveler, the common ground for Mexican kids, American kids, and kids like me, too. The better I did at baseball, the more comfortable I felt in my own skin. I knew there were some Mexican kids who wouldn't accept me because I had an American father and my name was Richardson, not Rodríguez or García. Maybe there were some American kids who didn't like the fact that we lived in a Mexican part of town and that I went to Pan American and hung out with Mexicans. These things bothered me because my place in society seemed to fluctuate depending on where I was, and with whom. Most of the time, I fit in with both sides pretty well. I'm still good friends with my Little League catcher, Ignacio Vázquez, who is now an architect in Cuernavaca, Mexico.

I developed into a very good right-handed pitcher who hardly ever lost a game in junior ball. I hit left-handed and was good at that, too. One year I won the pitching, batting, and home run titles. My father pressed and I tried to please him, while my mother told him to lighten up. After all, she'd say, Billy got three hits. Yes, he'd say, but he wasn't following through with his swing.

When I was eleven, I was in fifth place in the batting race near the end of the season. I went four-for-four in a game and moved up to second, behind this big American kid named Bob Ogden. He was hitting .390 and I was up to .386. I was very pleased with myself, and on the following Sunday morning, I crawled into my father's bed while he was reading the paper and told him how I'd moved up to second. Not good enough, he said. You should be first. I was crushed, but angry, too, and I was determined to show him. We played that afternoon; I went three-for-three and won the title.

One of my father's theories about batting was that you should never swing at the first pitch. He'd remind me of it every time I went to the plate, yelling at me not to swing. But I was an aggressive hitter who wanted to hack away at once. On one memorable occasion I wanted to shout something back at him when he was telling me to take a pitch. I paused on my way to the plate but I couldn't bring myself to respond. I just glared at him for a moment and took my stance. Then I swung at the first offering and deposited it over the right-field fence for a home run, breaking a window in the Squibb lab building in the process. Coming around third base in a slow trot, I kept my head down, not wanting to show him up. Later, with the hint of a smile, he ate a little crow when I brought up the subject. It was the first time I can remember getting over on him in even a small way.

My grandmother was a big baseball fan, but she regularly cautioned me that I had to stay close to God if I wanted to do well. Grandma gave me a St. Christopher medal to wear around my neck when I played; then she gave me a crucifix. My father said he'd gotten the crucifix blessed by the pope on a trip to Italy. I complained that the crucifix was too big to carry in my baseball pants, but she insisted. One time I executed a perfect slide into third and the crucifix tore up my butt. It was the last time I carried God in my back pocket.

By this time, I was confident on a baseball diamond, but I was still pretty awkward around the opposite sex. In sixth grade at the Pan American, for example, there was the matter of Donna Fletcher, the beautiful daughter of an American missionary who had every boy in school after her. One night, we were at a party playing Spin the Bottle. Donna spun and the bottle pointed at me; she came over and kissed me right on the lips. The next school day, I opened the top of my desk and found a love note from her. This was exciting! But what should I do? I had no idea and didn't want to reveal my naïveté by asking one of my friends. So I did nothing. Neither of my parents ever had the birds-and-bees conversation with me; later, I learned the way many boys do—from my friends.

One of the great lessons my parents taught me was to value people from all kinds of backgrounds. They practiced what they preached and welcomed a tremendously diverse crowd into their home. I played with wealthier kids in the Little League—and also poor kids around my house, and I went to movies with them. I didn't think of them as poor kids—they were just kids I played with. It wasn't out of charity that I brought them into the house. It never occurred to me not to.

The first time I knew that we might have more materially than other people was when I played on the neighborhood team, the Yanquis de San Francisco. They were all kids from humble backgrounds. I told my dad we were going to have a car wash to raise money for the uniforms, and he said, "No, no. I'll pay for that." We just got T-shirts and a cap, but I realized I had more than they did. I was nine at the time.

Without telling me at first, he began to set up Little Leagues all over Mexico. He would ask for donations from friends in the private sector, put up some of his own money, help to get teams organized, and start a league. Soon he was getting awards for his good works. My father did other charitable work as well. He was president of the board of trustees of Mexico City College, for example. My mother's main interest was in helping the blind, which she did by raising money to underwrite recordings of books for people who could not see. This was long before the phenomenon of books on tape.

The Pan American Workshop only went through grade six, so I spent seventh grade at the Crocker School, mixing more often with the American kids and starting to like what they liked—the fads, the music, and the girls. At Crocker, the kids came from more prosperous families, but my instincts were to diminish any suggestion of wealth. I'd work in a new baseball glove until it was weathered enough to bring out in public. I didn't want to show up anyone with shabby equipment. My father insisted that money was never to be flaunted. He never liked to discuss his finances or his charitable work. I learned later that he was lending his money, not the bank's, to relatives and friends less fortunate than he was, conveniently forgetting to demand repayment. He gave money to hospitals and schools. I found out that he'd bought a house for Felix, his longtime chauffeur.

My father disdained those who looked down on working-class people. Once, when he was driving me to a ball game, we were running late and a big bus was in front of us, jammed and moving at a crawl as the driver picked people up and dropped them off. I started to put my hand on the horn, but my father stopped me. Those people have jobs and need to get to work, he said. All you have is a baseball game. For him, work had dignity no matter what the work was.

My father was an intensely private man. When I was twenty years old and at Tufts, I looked up my father in the university archives and discovered some things I hadn't known. That he had been given the university's Distinguished Service Award in 1950. To my astonishment, I learned that he had been married before— on November 12, 1915, to one Mary Pescetto, daughter of Colonel and Mrs. Edward Pescetto of Genoa, Italy. Apparently, after graduation that year, he went to work for the bank in Italy, fell in love, and got married. I asked my mother whether she was aware of this. She said she was.

"Why didn't you tell me?" I asked.

"Because your father didn't think you needed to know."

But now I did know, and I confronted him with it. "Were there any children?"

"No, no children," he said.

"Well, where is Mary Pescetto now?"

"I don't really know. Probably still in Genoa."

"Why didn't you tell me?"

"Ah, that's the past," he said.

Two

THE CROCKER SCHOOL ran through seventh grade, so I spent much of that last academic year wondering what might be coming next. In retrospect, I needn't have bothered worrying, because my father knew where I was going. He was bound and determined to have me educated in the United States. I didn't want to go. My mother and grandmother didn't want me to go. Other members of my mother's family didn't want me to go. We had the votes, but this was my father's call. After considering military school, he settled on Middlesex School in Concord, Massachusetts, twenty-two miles from the center of Boston. Some of the Taylor side of his family had attended Middlesex and still lived in the area. They would look after me up there, my dad said.

So it was that in late August 1960 the Richardson clan— father, mother, son, and daughter—decamped for Concord. Middlesex was a small, strict New England prep school, founded in 1901. The campus was set on 350 acres three miles outside of town. The school's red brick buildings circled a green common with playing fields nearby. The place resembled an Eastern liberal

arts college in miniature. Apart from Easter and Christmas vaca-
tions and the summer, this was where I was going to be. It seemed
like a million miles from Mexico City. When it was time for my
family to leave, my mother began to cry. Weeping, little Vesta
dropped to her knees, wrapped her arms around my legs, and
begged our father to reconsider. I was tearing up a bit myself.

Here I was, not quite thirteen, the dark-skinned boy from
Mexico among a bunch of fair-skinned kids from cities like New
York and Boston and Chicago and their posh suburbs. A few of
the kids called me Pancho, but I didn't take it as a slur as much as
a recognition of the obvious: I wasn't one of them. I had a pretty
hard time my first semester at Middlesex because of the language.
My English wasn't nearly as strong as my Spanish. I was fluent
enough, but I couldn't speak idiomatic English as well as the
other boys. Back home, I could switch between English and
Spanish. I still processed information and reasoned in Spanish,
and it was tough to compete against kids who'd used English and
only English all their lives.

Here we go again, I thought. How am I going to fit in? How
am I going to be accepted? I felt out of my depth. School life was
regimented, with rules governing all student activities. There
were prescribed classes, compulsory study hall, mandatory chapel.
There was a house master in every dormitory, and proctors pa-
trolled the halls, enforcing the 10 P.M. curfew. Lights-out was
10:15 sharp. I was miserable the first semester. Classes were hard
for me, except for French and history, and I began to worry about
whether I was going to make it academically.

I called home almost every Sunday, but I kept my misgivings
to myself until I returned to Mexico City for the Christmas
break. I told my parents the truth, that school was tough. Maybe
I should come back and enroll in one of the good private schools
in Mexico City? Absolutely not, my father said. My mother was

sympathetic and asked my father what the point was of sending me to school so far away if it was just going to make me unhappy. But my father was adamant. He told me I had to buckle down, do the work, and stop whining. If I did, I'd make the adjustment. I might even like it there.

After the holidays, I tried to do what my father advised. John Briggs, an English teacher, took an interest in me and helped me work on my vocabulary and my writing. I still felt like an outsider. But as it had in Mexico, baseball rescued me.

My world at Middlesex was transformed almost overnight. In late winter, the school conducted tryouts for the varsity, junior varsity, and so-called third teams. It was too cold to play outdoors, so everyone went to the Cage, an indoor facility, for what they called "early baseball." The other kids knew I was a ballplayer and that I'd played Little League. Maybe it was my young imagination or baseball-centered ego, but when I stepped into the batting cage to take my first licks, I sensed that the place, filled with teenage boys, quieted just a bit.

I settled in, and proceeded to whack the hell out of everything the machine threw at me. After four or five pitches, a crowd gathered around the cage to watch the new kid work his bat. The same thing happened the next day and the day after that. On the last day of early baseball, Lawrence Terry, the school's headmaster, showed up. Now my classmates, upperclassmen, and even faculty members were treating this Mexican kid like a star. I was just grateful to be accepted after such a rough start.

Given my age, the best I had hoped for was a place on the junior varsity team. After dinner one night in the mess hall, the baseball coach, Thomas J. Quirk, announced the teams for the forthcoming season. Quirk was a giant of man at six-foot-nine and three hundred pounds. By day he was a math teacher. Now, before one and all, he announced that Bill Richardson was making school history by becoming the first eighth-grader to play varsity baseball—as a pitcher and first baseman.

My second semester at Middlesex, I played ball and my grades really began to pick up. I finished eighth in a class of forty, which meant that I was excused from study hall the first semester the following year. It didn't mean my father cut me any slack, though. If I told him I'd struck out twelve and was hitting .500, he'd want to know why I couldn't strike out fifteen and hit .800. Still, I could sense that he was pleased by my baseball prowess. On campus, there was still the occasional Pancho stuff and some jokes about Mexico, but I was now walking confidently across what had once been a hostile landscape.

As I was gaining acceptance in the United States, I was starting to get mixed messages back home. During the summer of 1961, I played Pony League ball in Mexico City. By now I was reasonably well known among the city's legions of baseball fanatics. They knew I'd been to school in the United States the previous year and some of them wanted to remind me of my desertion. Early in the summer season, I walked to the plate, settled in for the first pitch, and heard from the back of the stands *Poncha al gringo!* I was raised, if not born, in Mexico City, and Spanish was still my first language, but I was a foreigner to that guy and he wanted the pitcher to strike me out.

In the early 1960s, I was probably as aware of politics and current affairs as any other typical teenager. If there was a light on, the bulb was so dim that it illuminated little. At Middlesex that first autumn, we knew there was a presidential election and we knew it was a big deal. How could we not? We were less than a half hour from Boston, the heart of Kennedy country. John Fitzgerald Kennedy, the handsome young senator from Massachusetts, was running against Richard M. Nixon, Eisenhower's vice president. Kennedy won narrowly, Nixon didn't contest the outcome, my father grumbled, and life went on.

Even my father eventually conceded that the new American president was no ordinary politician. In 1962, the Kennedys paid a state visit to Mexico. They attracted huge crowds wherever they went, and Jackie won many hearts with her excellent Spanish. The couple attended Mass at the Basilica of Guadalupe, home to the shrine to Our Lady of Guadalupe, patron saint of Mexico, and considered by many to be the holiest place in the Western Hemisphere.

That particular Sunday, after the American leader had left for Washington, I was feeling rebellious. I told my father that I thought Kennedy seemed to be very good at this president business. Since it was over a weekend, Dad had seen much of the Jack and Jackie show, too. Yes, he said with a mix of admiration and disdain in his voice, he seems to have done well here.

Less than seventeen months later, I was sitting in a math class at Middlesex when President Kennedy was shot. My math teacher, William Hewitt (known as "Baby Huey" among the students), heard a commotion outside and opened a window to hear the news from a colleague. He turned from the window, already in tears, and dismissed the class. Along with the rest of America, I was devastated. I walked around in a fog for days, remembering Kennedy— he was my first political hero—and how he had fallen to his knees before the Virgin of Guadalupe. I liked all the Kennedys. I was very upset when Bobby was killed in 1968. Years later, Ted Kennedy came and supported me in my first run for office.

WHEN I WAS AT Middlesex, students were not permitted to have cars, and the school didn't provide transportation. You could walk the three miles to the town of Concord during the times we were allowed out, but most guys preferred to hitchhike. There were places on the campus and in town understood to be gathering spots for students looking for a lift, and it was a local tradition that permanent residents picked up the Middlesex kids.

Barbara Flavin was a local girl who lived across the street from the school. She went to the public school in town and would babysit faculty kids for 80 cents an hour. Barbara wasn't much of a sports fan, but her mother was a big supporter of Middlesex baseball and she'd seen me play. She mentioned the team's star pitcher to her daughter. "He's different-looking," Mrs. Flavin said, referring to my dark complexion and decidedly noncolonial features. I had returned to Middlesex in the late summer of 1965 for my senior year and was especially tan after ten weeks of nonstop baseball in Mexico. I was already tall—I'm six-two now—and I was very skinny in those days. It wasn't until I got to Congress that I lost my figure.

The way Barbara remembers it, she was downtown one day crossing the street when she saw this guy who fit the description her mother had given her of the baseball player. The first thing she said to me was, "You're from New Mexico, aren't you?" I said, "No, I'm from Mexico." To think where we ended up! She asked if I wanted a ride back to school. When I got in the car with this good-looking young woman, I decided I didn't want to go straight back to my dorm room at Hallowell House, so I said, "I really don't want to go back to school." We rode around awhile and then went back to her house and listened to records. I liked Elvis. Barbara was a little put off by that. We were now in the era of the Beatles and Bob Dylan, and Elvis was pretty retro. Anyway, Barbara's mother came home and I was sitting there.

We began dating. Because of the early school curfew, if we went on a date I'd have to take a weekend and stay over at Barbara's parents' house. She was one of five kids, the youngest of whom was one and a half, and I became the extra kid. I had a good friend who was a day student at Middlesex and lived in Concord. He had a car and we'd double-date with a friend of Barbara's. Sometimes we'd meet in the woods between her house and the school. A teacher would notice I was missing, and my roommate would come across the street and find me. "Bill, so-and-so's looking for you."

We broke for Christmas vacation and I headed home to Mexico City with Barbara Flavin very much on my mind. I did not come back to school empty-handed. One night in January, I walked over to her house and left a big Mexican sombrero on the doorstep with a love note. After that, we were inseparable. I was eighteen; she was seventeen. Apart from a brief period in college, Barbara and I have been a couple since we were teenagers. We've practically grown up together.

COACH QUIRK PITCHED ME almost every game because he hated to lose and he knew I could win. I did: I pitched for four years and won a lot of games. Although I didn't know it at the time, of course, I had my best year as a player when I was seventeen. I had a real good fastball and an effective curve, which might have been my eventual undoing given the wear and tear that throwing breaking balls puts on young arms. I pitched a no-hitter against the MIT freshmen that year. I was unhittable, striking out twenty-four of the twenty-seven batters. For that, I made the agate type up front in the *Boston Globe*. The paper took note of Bill Richardson from Mexico City. For my junior and senior years, I was Big Man on Campus at Middlesex. People looked up to me and I enjoyed the attention.

I was hot—and a hot prospect, too. Scouts for big-league

teams started to show up at my games. When I was a senior, the Pittsburgh Pirates wanted me to enter the draft. They said they'd draft me and send me to a minor-league farm club if I promised to forgo college. George Owen, the Pirates scout, was emphatic: I'd be a draft pick and get a small signing bonus. If I decided to go to college, Owen said, the Pirates might still draft me but the bonus would evaporate.

I'd grown used to making a lot of my own decisions since I'd been sent away to school. I was also a pretty independent spirit. This decision wasn't an issue with me: In my mind, I committed to a future playing ball. I was ready to sign on the dotted line right after graduation.

My parents arrived in Concord for graduation week, and everything went smoothly at first. Tufts had already accepted me as a freshman, partly because I was a legacy and partly because the admissions people recognized that my performance at Middlesex had been hindered by my early difficulties with English. I hadn't broken the news to my folks—my dad, really—that college would have to wait because baseball, professional baseball, was beckoning. I had my whole career ahead of me, an eighteen-year-old who could pitch and hit. I imagined myself moving to the big leagues as fast as Mickey Mantle.

After the graduation ceremony, our family repaired to the Flavin house for what was supposed to be a celebratory meal. Before we sat down for supper, I told my father the news: The Pittsburgh Pirates wanted to sign me to a minor-league contract. My father's face turned crimson. "No, no, no," he shouted. "You want to play baseball? You can play baseball in college, because that's where you're going." A phone rang and broke the tension. A coach from another college had tracked me down to tell me I should consider his school. I was noncommittal, thanked him, and returned to the living room. Dad didn't miss a beat. "Look," he said, the anger still visible in his face, "you can play baseball. But you'll play baseball in college, and that college will not be anything but Tufts. You have exactly one choice."

"What if I don't want to go to Tufts?" I asked.

"You're eighteen; legally, you can go anywhere you want," he shot back. "But if you go to Tufts, I'll pay for it."

I spent four days fuming, and I contemplated resisting my father. I suppose I could have defied him, gone elsewhere, and worked my way through school. But to what end? I think I knew he was right that college trumped minor-league baseball. He told me I'd never get anywhere without a college education. Maybe he knew before I did that I'd never make it as a pro. In retrospect, I wish I'd asked him that, but I didn't.

The prospect of a pro career did not end with the Pittsburgh Pirates. I spoke with scouts and representatives from other interested teams over the years, and made it clear that my father wanted me to pursue college rather than agree to be drafted by a major-league team.

The decision to go to Tufts was the last decision my father made for me. After I started going to Tufts, my mother noticed changes in him. She knew something was radically wrong. Finally, on a trip to Boston when he was being honored at Tufts, my mother made him an appointment at Mass General, where he was diagnosed with Alzheimer's right away. The doctor who diagnosed my father had cancer. He told my mother, "Your husband will live longer than I will, but you will go through hell." At the time, the public didn't know much about Alzheimer's. My mother didn't know what to expect other than the personality changes. She kept my father at home and she did go through hell. It is an enormous tribute to my mother that she persevered through this time.

My father died on July 27, 1972, at the age of eighty-one,

nine days before I married Barbara. He was buried two days later in Mexico City. Some of my friends and colleagues, familiar with the broad outlines of our relationship, have suggested that William Blaine Richardson was an emotionally abusive father. I can see how they might have drawn that conclusion, but they were wrong. He was stern and demanding and a strong disciplinarian who could reduce me to tears when I wanted to do something and he said no. But he never laid a hand on me or abused me emotionally. And what he taught me, by accident or by design, vastly outweighed his shortcomings. He taught me to respect other cultures and to learn from them. He taught me to be aggressive in work, to push for excellence, and to recognize that conciliation and compromise are not signs of weakness when they help you to achieve a worthy objective.

Years later, when my mother was seventy-two, she asked to meet with me face-to-face on a personal matter in San Diego, where my sister lived at the time. I was terrified that she was going to tell me she was ill. But she shocked me with something else. "Bill," she said, "I want your blessing to marry an older man."

I was so relieved she wasn't sick, I started laughing. "Well, how old is he?" I asked.

"Eighty-seven."

I said, "Well, who is it?"

"It's Salvador." I knew she had struck up a friendship with Salvador Zubirán. She told me they were very much in love and that she was lonely. She said she wanted my support.

"Of course I'll support you. You should get married if this will make you happy. That's the most important thing to me."

With that, my mother—as strong as she was gentle—burst into tears and gave me the biggest hug a small woman can give a big guy like me. "I was so worried," she said.

"What about?"

"I was worried that you would think I was dishonoring the memory of your father."

This woman, this positive and loving force in my life, is extraordinary, I thought, and not for the first time. She was very concerned about hurting my feelings at a time when her own happiness was at stake.

"No, I know you would never do that," I said. "The memory of my father is secure with me, as I know it is with you."

"What about Vesta?" she asked. Vesta, she told me, was against the marriage and worried that she would wind up caring for this elderly man, just as she had for our father in his last years, when the disease began to consume him.

"Ah, don't worry, I'll talk to Vesta. She'll be fine." We talked, and she was. Salvador Zubirán and my mother were married later that year in Chihuahua, Mexico. My mother didn't know how many years they would have together, and they wound up having twelve. He was an extraordinarily healthy man who kept working and played tennis. I liked him a lot and he made my mother very happy. He died at the age of ninety-nine. Dr. Zubirán was a very eminent figure in Mexico, and my mother was by his side in 1993 when he was awarded a medal for his early work on the importance of nutrition—the Presidential Medal, the highest honor a Mexican can receive.

My mother remains a stalwart supporter of both her children. Vesta became a doctor, and during her years in medical school, my mother would sit for hours on end typing her school papers. During my 1982 campaign for Congress, she went door-to-door to ask for support for her son. At one stop, a lady opened the door and asked Luisita if she was my mother.

"Yes," she said.

"Ah, what we mothers do for our children," the woman responded with an understanding smile.

Vesta and I often joke about our mother's pride. Whenever she met new people, she would introduce herself and add in the same breath that her daughter was a doctor and her son a U.S. congressman. And at ninety-one, she's still giving me advice.

Three

Tufts university's main campus sprawls across portions of two Massachusetts communities—Medford and Somerville—just past the Boston city line and no more than a half-hour drive from Concord. But compared with Middlesex, Tufts was a different world. College is always a step up from high school, but I for the first time encountered people from radically divergent backgrounds who'd had a multitude of life experiences. At Middlesex, the boys all seemed to be upper-middle-class or wealthy and white. There were plenty of prosperous white males at Tufts, too, but there also were kids from public high schools, from working-class families, from foreign countries.

My freshman roommate, John Bergstrom, was a conservative Republican who belonged to the John Birch Society. Bergstrom was a true believer, but his politics didn't affect me one way or the other. I simply tuned out. This was the fall of 1966, and student protests over the Vietnam War already were roiling some campuses across America. But Tufts was quiet and I was practically oblivious. Early on, my extracurricular interests were baseball, the linchpin of my life, and two new influences: One was the presence of young women on campus, the other was a fraternity I pledged at the beginning of my sophomore year.

Delta Tau Delta had been my father's fraternity when he was at Tufts, and he said he wanted me to join it because it was the best place for student athletes. "Jesus, is there anything else you want me to do?" I asked him in exasperation. My baseball exploits at Middlesex had not gone unnoticed by upperclassmen at Tufts's fraternities, and I was courted by them all. As it turned out, my dad was right: the Delts were the best fit for me. I lived in a dormitory for my first two years at Tufts, and then moved into the fraternity house in my junior year.

I became involved my sophomore year with a university committee, volunteering to show the campus to high school kids considering Tufts. One fringe benefit was a bigger dorm room at West Hall, actually part of a two-bedroom suite with old wood and high ceilings. I roomed with John Carco, a fellow pitcher on the baseball team, and we became great friends. Our suite became something of a salon, a place for prospective jocks looking at Tufts, Latin American students, and fraternity brothers. We'd talk, listen to the latest hot album, or watch TV. Old friends from prep school or even Mexico City would show up. I began to hang around with Steve Cary, an ROTC student from New York who played football and wrestled for the school. Steve later worked for me at the Energy Department in Washington and married one of my top New Mexico congressional aides, Melanie Kenderdine.

Meanwhile, my relationship with Barbara was blowing hot and cold. Barbara had been a year behind me in high school. The summer after I graduated, which was between Barbara's junior and senior years, she came to Mexico for the first time to visit my family. After she graduated from high school, Barbara went to

Colby Junior College in New Hampshire for two years and then to Wheaton College in Massachusetts to study psychology. We went back and forth, seeing each other every other weekend. At one point, we had a hiatus, and I got worried when Barbara started dating some athlete from Dartmouth. For years I had a spy in the Flavin house—Barbara's younger brother John, who'd report back to his friend Bill about his sister.

It was in my junior year that my priorities began to be rearranged. My hopes of a professional baseball career receded until they disappeared out of sight. It wasn't just my dreams that were fading: I was having trouble seeing period. Around the time I was eighteen, I realized I needed my eyes tested. I figured I'd strained my eyes at Middlesex studying under the sheets with a flashlight after lights-out—I wasn't hitting the books so much during the day—but there was more to it than that.

My mother took me to the eye doctor in Mexico City and he said I was nearsighted and definitely needed glasses. In the car on the way home, my mother had a little tear in her eye. She said the doctor told her my eyes weren't so good. "This isn't going to help your baseball career." I remember getting mad at her: "My eyes are not *that* bad." I felt I could get by on the baseball field well enough. I only needed two pitches, and I could read the catcher's sign for a curve, two fingers, well enough.

But my mother was right, it wasn't affecting me so much at the time but it might in the future. I didn't know of many players who pitched in the majors in spectacles or contact lenses. Yankee Ryne Duren, who played wearing thick Coke-bottle glasses, was one of my favorite players, but he was always pretty wild.

Still, I was good enough to pitch for the Cotuit Kettleers in the Cape Cod League in the summer of 1967, after my freshman year. Each player worked a day job—in my case, mowing lawns in the morning for $1.75 an hour—and lived with a local family.

I organized a trip for the Tufts varsity down to Mexico one spring break to play some local college all-stars. I raised the money, chartered the plane, and arranged the games. Five games were scheduled. Of the first four, I pitched and won two; we lost the other two. I pitched the fifth game on two days' rest and I came home with a 3–2 win. I also came home with a sore arm, sore enough that I couldn't pitch the opening game of the college season that spring. My throbbing elbow was sending me a clear message. I had to get cortisone shots to pitch, and even then I could only go five innings. Over three varsity seasons, I ended up with a 10–6 record and an average of eight and a half strikeouts and slightly more than six hits per nine innings. Still, I was getting hit and hit hard those last two years. My baseball dream was dying as my physical skills deteriorated, but it took time for me to accept it.

I started to devote serious attention to the school's academic program my junior year. My bachelor of arts degree was in Political Science and French. John S. Gibson, who taught introductory political science and public diplomacy, was particularly good at bringing his subject matter alive. Gibson brought in some fascinating speakers. The one who impressed me most was John Stoessinger, who at the time was acting director of the Political Affairs Division at the United Nations. A refugee from Nazi-occupied Europe before the war, Stoessinger had enjoyed a fine career as an academic. He wrote *The Might of Nations,* which won the Bancroft Prize in 1963.

Stoessinger talked to us about the United Nations, about the Universal Declaration of Human Rights of 1948, which grounded in no small part in the aspirations of our own Declaration of Independence, and about the workings of its General Assembly. What really caught my attention, I told Stoessinger years later, was how he explained the machinations of the UN Security Council and how its five permanent members (the United States, the Soviet Union, Britain, France, and China) dominated the international agenda. It opened my eyes to an institution I barely knew—one in which I would be privileged to participate three decades later as United States ambassador.

The other professor who had a significant influence on me was Seymour Simches, who taught romance languages at Tufts from 1954 to 1990 and who died in January 2003 at age eighty-three. Simches was the son of Lithuanian immigrants; his father was a tailor. Simches went to Boston University and received his master's and Ph.D. from Harvard. He was always kind to me and interested in what I was doing, and not because I was a baseball player. My grades were starting to pick up by my junior year, and his attitude toward me certainly helped. He would discuss the French philosophers with me—Camus, Sartre, Voltaire, Pascal, Rousseau, Descartes. He corrected my Spanish-accented French. He would invite me to his modest home in Medford and continue our talks over a bottle of French wine on a Sunday after dinner. He once told me I had the potential to be a good leader if I developed core philosophical values like the great French masters.

Simches was also one of the founders of Tufts' Experimental College. The college was started in 1964 to offer undergraduates access to expertise they might not encounter in regular coursework. People inside and outside the university—lawyers, architects, newspaper reporters, health care specialists, business executives, museum curators, even Tufts undergraduates—would propose courses to the Experimental College's board of faculty and student members. Perhaps twenty of the hundred or more proposals would be approved. The concept was central to what Simches believed: Education wasn't a one-way street; instructors could learn with their students.

Simches encouraged me to contribute to the Ex College curriculum. Between us, we came up with a two-part course that stretched over both semesters of my senior year. Steve Cary got a big laugh from the course titles, saying I was parodying myself. He probably had a point. The first part was "The Latin American Temperament and Personality"; the second, "The Charismatic Leader."

The third key element of my Tufts education came from my fraternity, Delta Tau Delta. By my junior year, I was becoming more involved in the fraternity's affairs. The Delts had a long tradition of civic responsibility and charitable work, but it seemed to me that the balance had shifted dangerously to the social side of fraternity life. I loved a party as much as the next guy, but I was concerned that we were becoming irrelevant. Seismic changes were taking place on our campus and hundreds of others across America. This was the 1968–69 academic year—after the assassinations of Martin Luther King Jr. and Robert F. Kennedy, after a summer of protests against the Vietnam War, after the riots and bloodshed at the Democratic Convention in Chicago, after a generation of kids returned to school suddenly politicized by what they had witnessed.

Three members of the fraternity approached me about running for fraternity president. One of them, Bob Karp, was a friend and fellow baseball player. Another was my buddy Cary, the straight-arrow jock. The third was Jack Darsch, a former president of the fraternity. These were pretty serious guys, and what they were saying dovetailed with my own evolving ideas about the fraternity. There was only one problem: Traditionally, the vice president got the top job if he wanted it, and Bob Fitts, the veep, definitely wanted to be president. I decided to run against him, and I won. My platform: You know Fitts damn well, but you don't know me—and I'm the guy who wants to change this fraternity. (Years later, when I was in Congress, I was in Bangkok on business and checked in with the U.S. Embassy, where I was assigned a liaison officer—Bob Fitts. We had a good laugh recalling the election at Tufts.)

After the election, we started a charity drive and instituted a speakers program. We invited a group of ten Black Panthers to come to our fraternity house at 98 Professors Row to talk to our members. They lectured us about the black power movement. They did right by the buffet table, and left an impressed and slightly unnerved audience behind.

I felt I was off to a good start as chapter president, but I soon took a stand that tested my developing political skills. I never tried marijuana or other drugs. Athletes, in my view, didn't do that sort of thing. I decided to clamp down on members' smoking marijuana in the fraternity house. This wasn't a terribly popular move. Still, even if as many people in the fraternity smoked dope as didn't, almost everyone understood it wasn't a good idea to risk getting the entire chapter busted and tossed off campus. Nonetheless, two guys challenged the president's executive order and tried to drum up support for a referendum to throw me out of office.

My opponents forced a meeting that drew nearly a hundred members and pledges. As it descended into chaos, David Swett, the chapter vice president, asked me to invoke *Robert's Rules of Order.* "What the hell is that?" I asked him. He meant General Henry M. Robert's century-old book of procedure for deliberative associations. I'd never heard of it. I finally prevailed when I threatened to invite the current dean of students, Alvin Schmidt, to arbitrate the dispute. My opponents backed down.

This was my first taste of politics, and I enjoyed it. I found the election, and the way I had prevailed over a huge favorite, exhilarating and fascinating. I liked all the organizing and the inside stuff, and I found that I was good at it. I started to appreciate that there was power that came with the office. Within the obscure world of student politics, I started to make a difference.

We worked to get our people into positions of power in other student institutions. Working behind the scenes, I got a guy named Tom Elliott elected to one of three spots on the Tufts Citizens Union, which was the most important arm of student government. And I pushed my friend Steve Cary to stand for election to the Inter-Fraternity Council. Cary won, too. This was my Lyndon Johnson moment, Bill Richardson as kingmaker, and I told them they had to look out for the fraternity's interests so long as our interests weren't inconsistent with the greater good. Cary got it. Elliott, however, went his own way on some issues, and I had to straighten him out. At one point, he said he wanted to turn fraternities into religion-focused cultural centers. I convinced him that while religion certainly played a role in the life of the campus, it shouldn't dominate the fraternity system.

My draft number in the lottery for military duty was 139, which everyone said was right on the bubble. I wasn't looking forward to service in Vietnam, but I decided to go if called up. The bubble burst and I got my notice early in the second semester of my senior year. I was classified 1-Y, a deferral that could be canceled only in the event of a declared emergency. The main reason was a deviated septum in my nose that caused a chronic breathing problem. It eventually required several surgeries and left me with an even bigger nose than I'd started out with.

By the early spring of 1970, I knew baseball was not a career option and I realized I had to figure out what to do next. Politics was intriguing me, not just within the fraternity but in the wider world outside. The country was going through great turmoil. And though I didn't fully realize it at the time, Gibson, Simches, Stoessinger, and others who brought the world outside America into their classrooms had influenced my thinking. I had some depressing moments when I realized I wasn't going to be a ballplayer. Politics would come to fill the void left in my life by baseball.

One day late in my junior year, Arthur House, a former fraternity president who was then a young assistant dean at the Fletcher School of Law and Diplomacy, gave a riveting speech at the fraternity house. House made three key points: Do something relevant with your life; consider graduate school, because it will serve you well; and think about public service. House impressed me tremendously. I was raised in a foreign capital and spoke fluent Spanish and serviceable French. I was interested in other cultures and wanted to learn more. Graduate school seemed to make sense, and the Fletcher School, on the Tufts campus I loved, seemed the perfect venue.

I approached House early in the second semester of my senior year and asked for his help. He told me flatly that I wouldn't get into Fletcher, not with the B-minus average I was carrying. Still, I applied late in my last semester. I was promptly wait-listed. My grades weren't on a par with the typical high achievers admitted to Fletcher. A friend of my father's, Edward O'Connell, who was a dean at Fletcher, said he'd do what he could to help me, and I had a good interview with Charles N. Shane, the Fletcher dean of admissions, who was a big baseball fan, but by late August, I figured Fletcher was not in my future.

September 4 was the day of enrollment. Early that morning, the phone rang. It was Charles Shane. "My boy," he said, "this is your lucky day." He was right: I was admitted to Fletcher when I really didn't deserve to be. I learned later that I got in thanks to the efforts of Shane, O'Connell, and House, in that order.

I chose a one-year program for a master of arts in International Affairs. That's what I received, but getting there wasn't easy. It was soon clear to me that I was out of my league. Some of the other students were mid-career businessmen or diplomats; others were Rhodes Scholars or career military officers on sabbatical. Compared with these people, I was woefully underprepared. One classmate, Barbara Bodine, was about my age, but she had earned a Phi Beta Kappa key as an Asian Studies major and had already studied abroad. She would go on to have a distinguished career in the United States Foreign Service, serving as ambassador to Yemen in the late 1990s; she was there in August 2000, when the USS *Cole* was attacked by al Qaeda terrorists as it was docked in port at Aden.

One assignment we received, from a professor of Asian Studies, Allen Cole, was to prepare a paper on contemporary China. Barbara Bodine saw me floundering. "Bill," she said, "with all due respect, you don't know shit." Barbara suggested I write about Chinese governmental control over particular issues in the press. I did middling well and made it through the course. Years later, Bodine needled me about her giving me my first assignment at Fletcher, and she was right.

There were a lot of foreign students at Fletcher, and they increased my interest in international affairs. One roommate, a Uruguayan named Elbio Roselli, would become an ambassador for his country. Another, Shotaro Yachi, is today the vice minister of the Japanese Foreign Ministry, although I don't recall ever seeing him attend class. The looming presence of Vietnam was also having an effect. The war came to Fletcher with explosive force one day when the dean's office was bombed, setting the entire administration building aflame. The dean, Edmund Gullion, had been United States ambassador to the Congo under President Kennedy. Gullion supported the Vietnam War effort and someone—the authorities never learned who—took violent exception to the fact.

I ran for and won one of three spots in student government at Fletcher. The big issues of the day included student financial aid, job placement after Fletcher, and the school's relationship with Tufts—whether Fletcher should go on its own or become part of Harvard. I was interested in politics and I was being elected to student office by my peers at school. But my focus was local and my political sympathies weren't oriented in any particular direction. Then, in what was a defining moment for me, I was offered a vision of a possible future for myself, crystallizing a lot of the thoughts I was having at the time into coherence.

In the spring of 1971, I went on a school trip to Washington. It was a whirlwind: We visited the White House, the Supreme Court, and Congress. Late in the day, we went to the Senate, and Senator Hubert Humphrey spoke to us. Humphrey had served as Lyndon Johnson's vice president following a long career in the Senate, then headed the ticket for the Democrats in 1968. But he lost to Richard Nixon, making him a guilt-by-association casualty of "Johnson's War." Humphrey returned to Minnesota to teach, but the Happy Warrior couldn't resist another turn on the stage. He ran for the Senate in 1970 and won, becoming his state's junior senator for a second time.

On this day in 1971, Humphrey walked into a Russell Office Building committee room, shed his suit jacket, and launched into a masterful political speech about values and the U.S. role in the world. About fifty of us political wannabes were transfixed by this incredible orator, who raised his voice and constantly waved his hands to add emphasis to what he was saying. Humphrey spoke to us about poverty and malnutrition and other social ills that he had dedicated his life to combat. These are vital issues, of course, but this wasn't what stuck with me. It was Humphrey's passionate sermon about public service that grabbed my attention. He didn't offer a partisan point of view but talked in general about the meaning of the words *public* and *service.* He said he was honored to work in government and to use its positive attributes on behalf of his fellow citizens.

I was sorry when Humphrey stopped talking. Our day in Washington drew to a close, but I remained enthralled by Humphrey and the force of his message. I felt as though he had been talking directly to me. Now, for the first time, I had an inkling of the real potential of political power in the country of my birth. And an inkling that I could succeed in this arena myself. I felt inspired to make politics and public service my life's work.

My aspirations were entirely unfocused. I had no way of knowing whether my enthusiasm for politics would ever be rewarded by a government employer or actual voters. But I did get a considerable confidence boost from an unlikely source just before graduation from Fletcher. I took a required course in International Law my second semester, taught by Leo Gross, a legendary figure at the school. Gross, who was Austrian by birth, had gotten his Ph.D. in Political Science from the University of Vienna and his law degree from Harvard. He arrived at Tufts in 1941, became a full professor at Fletcher in 1944, and taught there for nearly four decades.

Gross was a giant in his field. He was a formal man who never called students by their first names—it was always Mister This or Miss That. And he did not suffer fools kindly. Gross's technique for getting the best out of students was to insult them, to yell and call them stupid, to humiliate them. As a result, of course, everyone in his classes lionized him, yearning for the day Professor Gross would pay them a compliment or deign to address them at all. I got a B in his class, which was considered a triumph. An A came along from Gross about as often as a solar eclipse.

On graduation day, our eyes met and he walked over to me with a slight smile on his face. "Mr. Richardson," he said, "I hope you don't go back to Mexico. You're good at politics and you can

make a great contribution to this country." Although I managed
to mumble a few words of appreciation, I was blown away. I remember seeing an ad for Coca-Cola in the seventies in which
"Mean" Joe Greene of the Pittsburgh Steelers tosses his jersey to
an adoring kid. That's what Gross made me feel like that day.

Four

Hubert humphrey's speech had sold me on public service. Where better to start, I figured, than in Washington, preferably on Capitol Hill? There was only one problem: I had no contacts in the nation's capital, and my grades at Fletcher were little more than adequate, certainly not good enough to catch the eye of a representative or senator. But in the spring of 1971, figuring I had nothing to lose, I wrote nearly a hundred members of Congress with an interest in foreign affairs asking for a staff job or an internship. The response in most cases was a form letter thanking me for my application and telling me no openings existed at that time. In other cases, there was no response at all.

Next I asked H. Field Haviland, an International Affairs professor at Fletcher, whether he could write some letters on my behalf. He did. He also called someone he knew, the Republican congressman from Massachusetts's Fifth District, F. Bradford Morse. A couple of days before graduation, I got a note from Morse, acknowledging Haviland's recommendation and offering me a job—an unpaid internship for a few months starting in September, take it or leave it. I took it, happily.

In 1971, Morse was a long-standing member of the Wednesday Group, a loose association of liberal-to-moderate Republicans—Rockefeller Republicans, in the parlance of the day, named for Nelson A. Rockefeller, then in his fourth term as governor of New York. This kind of Republican is a much rarer bird in Congress today. The Wednesday Group numbered from fifteen to thirty. It met once a week to discuss public-policy issues and related legislation. Democrats controlled the House then, but they were at war with themselves: Starting with the death of House Speaker Sam Rayburn of Texas in 1961, liberals from the Northeast, Midwest, and West Coast had begun to challenge the Southern conservatives who had long held sway. The intraparty struggle meant that the votes of Wednesday Group members were in play as liberal Democrats searched for allies to support their legislation.

I was assigned by Morse to the Wednesday Group, and part of my job was to help arm its members for legislative battle. Usually on Thursday, the party whips would send out flyers listing the likely legislative agenda for the upcoming week. I had to research the bills and write summaries for Wednesday Group members by the close of business Friday. I'd check with the leadership and committee offices of the Democrats to get some sense of the prospects for the bills. Then I would hit the document room of the House to read committee reports and the proposed legislation. The work could be tedious, with very long hours, but it was invaluable training, because I learned how to synthesize information and to present it clearly and accurately in written form. I learned from some masters, including Patricia Goldman, who was the top staffer for the Wednesday Group, and Richard

Conlon, who was executive director of the Democratic Study Group, which worked for the liberal Democrats.

In December, Morse gave me an early Christmas present. The group's members liked my work and wanted me to join the full-time staff. The *salaried* full-time staff. This was my first job in government, and it paid $250 a week. Up to then I'd been living in a group house with seven other people, men and women, and I'd needed considerable help from home to pay my share. A paid job meant independence. It also meant something else. Barbara and I had wanted to get married—the guy from Dartmouth had long since left the picture—but I told her that we couldn't until I secured a paying job. She had gone to Boston to work at Mass General, while I looked for a permanent job in Washington. Now we could move forward.

I went to Barbara's parents' house to ask for her hand. Barbara's father, Jack Flavin, was all primed that this was the night. We had supper and then sat looking at each other. Barbara's father goes to bed very early, and after a while he said, "Well, nine o'clock. I'm going to bed," and off he went. I just couldn't do it. When I got up the nerve, I made Barbara go up and get her father out of bed. We went to the living room and had a very anticlimactic conversation. As Barbara recalls it, I said to her father, "Where's my dowry?" and her father said, "You ate it. I've been feeding you for seven years."

My own father was very sick by this time. Barbara asked my mother if it would help if we had the wedding in Mexico, but she said, No, we could be in the next room and he wouldn't know. We decided to get married in Goddard Chapel, on the Tufts campus my father and I cherished, and set a date for the end of July. Barbara's father had a golf tournament, so we moved the day to August 5, 1972. My father died nine days before. He was eighty-one and I was twenty-four. My mother insisted we go ahead with the wedding, and my father, I was convinced, would have been appalled by all the fuss if we had canceled. We toasted him, in Spanish and English, at the wedding, invoking a famous Mexican proverb in his memory: *"El respeto al derecho ajeno es la paz"*—in essence, respect your neighbor and there will be peace.

A lot of my mother's family came to the wedding in Concord. At the receiving line, a couple of people, noting my father's absence but not knowing what had happened, said to my mother, "I'm sorry Bill couldn't come." She just said, "Yes." She wasn't in a state to say, "Well, he died." She was just trying to get through the day. My mother hosted a dinner the night before at the Parker House, a Boston landmark hotel. We had our reception at Barbara's parents' country club, and we headed off to Lucerne, Switzerland, and to Crete for our honeymoon.

While we were away, my wonderful mother and my aunt went to Washington to clean up my bachelor apartment. On our return, Barbara and I went to Concord, picked up the wedding presents, and stuffed them into a U-Haul and then drove down to D.C.

In my new full-time position, I continued to prepare legislative summaries. The security of my position allowed me to begin moving into issue work. Latin America was a natural area of interest, and before long, I knew, or knew of, most of the Hispanic professionals on the Hill and on staff at nongovernmental organizations (NGOs) that promoted human rights in the region. In a sense, my foreign-policy career began one day early in 1973 when I was contacted by a prominent Latin American diplomat, Juan Gabriel Valdés. Valdés was a former foreign minister in the government of Salvador Allende Gossens, the Socialist who was elected president of Chile in 1970, to the consternation of the Nixon administration, which promptly began to do what it could to undermine him. Allende eventually was ousted in a military coup that began on September 11, 1973; he died in the presidential palace of a gunshot wound, either fired by his own hand or, as many people believe, by agents of Chilean general Augusto Pinochet, leader of the coup.

Valdés had been given my name by an NGO staffer who said I was Hispanic, spoke fluent Spanish, and had access to a couple of dozen liberal-minded Republicans in Congress. He was calling from New York, Valdés said, where he was working for the United Nations, and he wanted to pass along the gist of a recent conversation he had had with Fidel Castro. According to Valdés, the Cuban leader was interested in improving relations with the United States and with the Nixon administration. Castro, he said, would be willing to consider agreements liberalizing conditions in his country, up to and including human rights, if the United States relaxed the trade embargo it had imposed in 1960 after Cuba nationalized U.S. businesses without compensation. Could I pass along this entreaty to my principals and, through them, to the administration? Absolutely, I told him.

The core members of the Wednesday Group were Brad Morse, John Dellenback of Oregon, and Marvin Esch of Michigan. I wrote them a memo, summarizing my conversation with Valdés and suggesting that they get the message to someone in the Nixon White House or State Department. Instead, they directed me to write a formal memorandum to Charles A. Meyer, the assistant secretary of state for inter-American affairs, invoking their names and asking for a meeting. Meyer saw me, barely. In a meeting that lasted about ten minutes, he dismissed Valdés's report and insisted that the administration didn't have much interest in overtures from Castro anyway. I dutifully reported back and was delighted to see that my congressmen were pissed Meyer had blown off their guy. In the last year, Nixon had gone to China and signed the first Strategic Arms Limitation Treaty (SALT 1) with the Soviet Union. Those were the Communist giants. Why didn't it make sense to ease tensions with a Communist midget ninety miles from the United States mainland?

Meyer agreed to attend an informal gathering of the Wednesday Group, but he was no more forthcoming with congressmen from his own party than he had been with the twenty-five-year-old staffer, who was not a Republican but not yet a Democrat either. This is nothing, Meyer said with condescension in his voice. Consider the source. But the source was good. Valdés represented a democratic country with decent ties to Cuba. I urged Morse, Dellenback, and Esch to press ahead, and it didn't take much prodding: They were eager to follow up. They ordered me to write a paper for them, making the case for normalization of relations with Cuba, or at least the movement toward normalization. I didn't argue that Castro would suddenly become a democrat and a capitalist, but I believed that moving toward more normal relations, as the administration had done with China, would probably lead to some liberalization in Cuba.

When the paper was finished and edited, thirteen members of the Wednesday Group called in reporters and made their case. The press conference was well attended: These were members of the president's party, and the press likes to cover intraparty differences. What made my week, though, was when Walter Cronkite, in his sonorous voice, reported the story on the *CBS Evening News* that night: "Today, thirteen Republican members of Congress urged President Nixon to open relations with Fidel Castro. . . ." I thought, holy shit, I may have had an impact here. Nothing happened, of course, but still, to me, it was heady stuff.

My initial brush with American foreign policy, brief and

unavailing as it turned out to be, was provocative enough to start me thinking about opportunities at the State Department. I approached several members of the Wednesday Group to see if they would recommend me for a job as a congressional-relations specialist at State, and a few said they would do what they could. My background, command of Spanish, and work on Latin American issues, coupled with the backing of some moderate Republicans, were enough to sell the head of Congress Relations, Marshall Wright. In early 1974, I started work at the State Department's Foggy Bottom headquarters as a legislative management officer, congressional relations.

By then, the issue of human rights as an essential element in U.S. foreign policy was beginning to take shape under pressure from three forces: nongovernmental organizations such as Amnesty International and Human Rights Watch; human-rights advocates within the State Department itself, and a few insistent members of Congress. Within State, George Lister, the Department's first human-rights officer for Latin America, argued that the United States and its public officials could not parse human-rights abusers by their political orientation—that you could not condemn and penalize left-wing regimes and ignore abuses by right-wing regimes.

On Capitol Hill, two Midwestern congressmen, Democrats Donald M. Fraser of Minnesota and Tom Harkin of Iowa, led the way. In 1973, Fraser held the first congressional hearing specifically on human rights; Harkin and Fraser, meanwhile, introduced amendments in the mid-1970s that ended economic and military aid to chronic human-rights abusers. Senator Henry M. "Scoop" Jackson of Washington spearheaded the 1974 Jackson-Vanik Amendment that withheld most-favored-nation trade status from countries that denied their citizens the right to emigrate.

Don Fraser particularly impressed me; he was a dynamo, who

grabbed an issue by the ankle and wouldn't let go. Fraser had a dogged aide, John Salzberg, who lived and breathed human rights. With Salzberg behind him, Fraser had pushed for elevating the human-rights position at State long before Jimmy Carter was elected president. With Carter in the White House, Fraser had a powerful new ally. In March 1977, the new American president spoke to the United Nations General Assembly and announced to the world that human rights would move to center stage in U.S. foreign policy.

This was a few years off when I started at State. I was there to assist members of Congress, especially when they traveled to Latin America on official business. Early on, for example, Secretary of State Henry Kissinger brought several key members—House Speaker Carl Albert of Oklahoma, Senate Majority Leader Mike Mansfield of Montana, Senator Hugh Scott of Pennsylvania, and Representative Dante Fascell of Florida—with him to Mexico City, where they met with President Luis Echeverría and officials in his government. I went as unofficial translator, facilitator, and logistics arranger. Kissinger's star power was clear to everyone—his guests from Capitol Hill and his Mexican hosts alike. From my vantage point, the trip couldn't have gone better. I even got some attention in the Mexican press, with one magazine featuring me as a local boy who done good.

I learned that the congressmen had words of praise about me for Kissinger. Even though I didn't have regular contact with him, the secretary at least knew who I was. I usually was in the room when he met with members of Congress in Washington on matters related to Latin America and human rights. And once, he summoned me to his baronial sixth-floor suite for a meeting with Joseph Sisco, then undersecretary for political affairs. Kissinger recounted a conversation he'd had with Fraser where I'd been present and asked me, "Did I tell Fraser I'd consider cutting aid to

Chile? He's claiming I did. Will you check your notes?" I thought he had, too. This was 1974, after the coup, and Chile was inarguably a serious human-rights abuser. I went downstairs, found my notes, and returned.

"Well?"

"Yes, Mr. Secretary, you did tell the congressman that."

"Oh, shit." He didn't suggest we find a way to weasel out of it, but he clearly was angry that he'd gone further with Fraser than he apparently had intended. It was the sort of mistake Henry Kissinger didn't make very often.

My FORTUNES AT STATE IMPROVED. Asia and Africa were added to my portfolio at Congressional Relations, and I was traveling to places and meeting people I previously had known through newspapers, briefing documents, and hearings on Capitol Hill. Fraser went to Asia and took me with him, first to South Korea, where we met with Kim Dae-jung and other dissidents battling for democracy in their country. Kim spent much of the 1970s and early 1980s escaping assassination attempts and serving time in prison on charges invented by Seoul's ruling generals. He eventually would be elected president in 1997 and win the Nobel Peace Prize in 2000.

We also traveled to the Philippines on that trip, meeting with members of Ferdinand Marcos's government and with opposition figures such as Jaime Cardinal Sin and Benigno "Ninoy" Aquino, who was then in prison. Aquino was released and promptly assassinated in 1983; his death triggered a revolution that brought down Marcos and led to Aquino's widow's coming to power. Fraser would use these trips as additional fodder for his assaults on Kissinger's foreign policy, which balanced human rights against other national interests, such as a foreign country's antipathy toward the Soviet Union.

I was gaining a real sensitivity to human rights through work with Lister, Fraser, others on the Hill, and the nongovernmental organizations. Given our dedication to our nation's founding principles, to political pluralism and liberal democracy, we owed it to the people abused by brutal regimes to defend their human rights and use our economic power and foreign aid as a weapon when necessary. At however low a level, I was working for a Republican administration. The job was going well, but the added responsibilities, my own secretary, and what I regarded as a comfortable salary—a fat $18,000 a year—were bumping up against my political preferences. I was beginning to define myself, in my mind anyway, as a Democrat.

Human-rights issues at the State Department were what made me a Democrat. I'd voted for McGovern in 1972 as an independent. Now I was sympathizing a lot with what Don Fraser was trying to do. What helped seal the deal was a memo I saw that was written by Harold Geneen, the head of International Telephone & Telegraph, a multinational with big operations in Chile, in which he described some of the efforts under way or planned to screw Allende. This was written, as I recall, to Meyer, the inter-American affairs guy at State. ITT, it turned out, had offered the CIA $1 million in anti-Allende money during Chile's 1970 presidential election; the CIA turned it down, but the company still funneled $350,000 to Allende's principal opponent, Jorge Alessandri, a former Chilean president. I felt this just wasn't right. It was one thing to meddle in the affairs of dictatorships and authoritarian regimes. It was another to try to undermine an open and fair election in a foreign country or a freely elected government.

Pat Holt, then chief of staff of the Senate Foreign Relations

Committee and a specialist in Latin America, had expressed an interest in me and had even urged me to join his team on the Hill. I contacted him and told him about the Chile memo. I didn't feel I could leak the document to him, but he certainly could ask the State Department to produce it. Holt did, and the result was a hearing by the Latin American subcommittee. Again, I thought I actually might be having an impact.

I was casting around for a better job. Given how I was leaning politically, I wanted to work for a Democrat. One of them, Senator Frank Church of Idaho, was chairing the Select Committee on Government Intelligence Activities, and its hearings were digging into the CIA's dirty tricks in Chile and elsewhere. I pitched myself to Church's office, stressing my credentials as a Latin American specialist, and managed to get an interview with the senator. It may have been the shortest job interview in history. It lasted about a minute. He asked whether I had any investigative experience. I said no. He looked down at my résumé, then back at me sharply: "Wait, you're a Republican? You work for Republicans? The administration?" No, no, I started to protest, I'm not a Republican, but he was already on his feet with a curt thank-you-for-stopping-by. I was out the door.

Then I got lucky. Senator Gale McGee, a Democrat from Wyoming, was a colorful guy with a booming voice and a penchant for red and orange shirts and multicolored cowboy boots. He also was a foreign-policy conservative who chaired the Latin American subcommittee of Foreign Relations. One day, not long after the Church fiasco, McGee called me into his office and offered me a job on the Foreign Relations Committee staff as a staff associate. I could do some work on Latin American issues, but he had something else in mind, too. McGee said that he and Hubert Humphrey were going to form a foreign-aid subcommittee and that he would have his own person on staff. He wanted me to be his guy, one of four staffers handling the subcommittee's business, which also included arms sales.

It took a couple of months to work out the details, because Humphrey had a say in the staffing, too. In that period, pretty full of myself, I told a committee staffer, Bob Dockery, that McGee had asked me to do foreign aid *and* Latin America. There was only one problem: Dockery was already doing Latin America himself. He was upset enough to confront McGee. "You want to get rid of me?" he asked the senator. McGee wanted to keep Dockery on board and backed down. I joined the staff in 1976, but only as a specialist in foreign aid and arms sales. The episode yielded a valuable lesson: Don't talk too much and don't volunteer too much information.

Richardson's Rules

· Be discreet and don't volunteer too much information.

The two years on staff at the Senate Foreign Relations Committee meant a lot of foreign travel. I went to Iran on a fact-finding trip. I had dinner with Bill Sullivan, the U.S. ambassador, who said, "Aren't you kind of young for me to be giving you a dinner?" My job was to learn whether arms sales to the government of the shah, Mohammad Reza Pahlavi, should be maintained or whether human-rights abuses there meant that Congress had an obligation to cut off sales under section 502 (b)—a 1974 amendment to the Foreign Assistance Act that had been pushed by Fraser. Pressed by the United States, the shah had made some progress on human rights; there were fewer political prisoners and fewer reports of torture. In the end, both Congress and the

Carter administration kept up arms sales almost to the day the shah fled into exile in 1979.

The most astonishing trip in my time as a staffer in Congress or at the State Department unfolded in December 1976, when I accompanied Iowa senator Richard "Dick" Clark and one of his staff members on a thirty-six-day mission to Africa. Clark cared deeply about Africa and human-rights abuses there, whether they were perpetrated by old colonial rulers or by their black nationalist successors. It struck me as both an admirable passion and odd interest for an Iowa senator, summed up nicely when his wife Julie gently chided him just before the trip, "Dick, don't get too many headlines in Africa. You have to run for reelection next year as senator from Iowa."

But there were headlines aplenty. We traveled commercial, and it seemed as though we stopped in twenty different countries. Southern Africa was a politically volatile region with huge economic potential. We met with rebel leaders in Rhodesia, including Robert Mugabe, who would win the new country of Zimbabwe's one and only free election in 1980. Mugabe was a charismatic leader with penetrating black eyes who reflexively silenced his subordinates whenever they tried to participate in our talks. Although he talked about independence and democracy, Mugabe seemed to be demonstrating autocratic instincts.

Dick Clark was especially fixated on South Africa. He already had sponsored amendments to cancel aid to South Africa's apartheid government, although it would be almost another decade before Congress enacted sanctions against the country and overrode a veto by President Ronald Reagan to make them law. Clark asked for and got an audience with John Vorster, the prime minister and a major figure in the ruling National Party. The pleasantries quickly turned to anger as Vorster castigated Clark for his actions in

Congress and Clark upbraided Vorster for his government's racial tyranny. At one point, I was convinced Vorster was going to call guards and have us physically removed from his office.

Nelson Mandela was still in prison at this time. We asked to see him but were turned down. We did manage to meet a few black nationalist leaders who weren't in hiding or in jail, including Mandela's wife, Winnie, and Archbishop Desmond Tutu, who would later head South Africa's Truth and Reconciliation Commission after multiracial elections were held in April 1994.

One key figure we met was Stephen Biko, a founder of the black-consciousness movement in South Africa. Biko was at once intense and gentle, a giant of a man who talked passionately about democracy and the struggle for freedom among black South Africans. It was clear that he was in some danger. Biko was a "banned" person by then, which meant he was more or less restricted to his hometown, and he was regularly harassed by the South African authorities. He was picked up by security police on August 21, 1977, and "sustained a head injury during interrogation," according to a commission's report. He subsequently was moved twice, winding up on September 12 at the Pretoria Central Prison, where he died, naked and alone in his cell.

On the penultimate day of our five-week journey, Clark, his staffer Mary Ann Spiegel, and I were sitting on a beach in Cape Town, a beautiful city on the South Atlantic Ocean. Among other duties, I was handling the press on this trip, and we were getting plenty of it. Clark wrote a speech to give the next day to the Cape Town press association. He put something in it that, in retrospect, I wish I had red-flagged. He referred to the African National Congress, which he said was a revolutionary organization, and added that the United States had also had a revolutionary war. The local press interpreted that as an American senator siding with the militants and advocating revolution. The story got back to Iowa. Clark's opponent in 1978, Roger Jepsen, tried to make the case that Clark was more interested in Africa than Iowa—the senator from Africa, Jepsen called him. Clark became a one-term senator, losing his bid for reelection.

Five

IN THE EARLY MONTHS of the Carter administration, fresh job opportunities started to appear on my radar screen. Patt Derian, the new human-rights assistant secretary at State, was building a staff and asked whether I would be interested in a deputy assistant secretary's position in her office. The money was good, about twice what I was making on the Hill, and I believed in what she was trying to do. But I said no, figuring staff work for the Foreign Relations Committee would be a lot more fun with a Democratic administration.

There was another reason for my decision. I had worked with people who put themselves directly before the voters and I was steeling myself to run for public office myself. Staff work was satisfying, and you could have an impact on public policy by influencing legislation. My friends who were career staffers had great jobs, with travel and good salaries, and they made substantial contributions. But with rare exceptions, they were never recognized for their own worth. Staff work, I came to believe, was no substitute for the power to do good things for people that comes with elected office.

Unfortunately, the only places I could call home were Mexico City and the District of Columbia, neither of which is the fifty-first state, and Massachusetts, which I promptly abandoned for the nation's capital after graduate school. But an idea had begun to take shape in my mind. Starting with the Wednesday Group, I had been involved with Hispanic organizations and issues. The only Hispanic in the Senate was Joseph Montoya of New Mexico, until he lost his seat in 1976, and over the years, I had gotten to know members of his staff. The more I learned from them about the state, the more it seemed the perfect match.

I lost one mentor when Gale McGee was defeated by Republican Malcolm Wallop in November 1976. But another, Hubert Humphrey, the man who first inspired me to think about government service, was helpful when I told him that I wanted to run for office and that I was thinking of moving to New Mexico. He told me to see Montoya but also gave me a list of people to see in New Mexico—some of them "his people" from the 1968 campaign for president and some of them prominent politicos whom he didn't know well but who might respond to my dropping his name.

Barbara and I needed to talk this through. "I need to be from somewhere," I told her. She wasn't overjoyed by the prospect of a move west, to put it mildly. After a period of adjustment—Barbara had never lived in a big city before—she had grown to love Washington and had developed a circle of good friends. She was working for the Muscular Dystrophy Association on their summer camp and the Jerry Lewis telethon. The risks—emotional, financial, professional—of chucking a promising career in the federal bureaucracy for a crap shoot in politics were enormous. Barbara understood all that. But she also knew about my competitive streak and got it when I talked about testing myself in elective politics. Barbara now thinks the fact that I never got to play pro ball was a factor. One dream had been denied; if I never tried to run for office, I might always be wondering, "What if?" about that, too.

In August 1977, we flew to Albuquerque and I tapped the list of names Humphrey and others had given me. My pitch was that I wanted to move to New Mexico, work hard in Democratic politics, make a contribution, and eventually run for office. And not local or county or state office. With the confidence of my relative youth, I told one and all that my ambition was to run for the United States Congress because my half-dozen years working on issues at the federal level had prepared me in ways that other candidates could not match.

New Mexico in those days had two seats in Congress. The one I had my eye on was the First Congressional District, which essentially covered the northern half of the state and included Albuquerque, New Mexico's largest city by far, and Santa Fe, its capital. It had a mix of liberal and conservative areas, incorporated a large part of the Navajo Indian reservation, and was 25 percent Hispanic, Hispanic like Republican incumbent Manuel Lujan Jr., then serving his fifth consecutive term. I was prepared to pay my dues on behalf of the party, but one day, maybe a half-dozen years from then, I wanted to run.

The response to my audacity varied from puzzled skepticism to outraged disbelief. New Mexico, "the Land of Enchantment," was welcoming to tourists, retirees, and companies that wanted to relocate, but its political establishment didn't look kindly on what it regarded as carpetbaggers. Ed Romero's reaction was typical. Romero was a pillar of New Mexican politics who traced his ancestry back to the Conquistadors. He was then serving as Democratic chairman for Bernalillo County, which includes

Albuquerque, and Humphrey had given me his name. I met Romero in his office for what was a relatively brief interview. He was polite, but I sensed what he was thinking, confirmed by Romero himself years later: *The nerve of this kid! He's a visitor, doesn't even live here, and he comes in and says he wants to run? Fucking nuts!* There were several like that, including Ben Alexander, then chairman of the state party. I met Alexander for coffee at the La Fonda Hotel in Santa Fe and told him of my plans. There were others who had the same idea, Alexander told me. You'll probably have to wait in line.

Still, although Barbara remained leery of what she sensed was inevitable, we both fell in love with New Mexico. I returned to Washington convinced a move was the right thing to do, and I started taking weekend trips back to New Mexico to look for a job in politics. At one point late in 1977, Governor Jerry Apodaca introduced me to Dan Croy, a former New Mexico health secretary who by then had replaced Alexander as state Democratic chairman. Croy and I stayed in touch.

On January 13, 1978, Hubert H. Humphrey Jr. succumbed to a long battle with cancer. America lost a great man, in my judgment, and I lost my second mentor in the Senate. Soon after Humphrey died, my persistence in New Mexico paid off. The job of executive director of the state Democratic party, the top staff position, had become vacant. One day in February, Croy and Romero, who had warmed to me after my repeated visits to the state, walked into the living room of our house in Washington and offered me the job. I accepted on the spot.

Barbara and I had decided we weren't going to move to New Mexico unless I got a job. Now that that had been taken care of, we made our arrangements. In May, I loaded up our Alfa Romeo with as many of our possessions as I could fit in, got my best friend from Tufts, Steve Cary, to tag along, and headed west. The plan was for Barbara to settle our affairs in Washington and fly out for good in a couple of months.

This was a risky move for a number of reasons. I was giving up one career and was by no means assured that my job would last very long. Apodaca, who had signed off on my appointment, warned me that he would be a lame duck as soon as the June 6 gubernatorial primary was over. The winner, either his lieutenant governor, Bob Ferguson, or a former governor, Bruce King, would immediately become head of the state Democratic Party, with authority to pick a new chairman and executive director. He said he'd have a word with Ferguson and King but could guarantee nothing.

King won the primary. Sure enough, he immediately replaced Croy with a new state chairman. I had barely arrived in the state and my job was on the line. So I did what has become my political trait: I got up close and personal. I jumped into my car and visited every county in the state in a week. I just hit everybody, boom, boom, boom, all thirty-three county chairmen, asking them to urge King to keep me as executive director. I thought it had been an effective blitz, effective enough that when Toney Anaya, another big politico in New Mexico who was running for the U.S. Senate, offered me a job as his campaign manager, I said no. (I knew Anaya faced a very tough run in November against the incumbent, Senator Pete Domenici. Toney lost, although four years later, he ran for and won the governorship.)

Finally, about two weeks after the primary in June, I got to see King myself. He seemed like a decent guy, and I came away from the meeting feeling pretty good, as if King had made a commitment to me.

Within days, however, a reporter asked me if I was going to be replaced as executive director. The reporter had heard that the new state chairman, Larry Ingram, was going to fire me. I told the reporter that I thought the candidate had committed to me, and I told him that Mike Anaya, Toney's brother, who was there at my meeting with King, could substantiate what I said. So the reporter called Mike, and Mike said he didn't remember it that way. As he remembered it, King had made no commitment. He sold me down the river.

I was history, gone by the end of the month in a well-publicized firing. Barbara, who came out on July 4, had only been in Santa Fe about two weeks and she'd had no time to settle in when I lost my job. Our furniture hadn't even arrived from Washington.

Later, I got to talk to King. "I thought I had a promise from you that I could continue as executive director," I said.

"I never made such a promise, Bill," King responded.

"Yes, sir, you did. I'm sure you made a commitment to me."

"Bill," he said, "a commitment and a promise are not the same thing." You could have fooled me. I heard it as yes. He meant it as maybe, but don't take it to the bank. Another political lesson learned.

Fortunately, I caught the eye of the chairman of the Bernalillo Democratic Party, Bert Lindsay, who was in his sixties and a card-carrying member of the American Civil Liberties Union—in short, a classic liberal. Bert had taken over the party in Bernalillo late in 1977, succeeding Ed Romero, and he wanted me to come aboard as executive director. He said he'd been watching me and thought I knew something about politics. He could care less about my being fired by King. Bert said he'd pay me what the state job paid, $1,000 a month, which he could afford to do because he ran the biggest county. "But you have to do the job in Albuquerque," he insisted. I took the job and commuted every day from Santa Fe—about sixty miles, door to door.

We worked hard, rounding up the Democratic votes for King. At one point, Ed Romero asked me to meet with Anastasio Somoza, the president of Nicaragua. I told Romero that Somoza probably wouldn't want to see me. I told him I'd been one of the staff people advising members of the Senate Foreign Relations Committee to cut off aid to Nicaragua because of its human-rights abuses, and I'd helped to draft the legislative language that did so in 1977. No, Romero said, that's why he wants to see you. Vastly overestimating my influence in Washington, Somoza wanted me to try to reverse administration policy. I knew it was a waste of time, but out of courtesy to Romero I met with Somoza, and his army of security guards, in a hotel room in Albuquerque. Somoza made his case for renewed military aid— essentially, that the Marxist Sandinistas fighting him would turn Nicaragua into another Cuba if Washington didn't relent. I told him I couldn't help, as politely as I could.

On November 7, 1978, King was elected governor by a margin of one percent. What put him over the top was the work we did getting out the Hispanic vote in Albuquerque, particularly in the South Valley, where I went door-to-door from dawn to dusk, speaking Spanish and often staying for hours at voters' homes chatting up King.

Getting fired by King hurt me politically, but it was partly offset by the respect I got for helping the party get its man elected. I had survived a tumultuous beginning in my new home state. But it was more than that. Running the state party, however briefly, and the Bernalillo County party had given me the chance to get to know all the key political players in the state. It was an amazing short course in New Mexico politics that kept me in the game and allowed me to move to the next level.

BARBARA REMAINED NERVOUS about our financial security, and I couldn't blame her: We didn't have much. But in late 1978, I established the Richardson Trade Group, a consultancy in Santa Fe, and got a couple of contracts that provided a decent income stream. One was from the United States Agency for International Development, USAID, thanks to its assistant administrator, Abelardo Valdez, who later became President Carter's chief of protocol. I looked at Latin American aid programs in the government—programs in nutrition, education, and civil society that encouraged democratic political development—to see if there were ways to justify increases.

I went to Washington every couple of weeks to meet with USAID people and to work the Hill. Representative Dante Fascell, the Florida Democrat I had accompanied to Mexico with Kissinger, had become a good friend, and I managed to persuade him to engineer an increase in the aid appropriation for Latin America in the next fiscal year. The people at USAID were delighted.

With another contract and a modest position teaching politics and government at a community college in Santa Fe, I was doing well. Although we kept the house in Washington and rented it out, we bought a small place in a historic area of Santa Fe. Santa Fe is very different from anywhere back East where Barbara was from—no water, no leaves, as she puts it—but she settled in quickly. She started working at an antiques store. All in all, we were pretty happy. Nevertheless I was getting itchy feet, even though it was 1979, an off year in the political cycle. I had come to New Mexico to run for office, and I began to talk to political people about the prospects, even for local races. But I hadn't moved 1,900 miles to run for city council.

The carpetbagger charge was raised again. They had a point—I'd lived in the state less than a year. But in politics you have to take advantage of an opportunity, and I thought I saw one in

New Mexico's First Congressional District. Later, John McCain would be elected to Congress after living in Arizona for two years.

The incumbent, Manuel Lujan, was a huge figure in the state. He'd been seriously challenged only once, in 1972, by Gene Gallegos, a lawyer in Santa Fe. Gallegos told me he'd run a great race against Lujan and had still lost by 5 percentage points. He thought Lujan was unbeatable. Lujan had the best casework operation of any member of Congress. If you went to one of the five offices he had set up in the district, his caseworkers would get your Social Security check, help with veterans' benefits, find a long-lost brother in the old country, polish your shoes, and wash your pickup truck. Then they'd buy lunch.

But Lujan was an almost invisible presence in Washington, and as a very conservative Republican, he often voted against the interests of his district, I thought. I kept checking to see if anyone had filed to run and no one had. When I hinted I might run, the politicos in the party said Lujan would kill me. My argument was that we had an obligation to run *somebody* against him. Lujan shouldn't get a free pass to Congress.

I filed on the last day, picked up the newspaper the next morning, and read that *two* Democrats were taking on Lujan. Willie Orona, a longtime activist among Hispanics in the South Valley of Albuquerque, also had stepped forward. It was the best thing that could have happened, because it meant I had to work my butt off immediately to get votes. I went to festivals and ball games, held small town meetings, and shook every hand within reach—two thousand of them in one night at an Emmylou Harris concert. I worked neighborhood streets and major intersections. During rush hour, I'd park myself on the corner and dart out to shake hands with every driver waiting for the stoplight to change.

On June 3, 1980, Democrats in the First Congressional District cast ballots. The outcome wasn't close: I took 80 percent of the total vote. Thousands of people—60,000 people—had selected me to represent them. It was my first victory in elective politics, and it was a humbling experience. But the rush of adrenaline was staggering. I was over the moon.

Keep doing what you're doing, a pollster I hired told me, and I did. I went to the Albuquerque racetrack during its multiweek run and shook every hand. I did the same thing at the state fair. Lujan simply ignored me, pretending I didn't exist as an opponent. But other players in the district's politics were paying attention. One of them was Donaldo "Tiny" Martinez, a wiry Hispanic activist who desperately wanted to defeat Lujan. Martinez was a lawyer and an old *patrón* whose base was San Miguel County, but he also exercised enormous influence in adjacent counties, such as Mora and Guadalupe.

I paid a call on Tiny in his office in Las Vegas, the San Miguel County seat. It was as if I were talking to a god. No matter what I said, he would contradict me, absolute certitude in his voice. Your Spanish will not help you, he said. What matters is what's in your heart. I asked for his endorsement, knowing that *patrones* in northern Democratic counties had sometimes endorsed Lujan. He said he'd get back to me.

But by early July, I hadn't heard a word. Martinez threw a big Fourth of July party each year, an event that was part barbecue and all political rally. At the party I asked one of Tiny's underlings whether I could speak. No. I approached Martinez himself, complimented him on the turnout, and asked very politely whether he would permit me to speak. He didn't say no, he didn't say yes. Speakers came and went and I wasn't called. Tiny himself was always last, and when he rose to speak, I figured, Well, he's made up his mind: I'm not a part of this picture.

I was wrong. "Today, northern New Mexico is going to take a new direction," Martinez said to the crowd. "There's a young man here who came to see me, who has the right idea, and I believe has a future in politics. He's a little green, but I want us to get behind him. Now here's Bill Richardson." He called me up to stand beside him. Pictures were taken. The crowd went nuts. I'd been working these people, and many of them were for me, but they couldn't commit, not publicly anyway, without the word from the *patrón*. That's the way it worked among Hispanics in those days. We still thought we needed the other big *patrón* up north, Emilio Naranjo of Rio Arriba County, but the endorsement from Tiny Martinez helped me. It taught me another one of those lessons: Show proper respect, which I didn't always do.

Richardson's Rules

· **Your style can be informal, but you must show proper respect.**

More than two decades later, Martinez's son applied for a state job. I talked to him and he told me his credentials. He was as qualified as the other candidates. I told him he was getting the job because he was his father's son and because his father did a fine thing for me many years ago.

It's very important to remember who your real friends are. On my first campaigns, Butch Maki, a volunteer who was a former pilot in Vietnam, flew me around the district in his single-engine plane. You just don't have time to drive everywhere. During my second campaign, Butch and I went to Las Vegas (the bigger one in Nevada) to see a fight. On Sunday, we took a detour on the way back and stopped in Grand Junction, Colorado, to speak at the Rural Electricity Co-operatives annual meeting. I was looking for the endorsement of Carl Turner, who was from my region. Turner said he'd endorse me and gave me a $1,000 check for my campaign.

We had started to leave when Butch said to me, "We got a problem."

"What is it?" I wanted to know. "We got our thousand dollars."

"Well, it's Sunday."

"So?"

"You know any banks that are open Sunday? We need cash for gas, or we're here." We were a cash-poor operation in those days, and neither Butch nor I had enough money to fill up the airplane. So I went back to Carl Turner and said I had to borrow a hundred dollars for gas. He was shocked I needed so much money till I told him it was for my plane, not my car.

When you're congressman, or ambassador, or governor, you've got lots of friends. The true measure of a friend is someone who was behind you when you weren't doing so well, when you were floundering. I was going nowhere my first campaign, at least according to the polls. So you remember those who were with you then. And then you remember those who stuck with you between the first campaign and the second campaign. You should remember people like Tiny Martinez, Carl Turner, and Butch Maki.

When I was eventually elected, Carl Turner said he wanted to be appointed to the Cumbres & Toltec Scenic Railroad Commission, which oversees a little railroad that runs a short distance between Colorado and New Mexico. I was happy to be able to return the favor.

Richardson's Rules

· Remember who your friends were when things weren't
going so well.

I was campaigning twelve or fourteen hours a day, seven days
a week, and Lujan was doing nothing. The first poll put Lujan at
70 percent, Richardson at 15 percent. No wonder he wasn't paying any attention to me. I wasn't discouraged, but I thought,
Well, if something doesn't change the equation here, I'm going
to get my ass whipped.

My father left each of his children $100,000 when he died. I
went to Barbara and said, We have to use this. If we spend it
right, I can win. I worked with Crawford Cook, who operated a
media firm out of South Carolina. One of his guys came out to
help and taught me an important rule: When you're a big under-
dog, you've got to go after the other guy's record. We did, high-
lighting Lujan's ties to big energy companies and his spotty
attendance record in Congress, where he missed 25 percent of
the votes. We stuck mostly to the radio, with a professional doing
the ads in English and yours truly doing the ads in Spanish.

I did one television ad in Spanish, a positive, thirty-second
spot in which I spoke about respecting New Mexico's culture and
tradition and how I was going to help senior citizens, veterans,
small businessmen, neighborhoods, families, and the land. The ad
broke with tradition. There was an unspoken assumption that if
you did ads in Spanish, you'd lose Anglo votes. That's the way the
political pundits first reported it—good kid, working hard, but
now he's run this stupid ad that's going to cost him. The ad

caused a sensation, capturing the Hispanic electorate. The question was how it played among Anglos.

We went on a TV barrage the last month of the campaign, and people started to notice. Lujan accepted a couple of debates, including one on radio where I just ripped him, but he wouldn't debate on TV. I appealed for help from some big guns. I'd endorsed Senator Edward M. Kennedy in his run against President Carter. Kennedy made several trips to New Mexico to campaign for his own candidacy, but he wouldn't campaign for me because his staff people said I didn't have a prayer. I did get a nice boost from another giant of Massachusetts politics, the speaker of the House, Thomas P. "Tip" O'Neill.

During college, I'd gotten to know Thomas P. O'Neill III, Tip's son, nicknamed Kip, through Barbara's college roommate and her boyfriend. Kip and I met up again in Washington, and we became good friends. Now I asked if he'd approach his dad about campaigning for me. Tip wasn't too keen on it, because Lujan was an entrenched incumbent and, by O'Neill's lights, not a cut-throat partisan. But he was planning a swing west to campaign for Morris K. "Mo" Udall in Arizona and said he'd stop in New Mexico and make some appearances on my behalf. There was only one caveat—I had to provide air transportation to get him from New Mexico to Arizona. No problem. Except that the plane I arranged for him at the Albuquerque airport after he was done wasn't where it was supposed to be. O'Neill started to steam, but someone recognized him and ferried him over to Phoenix. Still, Tip was pissed off, and he didn't let me forget the episode when I finally got to the House.

A week before the election, the polls showed Lujan at 65 percent, Richardson 18 percent. I couldn't believe it but there it was. I was getting creamed.

So much for polls. Election night arrived and the returns

started to come in. The first count out of northern New Mexico: Bill Richardson, 7,300 votes, Manuel Lujan, 7,000 votes. It went like that until midnight, a deadlock; Lujan, on TV at his campaign headquarters, looked as though a lightning bolt had hit him. About one in the morning, Lujan started creeping up because the Albuquerque vote was coming in. I was winning the Hispanic South Valley, but I was losing the white vote—overwhelmingly—in Albuquerque and Los Alamos. By first light on Wednesday, November 5, 1980, it was clear that Lujan had won by less than one percent. The Democrats' National Congressional Campaign Committee had written me off: I was in the category of "Deserves No Help" because they thought I was certain to lose. A guy from the committee, Bill Sweeney, called to apologize for bypassing my race and offered to pay for a recount if I wanted one.

I declined. Richard Nixon might have resigned in disgrace, but he did the right thing when he begged off a recount in 1960 after the tight race with John F. Kennedy. Besides, I was ecstatic. I had prepared myself to lose: All I wanted was to lose respectably so that my political prospects were not foreclosed. There was talk of redistricting, which would expand my options for next time. And the rush when those first returns came in, that was an extraordinary feeling. On balance, this had been a wonderful political experience. An *Albuquerque Journal* cartoon portrayed me as a giant killer despite the loss, and even Barbara was pleased, although she worried like crazy about the hundred thousand we'd spent.

I REOPENED MY consulting company, gave up teaching because it was taking up too much time, and awaited what the United States Census Bureau's figures would reveal about apportionment. Sure enough, in early 1981, the papers reported that New Mexico would get a third congressional district, effective with the 1982 election. It was great news. But subsequent stories were alarming: They said northern New Mexico's Hispanic leaders were jockeying for the most favorable congressional seat, and my name was conspicuous by its absence. Apparently, I was yesterday's story—a political star on the rise right after the election, a political nobody a few months later.

The Third Congressional District, the New Mexico legislature decided, would be the northern half of the state, except for Albuquerque, which became almost all of the refashioned First CD. The new Third was tailor-made for a Democrat and a Hispanic, since it included the Navajo reservation and counties with substantial Hispanic populations. And that made it perfect for the current lieutenant governor, Roberto Mondragon, one of the most prominent Hispanics in the state. I thought I had paid my dues by running well against Lujan, but not when the state's long-time political leaders had a chance to elect one of their own to Congress.

Then Bruce King, the guy who fired me in 1978, did me a favor. The governor, it seemed, didn't get along with his lieutenant governor, so he pushed a district judge, George Perez, into the race to diminish Mondragon. With me, that made three Hispanics gearing up for the primary fight. Then an Anglo got into the race. And not just any Anglo, but Tom Udall, whose father, Stewart L. Udall, was a former Arizona congressman and interior secretary to Presidents Kennedy and Johnson. His uncle, Mo Udall, was a sitting Arizona congressman. Tom, a Mormon, was an assistant U.S. attorney, six months my junior and the fair-haired boy of the Udall clan. His strategy was transparent: The Hispanic candidates would carve up the Hispanic vote, he'd get white moderates and conservatives, and maybe that would be enough to win.

The primary was the ball game, given the heavy Democratic tilt in the new district; whoever won, we knew, probably would coast to an easy win on election day, set for November 2, 1982. I was doing my thing, which was as much retail politicking as I possibly could. I showed up at every town and village meeting I could manage, shook every hand I could, went to every plant gate, every festival—anything and everything.

It was a very tough campaign. We weren't flat broke but pretty close to it, so I had another one of those money conversations with Barbara. We took a loan, for $100,000 at 18 percent interest. Through his surrogates, Udall pounded me—a *Mexican* national guaranteeing a loan for a United States congressional candidate. The first poll comfirmed Mondragon as the frontrunner: He led with 35 percent; Richardson, 25 percent; Perez and Udall in the high teens. I'm going to lose this, I thought, unless I change tactics.

We made two course corrections. My campaign had concentrated heavily on Hispanic voters, and I needed to extend my reach. I started working the Anglo vote in cities like Farmington and Gallup; these were conservative Democrats who would be hard to keep in our column in the general election, but they also wouldn't stay home in the primary. I'd happily take their votes now and worry about the general later on. In the 1980 campaign, I had done well among the Navajos in northwestern New Mexico; now I vowed to get every single Navajo vote if I could. I became a regular presence at Navajo chapter houses, sitting and waiting my turn to speak, then waiting longer because the Navajos insisted that someone translate my words into their language before the floor was open to questions and discussion.

The last poll came out the weekend before the election: Mondragon, 31 percent; Richardson, 29 percent; the others still in the teens. The last three days were a blur. I never slept except for cat-naps between stops. I'd show up at bars at one in the morning, stand on street corners at three in the morning, move to highway off-ramps to catch early-morning drivers. In three days, we logged hundreds of miles of travel around the new Third, shoring up the Hispanic base, reinforcing my interest in Anglo voters, telling the Navajos that I meant it when I said I'd work for their interests in Washington.

It was on one of those whirlwind schedules that the campaign almost ended for good. Butch Maki was flying me around and he'd upgraded to a twin-engine plane, but he had to fly with an instructor for a time before qualifying to fly solo. We were coming in to land at the Las Vegas, New Mexico, airport when the plane's warning buzzer sounded. Alas, neither Butch nor the instructor had remembered to lower the landing gear, so we had to make a wheels-up landing. We came to a halt, the propellers both twisted way out of shape. Then there was a smell of burning. "Get out fast," Butch yelled, and we did as told, untangling ourselves from the seat belts and running from the plane. We hopped into a car in time to get to the next rally, as if nothing very eventful had happened.

Butch says he was embarrassed that he was waiting for the plane to blow up. It didn't, though Butch didn't fly much after that. He decided he liked the view better from the back of the plane. He and I became good friends. Hell, I was grateful he didn't kill me. Later, I hired him to help organize town meetings in the district and work on constituent service. Butch is now a successful consultant and lobbyist in Santa Fe.

Election night finally arrived and the early returns showed me ahead of Mondragon by about a thousand votes. But as the counties across northern and east-central New Mexico continued to report, my lead began to shrink. With two counties left to report, I was leading by a mere 200 votes. The two counties, San Juan and Rio Arriba, sit beside each other in the northwest corner of the state, bordering Colorado. Mondragon won Rio Arriba by a hundred votes. I was left with a hundred-vote edge and San Juan County left to report. I'd made a big bet on this county, with its substantial Navajo population and its conservative Anglo enclaves in Farmington and Gallup. But I was worried. Udall had appealed to the Anglos, and his uncle, Mo Udall, had campaigned on his nephew's behalf among the Navajos. Just before midnight, the results came in, and my bet had paid off. We carried the county with plenty of room to spare, thanks to overwhelming support from the Navajos. In the end, Mondragon won the Hispanic vote but lost the election to me by 4,000 votes. Udall finished last. Years later as governor, Mondragon came to see me hurting financially, and I gave him a job.

The general election in 1982 was a breeze compared with the primary. My opponent, Marjorie Bell Chambers, was an accomplished activist—a moderate Republican from Los Alamos. But she came at me from the start with an odd and out-of-character appeal to bias: Let's send this guy back to Mexico. This might have attracted some of the Anglos in the district, but it didn't go over well with Hispanics and Indians. I cleaned up among those voters and did well enough among the Anglos to win with 64 percent of the vote.

I was a couple weeks shy of my thirty-fifth birthday and the U-Haul was headed back in the other direction. I was going to Congress.

Six

THE CONVENTIONAL WISDOM in Washington is that new members of Congress are supposed to be seen and not heard. Congress does have a lot of arcane rules, and the seniority system is inviolate. A first-term representative might be prudent to take time to learn the ropes from the masters. Not me.

I'd already spent a half-dozen years on the Hill, working with staff and elected officials alike. I felt comfortable in Washington's corridors of power. I was sworn in on January 3, 1983, to represent the state's Third Congressional District. My philosophy was then and remains today this: Err on the side of trying to do too much rather than the side of doing too little. I came to Washington with an agenda and I intended to press it aggressively from day one.

Richardson's Rules

· Aim big. Always try to achieve more than you have to.

· Know where you can settle. Identify eight essential goals and achieve five.

· Take advantage of goals you share. Agree on them and move on from there.

When you're a freshman, the most important task is to get on the right committee—one of the major ones, where you can really help your district. The most important committees are Ways and Means, which deals with taxes, Appropriations, which deals with money, and Energy and Commerce, which, they used to say, deals with everything that needs to be regulated and everything that moves. In my case, the key was the Committee on Energy and Commerce, then chaired by John Dingell, one of the dons of the House, who was elected to his Michigan seat after the death of his father, Congressman John Dingell Sr. Between them, the Dingells had held the seat for the Democrats since 1933.

Energy and Commerce dealt with many things that counted in New Mexico—the Los Alamos and Sandia national laboratories, railroads, telecommunications, the environment, and, of course, energy. Most Americans don't realize it, but New Mexico is a major energy-producing state. For example, New Mexico's part of the San Juan Basin, nearly 10,000 square miles in the northwestern part of the state, produces about 10 percent of the entire nation's natural gas. Oil and gas companies are major employers in New Mexico, and through taxes and royalties, they contribute significantly to the state budget.

I started lobbying for a seat on Energy and Commerce even before I was sworn in. My first executive assistant, Melanie Kenderdine, who later became my legislative director and chief of staff, swears she saw me grabbing senior members of the committee by the lapels to make my case. I probably did. Hands-on is my style, whether I'm running for office or lobbying for a committee assignment. It didn't hurt that I had some very important people looking out for me. Tip O'Neill was speaker of the house, and Jim Wright of Texas was the majority leader. Both men had campaigned for me, first when I lost in 1980, then when I won in 1982. The airplane snafu in '80 was ancient history as far as O'Neill was concerned, but he still kidded me about it. Now they supported me for Energy and Commerce on the Steering and Policy Committee that made the appointments.

I got the coveted seat and immediately took the lead on a critical issue: deregulation of the energy industries—in particular, natural gas. The time was right. President Ronald Reagan had swamped Jimmy Carter in November 1980 in part because he supported less government intrusion in the private sector. I promised the oil and gas guys in my state that I would listen to their arguments for deregulation—or about anything else, for that matter. I told them we wouldn't always agree, but my door would always be open. So in 1983, the first year of the 98th Congress, I sponsored a bill to deregulate the natural-gas industry. Dingell, the committee chairman, wasn't happy. I hadn't cleared it with him and he was opposed. In committee, I had the votes to win, because all the Republicans and a few other Democrats from energy states were for it, but Dingell gaveled the meeting to a close so he wouldn't lose. I had irritated my chairman. But I had established my bona fides with the energy guys back home.

Dingell and I also tangled in 1987 when I proposed an amendment to the Clean Air Act that mandated cleaner reformulated gasoline. Dingell, from the automotive state of Michigan, objected, but my side won, with strong backing from one of the biggest environmentalists in the House, Representative Henry

Waxman of California, who was also Dingell's chief Democratic rival on the committee. The chairman was a tough old buzzard and not easy to challenge, but I think I gained his grudging respect over the years. And later, when I campaigned for some of his candidates in Michigan and befriended his influential wife, Deborah, he softened. Today, both John and Deborah are among my closest allies.

I could do far less with my second committee assignment, Veterans' Affairs. Of course, veterans are a vital group, but the committee has little clout because the purse strings are held by Appropriations. I did what came naturally: I started plotting to get a seat on the other major committee critical to New Mexico—Interior. Its issues were the environment, land use, water, and, crucially, Indian affairs. I would not have made it to Washington without those big votes from the Navajos and many of New Mexico's nineteen Pueblo Indian tribes, and I intended to advance their interests if I could. Besides, the Indians had been getting screwed by the United States government for two centuries. I couldn't even the score, but I could try to do what was right. I went back to Steering and Policy, but they told me I had to learn to wait.

On Commerce, I'd struck up a friendship with New Jersey's James Florio, who ranked fairly high on the Interior Committee. Jim had run unsuccessfully for governor in 1981 but was already thinking about another try. For him, Veterans' Affairs would burnish his credentials with his constituents in populous New Jersey the way Interior would with my folks. So with the approval of the leadership, we arranged to swap. Florio did run for governor again, in 1989, and won.

So within six months, I had seats on two major committees that were vital to my district and my state. But I also made my first big mistake: I hadn't told my constituents why a seat on Interior was better for them and for the state. I'd campaigned as a big supporter of veterans' issues and I'd been active my first few months, holding hearings and raising veterans' issues at town meetings in the district. My dumping "their" committee angered a lot of vets, and I couldn't blame them. That error was the main reason I had a primary opponent in 1984 and had to deal with the charge that Bill Richardson didn't care about veterans.

Well before I made the announcement, I should have prepared the ground by telling veterans' groups what I was proposing to do. It wouldn't have eliminated criticism, but it would probably have diminished the damage. After I left the Veterans Committee, I went back home and faced them. I also promised to join the Select Committee on Aging and specialize in older veterans' issues.

Richardson's Rules

· When you're about to make a major change, cover your bases.

My freshman class in Congress was huge and included several members who went on to bigger things. Barbara Boxer of California, Harry Reid of Nevada, and Richard Durbin of Illinois, for example, are now in the Senate. Tom Ridge of Pennsylvania became governor and then President Bush's first secretary of homeland security. It was considered an active and ambitious class, and many of us felt competitive against one another. But if anyone was pushing harder than I was, I wasn't aware of it.

Late in my first term, I asked Jim Wright whether he'd put me on the Select Committee on Intelligence, because I wanted to build on the international experience acquired during my work for the Senate Foreign Relations Committee and at the State Department. He said no, not right now, but he did get me a spot on the Helsinki Commission, the group established in 1976 to monitor human rights and security issues in Europe. O'Neill and Wright put me on the Select Committee on Aging that first term and, for a short time, on the House Education and Labor Committee, which was valuable because the Elementary and Secondary School Act and the Higher Education Act were up for revision. In 1987, during my third term, Wright came through and put me on the Intelligence Committee. For a time I was known as the man in the House with the most committees to his name.

In my House office, I was moving a thousand miles an hour, hustling on all my committees and working my staff to death. I was becoming known as Mr. Amendment because of the attachments I proposed to the big bills. I have tried never to ask more of my people than I ask of myself. My energy level in those days was 93-octane—it's still in that area—and that made it rough for some employees. I've always believed in getting the best out of everyone.

I established regular contact with the people in my district back home. Too many members of Congress stay in Washington and only show up in their district when they need to ask for re-election. I'd been in New Mexico less than five years when I was elected. Some people still thought of me as a carpetbagger, so it was politically wise that I be a regular presence. But more than that, I've always believed you can learn an awful lot from the folks directly and indirectly affected by decisions politicians make. I needed to hear from them, and they needed to hear from me, face to face, not through intermediaries.

I set up service offices outside my Santa Fe base—in Gallup, at the western edge of the state, ten miles from the Arizona border;

in Las Vegas, sixty-five miles east of the state capital; in conservative Curry County, adjacent to West Texas; and in Rio Rancho, a fast-growing community attached to Albuquerque. I returned to the state as often as I could. During my fourteen years in Congress, I averaged at least a couple of weekends a month in my home district. It was tough on Barbara, because I was in the office all week and in New Mexico all weekend. There was a plane that left Washington at eight o'clock that often got in late, sometimes at one in the morning. I'd hold a town meeting the next day at seven. We'd take six or seven meetings a day. I must have done two thousand town meetings when I was in Congress. Al Gore was a contemporary of mine, and he was proud of the number of town meetings he did. When I told him I did more, he got mad at me.

At a meeting there might be a few hundred people in an auditorium or six people in a coffee shop or small-town hall or Navajo chapter house. On any divisive issue—local, regional, state, or even national—I'd try to bring competing sides together to air out debate. I'd tell the crowd I had my staff with me and we were ready to resolve problems on the spot if we could. We'd bring my caseworkers from local offices and outside experts if necessary. There might be a water dispute between Hispanic and Indian farmers. I'd say, "What do we need to do?" I'd be told there had to be an easement. Often someone from the federal Bureau of Land Management would be with us and they'd say, "We'll get some people together and see what we can do, congressman." Frequently, I would establish task forces of citizens to try to resolve disputes. Often, they did; my job then would be to secure the funding for their compromises. Always, always, I would insist on taking any and all questions and I would listen hard to what people had to say.

Unless it's absolutely necessary to the objective you seek, never give individuals or groups 100 percent of what they want. Former congressional icon Dan Rostenkowski once told me you have to screw your friends once in a while to let them know you're around. It's critical that no one thinks they own your vote and that you remain your own person. In any dispute, even the relative loser in a compromise should come away with something, a stake in the outcome. The energy and mining guys in my district understood that better than the environmentalists did, even though I got high marks from the latter and just fair marks from the former.

Richardson's Rules

· **Don't concede absolutely everything the other side is requesting. Get something in return, even if it's minor.**

Holding town meetings helped me develop a style of negotiation that proved useful later on when I was a diplomat, cabinet officer, and governor. They also brought me face-to-face with individuals who needed help. It's a vital part of any elected official's job to help his or her constituents. It sounds obvious, but some politicians don't get it. I met a woman at a town meeting in the Las Vegas area. She said she was a ninth-generation New Mexican and not once had ever had to ask for help but now she needed it. She was widowed with a couple of kids and couldn't get started in life because she couldn't afford day care for the kids and she couldn't afford clothes to go for interviews. We got in touch with a church and arranged day care for her, we contacted stores and got her some clothes, and we called employers to get her interviews. We couldn't do this every time, of course, but she was very sincere, so I was happy to help.

I always thought *The Almanac of American Politics* had a pretty accurate take on me. The 1992 edition called me "a political anomaly as well as a political dynamo . . . an ambitious and often pushy politician who has sometimes taken impolitic stands for no apparent reason except the conviction that they were right." Isn't that what we were supposed to be doing in Congress? I voted *against* the Brady Bill, which mandated background checks for the purchasers of handguns, and *for* the ban on assault weapons, which got both gun-control and anti-gun-control people in my district pissed at me. After the vote on the '94 crime bill that included the assault-weapon ban, some ominous-looking guy showed up at a town meeting with a shotgun, not to threaten, he said, but just to show how upset he was with my vote. I also voted on more than one occasion for a balanced-budget amendment to the U.S. Constitution and against cutbacks in Reagan's Strategic Defense Initiative, and I backed the constitutional amendment banning flag-burning, angering liberals. Many of these were not votes that warmed the hearts of leaders in my party.

Sometimes I made the wrong call. In 1991, my district overwhelmingly opposed going to war against Iraq. I voted against going to war, arguing that we should give sanctions more time to work. In retrospect, that was a mistake: The right vote was the one cast by a majority of my House and Senate colleagues, who supported the first President Bush's request for the authority to remove Iraq from Kuwait by force if necessary. During my time as UN ambassador, I became convinced of Saddam Hussein's deceptions.

I learned that seemingly arbitrary decisions by unelected bureaucrats need to be challenged, sometimes with the application of political muscle or the threat of it. In 1993, for example, we asked the Federal Aviation Administration to authorize and fund radar at Santa Fe Municipal Airport. The airport had a tower and it was capable of handling commercial flights for planes carrying thirty or fewer passengers, but it had no radar. I thought it should, given that Santa Fe was the state capital, had a booming economy, and was an internationally renowned tourist destination. The FAA turned us down flat, saying the airport was simply too small to warrant radar. I called up the administrator, David Hinson, and asked him to reconsider. He invoked his friendship with President Clinton and told me, in effect, to get lost. Fine, I told him, but you'd better keep your eye on the House floor over the next few days.

Two days later, I went to the House floor and said I would offer an amendment to an appropriations bill, substantially cutting the staff of the FAA administrator. The morning before the scheduled vote, one of Hinson's people called to say the administrator was reconsidering our request for radar. Reconsidering? No way. I told him I wanted a letter on Hinson's stationery with Hinson's signature saying that the FAA has authorized radar for the Santa Fe Municipal Airport.

"You're going to lose on the floor," the guy said to me.

"Wait a minute," I said. "I've got my ducks lined up and I'm going for it." The truth was I was bullshitting: I knew I'd get beaten on the floor. But I told him that I was going to give a real impassioned speech in advance of the vote that was bound to change some minds. The vote was scheduled for two in the afternoon. About 12:30, I went to the floor and gave one of those sixty-second speeches you can read into the Congressional Record and maybe get covered by C-Span before the formal session begins. It went something like this: "Today, we are going to vote on an amendment I plan to offer to reduce the size of the FAA administrator's staff by twenty-five percent. I want my colleagues to know that the FAA administrator has increased his staff by twenty-five percent, but in rural areas, or even in the capital city of my state, we cannot have life-saving radar at our airports. I ask fellow members for their support."

Half a hour before the vote, Hinson called to tell me he'd put Santa Fe on the radar list. Good, I said, I need the letter in an hour because I'm going to announce it this afternoon. Needless to say, I didn't offer the amendment. We were approved for radar, but we still await the funding, so it was a partial victory.

In 1985, Amtrak announced that the L.A.-to-Chicago would bypass New Mexico to save money. Everyone in our delegation went ballistic, and I offered an amendment to cut Amtrak's budget by 30 percent, getting Republican Dan Coats of Indiana to cosponsor it with me. The Amtrak people said we'd lose, and we did, by 20 votes. Then we proposed a motion to send the bill back to committee, which would have effectively killed it. Now it was Amtrak and the subcommittee chairman Jim Florio, my old friend, who were steamed. But the Southwest Chief still runs daily between Chicago and Los Angeles and makes stops in five New Mexico cities—Raton, Las Vegas, Lamy, Albuquerque, and Gallup. Amtrak is put on the chopping block every year by the administration in power. But at the end of the day, Amtrak always survives because of congressional pressure.

Working on behalf of the Navajos and New Mexico's Pueblo Indians was a critical part of my job in Congress. Over the years, I sponsored or cosponsored legislation that got land added to Pueblo holdings; improved tribal courts, health care, and education; provided incentives for business development; ensured religious freedom for the Navajos; and funded environmental restoration. Much of this came in the early 1990s, when I became the first chairman of the new Subcommittee on Native American Affairs. But the sad fact was that so much was left to be done—not least a complete transformation of the Bureau of Indian Affairs, which I said then and still say is the worst agency in the United States government because of its mismanagement of Indian trust funds.

Environmental and land-use issues also ranked high on my legislative agenda for New Mexico. My state was the nation's fifth largest, when measured in total square miles, but it had a small population, barely one and a half million people in 1990. Even so, New Mexico was beginning to grow rapidly, and in my view, its natural wonders, key reasons people wanted to visit or resettle in the state, needed permanent protection. I quickly became active on these issues and learned just as quickly that Bill Richardson was not the dominant New Mexican in Washington. That honor belonged to Pete Domenici, the state's Republican senior senator. Domenici was elected in 1972 at the age of forty, and quickly rose to prominence. I toyed with running against him in 1984, but some discreet polling strongly suggested that a second term in the House made more sense. "Saint Pete," as he already was known in New Mexico, would have whipped me.

Domenici and I wound up having some big fights, but more often than not we found ways to compromise and got good legislation done on behalf of the state. He tended to advocate a more conservative approach to setting aside public lands; my position usually was more aggressive. In 1984, during my first term, I introduced in the House the San Juan Basin Wilderness Act, an effort to protect three wild areas in northwestern New Mexico, the so-called Bisti Badlands, the De-na-zin Wilderness, and an area called the Fossil Forest. Domenici wanted a study conducted of the appropriate use of the Fossil Forest area, which also was rich in minerals. He prevailed, but the Fossil Forest was later designated a "research natural area" limited to research and educational projects and made off-limits to most motorized vehicles.

In 1987, I introduced legislation to designate the El Malpais National Monument and Conservation Area. El Malpais, which is Spanish for the badlands, is a beautiful tract of volcanic craters, lava tubes, ridges, cliffs, and mesas about fifty miles east of the border with Arizona. Domenici was behind El Malpais, too, but he resisted my idea that the newly designated monument be run by the National Park Service and the Bureau of Land Management, both of which are arms of the Interior Department. The senator knew I was right; he just wanted to see me sweat. We finally compromised, with the Park Service managing the land.

We also mixed it up over something called the Waste Isolation Pilot Plant, or WIPP. WIPP was a plan to safely store low- to intermediate-level transuranic nuclear waste. (*Transuranic* signifies anything with an atomic number higher than uranium, like plutonium.) In the 1970s, the search settled on southeastern New Mexico in an area twenty-six miles from Carlsbad—more precisely, a geologically stable giant salt formation 2,150 feet beneath the Chihuahuan Desert. The Department of Energy began to build WIPP after Congress authorized construction in 1979. The idea was to consolidate the nuclear garbage currently stored at sites in ten states and put the stuff in thick stainless-steel containers for transport to WIPP on specially designed trailers hauled by diesel-engine tractors.

By the time I got to Congress, underground excavation had begun. But another piece of legislation was required: The 10,240 acres of federal land designated for WIPP had to be transferred by law from the Interior Department to the Energy Department. That proposed legislation came in May 1987, when the plant was within a couple of years of completion. Because WIPP was on his turf, Joe Skeen, the Republican representing New Mexico's Second Congressional District, was the bill's chief sponsor. He and the other members of our delegation—Domenici and Democratic Senator Jeff Bingaman, and Manuel Lujan, representing the state's First Congressional District—were enthusiastic supporters of WIPP, which would generate hundreds of permanent, well-paying jobs.

But my constituents, particularly in Santa Fe and northern New Mexico communities such as Taos and Las Vegas, were not thrilled about having WIPP anywhere in New Mexico, especially to the southeast, even if it was 270 miles from the capital. A lot of waste would be heading for WIPP from Los Alamos Nuclear Laboratory 35 miles northwest of Santa Fe, which meant the logical route for the stuff would be right through their backyards—down St. Francis Avenue, one of the city's principal thoroughfares. I had other issues with WIPP: What about the other towns along the route? Would local authorities get money to train people in the event of an accident or an emergency? Who would be the first responders? I also wanted the Environmental Protection Agency to write a set of regulations and to demand that the Department of Energy demonstrate that it could live by those regulations before WIPP opened its doors.

The Republicans wanted the entire New Mexican delegation—all five of us—to come together and support the bill. The night before the delegation met to discuss WIPP, I told my chief of staff, Melanie Kenderdine, that I wouldn't support Skeen's bill unless money was allocated for a road to bypass Santa Fe that would be built before any nuclear-waste shipments to the WIPP plant. Kenderdine and my other people told me I had to go along with the vote. No I don't, I told her.

I hosted the delegation the next day and it was not a moment of bipartisan comity. My Republican colleagues were angry with me about the Santa Fe road and my environmental concerns. We agreed to disagree, and did so more or less continuously for the next five years. For that period, I was the WIPP-ing boy, accused of doing anything I could to torpedo the project. But I felt New Mexico state officials had made a deal with the devil when they agreed to be home to a nuclear waste dump, and I just wanted to make sure we could live with the transaction.

The project became bogged down over the transfer of land from Interior to DOE. The departments wanted to execute an "administrative transfer" of the land, bypassing Congress, a move that no one in the delegation supported. So it went in fits and starts, through imminent openings and indefinite delays. There was a time when hundreds of WIPP workers, anticipating the first shipments, were wearing buttons reading "Ready for waste— October '88." But it would take until the summer of 1992 for bills to pass the House and Senate and until October that year for the two chambers to approve compromise legislation produced by a conference committee. On October 30, 1992, President Bush signed the land-transfer legislation into law. I got my bypass road and some of what I sought on safety-related and regulatory issues such as EPA oversight. But the story wasn't over. Lawsuits continued to plague WIPP, and the plant wasn't licensed to operate until May 1998. It didn't receive its first shipment of nuclear waste from Los Alamos until March 26, 1999, fully twenty years after Congress first authorized the plant.

WHEN I WORKED as a staffer in Washington during the 1970s, I got to know many of the top Hispanics in town, including most of the Hispanic members of Congress. Now that I was one of them, I wanted to raise my profile. I was not interested in becoming a professional Hispanic, but my heritage was central to my identity, and I was proud of it. Hispanics made up a significant portion of my district, and to the extent they had issues that I could reasonably promote, I was eager to do so. I fought to legitimize the Hispanic land-grant families in my state—people who laid claim to land acquired when New Mexico was administered by the Spanish and Mexicans that was taken over by the federal government—as well as the historic *acequias,* or irrigation ditches, so important to Hispanic farmers and landowners.

The 1980s and early 1990s also brought the beginnings of sweeping change to much of Latin America. Countries in a vast region stretching from Mexico to Cape Horn were going through various degrees of democratic reform. Military dictatorships were being cast aside (Argentina, Chile, Guatemala), one-party rule was getting competition at last (Mexico), and new leaders committed to free elections were emerging almost everywhere. These were developments to be encouraged by the United States, which wasn't always subtle or skillful in its application of carrots and sticks.

Late in my first term, I was elected chairman of the Hispanic Caucus. This was something of a coup, because the caucus included several members with some seniority in Congress. Two of them, Edward Roybal of Los Angeles and Robert Garcia of New York, essentially settled on me as chairman, despite my rookie status, to avoid a divisive fight. I owed both of them for other reasons, too: Garcia had campaigned for me and had helped line up votes on the Energy and Commerce Committee; at my request, Roybal had secured a $10 million appropriation to build the Crownpoint Hospital for the Navajos in McKinley County, New Mexico.

It was important, I thought, to show as quickly as possible that I took this new role seriously and to link it to my continuing interest in foreign affairs. I asked Tip O'Neill, the speaker, whether he would authorize a fact-finding trip to Latin America organized by the Hispanic Caucus. He agreed and helped to arrange for an Air Force plane to take a delegation of Hispanic members in December 1984 to nine countries in eleven days.

In Nicaragua, I met with Daniel Ortega, who had led the Sandinistas in their overthrow of Somoza in 1979. Ortega had come to power promising land reform and an inclusive government, if not precisely a democracy. Instead, he ruled as head of a junta that consolidated power and ran roughshod over all opposition. In November 1984, Ortega was elected president with 63 percent of the vote—an election that the Reagan administration considered a fraud. When we met a month later, Ortega was pretty full of himself. We had a verbal fight: He defended his policies and I attacked his deteriorating record on human rights. I reminded him that I had opposed the Somoza regime, but not to see it replaced with a Marxist autocrat who got his inspiration from Fidel Castro and his arms from the Soviet Union.

Since 1981, the CIA had been sending covert aid to the so-called Contras—English shorthand for *contrarrevolucionario* rebels fighting the Sandinistas from sanctuaries in Honduras. But authorization had expired in September 1984; unless Congress renewed its approval in 1985, the Contras would have to rely on private funds or arms from other governments. I told Ortega that my instinct was to vote against new aid, but my decision and that of other members of Congress might well depend on Nicaragua's performance on issues like press freedom and political dissent. Speaking in Spanish, Ortega and I sparred mercilessly to the point where Arcy Torres, wife of Representative Esteban Torres of Los Angles, pinched my arm and asked me to cool it.

Ortega made no commitments; in fact, he was openly hostile. The following spring, I voted to approve humanitarian aid to the Contras in part because I thought President Reagan meant it when he said before the vote that he was determined "to pursue political, not military solutions in Central America." Not much later, the outlines of what came to be known as the Iran-Contra Affair, the selling of arms to Iran and diversion of funds to the Contras, started to appear in press reports. Iran-Contra was a real blemish on U.S. foreign policy and a stain on Ronald Reagan's legacy. My next vote, in 1986, was against aiding the Contras.

After the bloody civil war ended, Violeta Chamorro, a member of the original Sandinista junta, was elected president. Daniel Ortega stood for election in 1996, and I was briefly pressed into his service as an unwitting supporter: Using a picture taken on my visit in 1984, an ad appeared of a smiling Richardson flanking Ortega. They must have found the only photograph I cracked a smile in. It appealed to moderate, even pro-American, voters. As the British royals say, we were not amused. The U.S. State Department demanded that the ad, which conveyed an "inaccurate" American connection to Ortega, be taken down—and a day later, Ortega's campaign complied. Ortega lost again, this time to Arnoldo Alemán, the former mayor of Managua.

DESPITE MY ARM PROBLEMS, I did eventually make it into the baseball hall of fame—the Congressional Baseball Hall of Fame, not Cooperstown. There was a congressional game that I used to play in. A few players had been pretty good in their prime. Jim Bunning, the senator from Kentucky, was in the real Hall of Fame. He had been a big-time major-leaguer with the Tigers and Phillies, among others, and pitched no-hitters in both leagues, including the National League's first perfect game of the twentieth century, in 1964. But boy had he lost his fastball by the time we played in Congress. He still had great form, but he'd lost his velocity. Bunning pitched for the Republicans. I wore my Albuquerque Dukes uniform and played third base. (We all played in the uniforms of our local team.) I loved it when Bunning pitched, because I hit him a ton. Bunning got mad when he got hit.

Wilmer Mizell (who was known as "Vinegar Bend" Mizell when he played, after the town in Alabama where he was born) was another ex-major-leaguer who pitched for the Republicans. He'd been a congressman from North Carolina and went on to take positions in the Reagan and Bush administrations. Mizell was so good the Democrats formally asked the Republicans to not let him play. Steve Largent, the great pro football receiver for the Seattle Seahawks, was a superb athlete who had a good fast-ball, but it was straight and I could hit it. He always managed to beat us anyway.

A month beforehand, we'd be out practicing at 7 A.M. Our coach was Martin Sabo of Minnesota; the Republicans had Mike Oxley from Ohio. Everybody was very determined. The games themselves were very competitive. We had one major weakness: the Democrats' pitching was always just awful.

IN LATE 1987, Jim Wright, speaker of the House, named me to the Select Committee on Intelligence, fulfilling my dream to have an official outlet for my interest in foreign affairs. The committee's brief was the broad oversight of the fifteen different departments and agencies that made up the so-called intelligence community. The committee's legitimate concerns included friends and foes alike in every region in the world. Fact-finding trips, it seemed to me, were not discretionary adventures; they were essential to our roles as members of this important committee of the Congress.

My first committee meeting, in early January 1988, was un-eventful in all respects except one: It resulted in a new friendship and professional association that made my life more productive in many ways. It's the way of Washington that congressional committee members sit at a large rectangular table and staffers—their own aides and those who worked full-time for the committee— fill chairs lined up along the walls. Among the couple of dozen white faces along the walls was one African-American, who looked slightly uncomfortable. I'd heard about this young man from Congressman Louis Stokes of Ohio, who said I should get Calvin to help me. I walked past the row of staffers along one wall, put my hands on this young black guy's shoulders, leaned down into his face, and said in mock seriousness, "Are you a soul brother?"

For a brief moment, Calvin Humphrey, who was born and raised in Georgia, was flummoxed. Here's this big, hulking congressman leaning over him, blurting out a teasing racial reference. When I say something like this, it's my way of establishing a connection. We both broke into smiles and I extended my hand. Calvin shook his head and laughed and told me he was an associate counsel to the committee, appointed by the Democratic leadership. I told him I looked forward to working with him. Before long, I was.

I was anxious to return to South Africa. The Reagan administration supported a policy of constructive engagement with the Republic of South Africa, a diplomatic approach to the lingering problem of apartheid. I'd been there and seen the horrific system of massive discrimination and oppression for what it was. How could you "engage" South Africa's white bosses with carrots absent one very large stick? The stick was economic sanctions, which I helped push through Congress in 1986. Reagan vetoed the legislation, and we overrode the veto to turn sanctions into law.

I also wanted to visit Angola, which had been embroiled in a long civil war. Late in 1988, Calvin and I left for South Africa. We checked into our hotel in Pretoria, the capital. The hotel staff at reception was entirely black; Calvin, who had been there with a congressional delegation the previous year, was greeted with open arms—"my black American brother," as one guy put it. I was admiring my plush accommodations, quite a grand affair about the size of my 800-square-foot congressional office, when the phone rang. It was Calvin: "You've got to come up and see my room," he said. I did and discovered they'd put him in the Presidential Suite, which made my room look like a closet.

Just for fun, and maybe to learn something, too, we went downstairs and buttonholed the man who greeted us at reception. "I'm the U.S. congressman and he's the staff," I said. "Did you give him that big suite just because he's black?"

"Absolutely," he said, "he's my African-American brother so he should get the room." Calvin grinned and I had to smile, too. This was a small rebellion against the protocols of apartheid, and it was just fine with both of us.

Early the next evening, we left for Angola on a small plane. Our South African pilot flew on instruments, using no lights, so as to avoid the Soviet-made surface-to-air missiles used by government forces. We flew not much higher than treetop level, almost the entire 1,100 miles to a destination near Jamba, headquarters town for UNITA. We hit the ground hard and taxied only a few yards before the lane ahead of us blazed into light, revealing a serviceable runway. A jeep took us to meet Jonas Savimbi and his aides. The plane gassed up and was gone less than five minutes later. He would be back in two days, the pilot said. I looked at Calvin and thought I saw skepticism in his eyes. Maybe it was a reflection of what he saw in mine.

UNITA, the Portuguese acronym for the National Union for the Total Independence of Angola, was headed by Savimbi, who had been fighting the government of José Eduardo dos Santos for more than two decades. This was one of the world's most painfully enduring proxy wars. Dos Santos was supported by the

Soviet Union and Cuba, Savimbi by the United States and South Africa.

The night we arrived we talked with Savimbi and Tony Fernandez, one of his chief aides. We asked about the state of the conflict and were told UNITA was making progress against the government. I asked him about Tito Chingunji, a UNITA veteran who had served as the organization's envoy in Washington earlier in the '80s. Many of us had gotten to know and like him; now there were rumors that he had broken with Savimbi and even that Savimbi might have killed him. "He's at the front," Savimbi said.

I nodded. "Can I ask you another question?"

"Certainly," Savimbi said.

"But let me ask you this," I said, edging closer to my host. "Does he still have his fingernails?" Calvin looked aghast, but Savimbi howled with laughter, not quite answering the question.

Savimbi kept talking up democracy, how all he wanted was free and fair elections and an end to dos Santos's one-party rule.

"Let's say there was a free and fair election and you lost," I asked him. "What would you do?"

"We wouldn't lose."

"But hypothetically, what if you did lose? What then?"

"We won't lose."

I gained a couple of valuable insights—not unassailable facts, but solid hunches. One was that Savimbi and the clique of men around him were no democrats. "These guys are not ready for prime time," I told Calvin after we were delivered to our tiny guest house. The other was that Tito Chingunji was either dead or a marked man. Both hunches turned out to be right. Chingunji and his family were murdered by Savimbi henchmen three years later, in 1991. A year later, multiparty presidential and parliamentary elections were held; UNITA and Savimbi came in a close second to dos Santos and his party. Neither side got a majority. But even before a runoff could be scheduled, Savimbi blew off the results and went back to war. He never stood for election again. A decade later, on February 22, 2002, Jonas Savimbi, sixty-seven years old, was killed in a battle with the government troops he had fought for nearly four decades.

Seven

IN PRESIDENTIAL POLITICS, New Mexico almost always goes with the winner. Since 1912, when we got statehood, the winning presidential candidate carried New Mexico every time until 1976, when voters gave the edge to Gerald Ford over Jimmy Carter. But New Mexico went back to being a bellwether in 1980 and also went with the victor in 1984 and '88. In 1988, I headed Michael Dukakis's Hispanic outreach program, campaigned in thirteen states, and helped to nudge up my party's share of the national Hispanic vote from 66 percent to 70 percent. But in New Mexico, Mike Dukakis wasn't the candidate to buck the reestablished state trend.

In 1991, Bush seemed unbeatable, certainly after the Persian Gulf War. But a stalled economy and the perception of a president inattentive to the plight of those affected by the slump began to erode Bush's numbers. By the time Arkansas governor Bill Clinton had sewn up the nomination the following spring, the sitting president was vulnerable.

No Democratic candidate had carried New Mexico since President Lyndon Johnson managed it in 1964. I vowed to do what I could to put my state in the Democratic column and Bill Clinton in the White House. I hadn't met the candidate yet, but he called me from his campaign plane to ask for my support; his voice was soothing and inspirational on the phone, and I told him he could count on me. We met face-to-face later in the campaign, when I arranged for him to meet Hispanic leaders in Miami. It was the first time I was the object of that penetrating Clinton gaze: When you spoke, he gave you the feeling that he was totally focused on everything you said.

November 3, 1992, election night, was sweet. Bill Clinton won a comfortable victory. Typically, New Mexico was close to a template for the national totals: Clinton, 46 percent; President Bush, 37 percent; independent Ross Perot, 16 percent.

The night was sweet for me, too, since I was reelected with 67 percent of the vote. I got another boost in early December when my party's leaders formally elevated me to their ranks by making me a chief deputy whip. Now I was one of four members charged with working the corridors and the House floor to align our side's votes with the leadership's position. Between us, the whips covered most of the party's demographics. I was a centrist Hispanic from the Southwest; John Lewis of Georgia was an African-American, a legendary figure in the history of the civil rights movement; Butler Derrick of South Carolina was a Southern conservative; and Barbara Kennelly of Connecticut was a Northeastern liberal. I felt honored and excited, but the truth was that I already had launched another campaign, for a position in Clinton's first cabinet. It was no secret that I wanted to be the next secretary of the U.S. Department of the Interior.

My years on the House Interior and Energy committees had provided plenty of preparation for dealing with the issues central to Interior's work. These included management of half a billion acres of public lands, oil and gas leasing and mineral rights, the national parks and wilderness areas, and the Bureau of Indian Affairs. I knew BIA needed to be reinvented, and I thought I was the one to do it.

Shortly after the election, Warren Christopher, the lawyer and diplomat running the Clinton transition team, called and told me officially that I was under consideration for an appointment. He said I should begin to get my paperwork in order. Filling out the background forms and locating all the documentation required takes time, but I went into overdrive and got it all done as quickly as I could. Meanwhile, I was getting winks and nods from Clinton people that a cabinet job—either Interior or perhaps secretary of energy—was all but mine. At one point, I was fingerprinted by the FBI. Afterward, the agent smiled and called me "Mr. Secretary." I thanked him and said he was a bit premature. But he insisted that everyone who made it to fingerprinting got nominated.

On Wednesday, November 25, 1992, I met with the president-elect in Little Rock. It was all very hush-hush, but the papers had the story the next day. I was one of at least three people Clinton saw that day; others included former Arizona governor Bruce Babbitt and Colorado senator Tim Wirth, who did not stand for reelection that November.

My meeting with Clinton lasted an hour and felt wrong almost from the beginning. We usually got along well together, but the chemistry was off this day. Maybe it was because he was now the president-elect, not just a small-state governor, or maybe it was something else. But we kept interrupting each other, and he was doing what he can do, proving that he's always the smartest guy in the room. Hell, he knew as much as or more than I did about the craziness at the BIA.

I was barely out the door before Clinton's old friend Bruce Lindsey told an Associated Press reporter that the Richardson interview didn't go well. The next month was like that, with stories that my star was rising or falling, that Babbitt was the front runner for Interior, or that the environmental groups were aligned against me. My record in the House had gotten fairly good marks from environmental groups over the years, although I wasn't as green as Babbitt, who was then president of the League of Conservation Voters, one the most powerful environmental lobbies in Washington. But I still thought the omens looked good: It was clear that Clinton wanted Hispanics in his cabinet, and my home state governor, Bruce King, a friend of Clinton's from their work in the National Governors Association, was pushing hard for my appointment.

Christmas week was nuts. The papers had me out of the running for Interior. Then my friend Henry Cisneros, the former mayor of San Antonio, who had been named secretary of housing and urban development a few days earlier, called me. Cisneros was calling at Clinton's behest, asking that I withdraw my name from consideration for a cabinet position. "That's bullshit, Henry," I told him. If Clinton didn't want to appoint me, I thought, he ought to have the guts to call and tell me himself.

Then, on Wednesday, December 23, 1992, the *New York Times* ran a front-page story by political reporter Adam Clymer saying that Clinton was under pressure to add more minorities to his cabinet and was now leaning my way over Babbitt. But by the end of that day, word came from Little Rock that Clinton had picked Babbitt for Interior after all. A second Hispanic in the cabinet would be Federico Peña, the former mayor of Denver, later named secretary of transportation. The new secretary of energy was Hazel O'Leary, an African-American power company executive.

By then, Barbara and I were in Mexico to spend Christmas with my mother. The president-elect called on Christmas Eve, and Clinton and I talked for fifteen minutes or so. "Sorry, man, the enviros killed you," he said. By that, he meant both the groups and his vice president–elect, Al Gore, who wasn't so much anti-Richardson as he was pro-Babbitt. Babbitt would be formally named later that day, Clinton said.

In the administration's musical chairs, two other people expected to get cabinet positions were left standing: Jim Blanchard, the former governor of Michigan, and Bill Daley, the brother of one Chicago mayor, the son of another, and a formidable political intelligence in his own right. If you had to be among the losers, this was good company to keep.

Clinton asked how I felt. "I'm hurting," I told him. I was—and I was pissed off, too.

"Look, you got screwed. I'll move some people around later on and give you a shot."

Bill Clinton is the best natural politician I ever met. He's got a great mind and an encyclopedic memory for detail, and he knew the issues like no one else. Sometimes he wanted to be loved by everyone and he wanted to please his critics too much. The Interior business may have been a reflection of that, maybe not. But for the most part, he treated me very well, and he more than delivered on his promise to look after me down the road.

Barbara and I did a postmortem on what had transpired. She said that despite the hard landing, it probably was the best outcome. Timing is important, she said, and this wasn't the best timing for me. How she could have known that was beyond me, but her political sense turned out to be flawless, as usual.

.   .   .

WHEN YOU'RE a chief deputy whip in the majority party, you get a tiny office in the Capitol and the funds to hire a floor assistant. I interviewed a dozen people over several weeks and finally picked a young guy, David Gillette, who had done legislative affairs work at the State Department and who was currently at the American Israel Public Affairs Committee, the pro-Israel lobby in Washington. We needed to make a good team, and over the next two years, we did.

Two legislative issues dominated Clinton's first year: his economic and budget plan and the North American Free Trade Agreement. The Clinton budget was red hot from the moment it was introduced in the spring, and it stayed that way until the very end. George Bush had paid a huge price for raising taxes after his "read my lips" promise in 1988 to hold the line. Now here was the new guy proposing to cut the deficit by raising personal income taxes immediately but delaying most spending cuts until 1996.

In his first State of the Union Address, on February 17, Clinton introduced one of Al Gore's ideas—a proposed BTU tax. The BTU, the British thermal unit, is a measure of energy. Whatever it was called, this was a new tax on fossil fuels—the gasoline people used in their cars, the heating oil they used to heat their houses, the gas they used to fire their kitchen ovens. The idea was partly to raise revenue and partly to encourage conservation. It might have had something going for it at a different time and place, but the BTU tax took dead aim at Main Street America. By most estimates, it would have cost an average family around $400 a year.

We whipped our members and passed the Clinton budget on May 27; it was still close, 219 yea votes and 213 nays. But our guys weren't thrilled. When the Senate passed its version of the

Clinton budget plan, jettisoning the BTU tax, there weren't a lot of tears in the House. The final bill before the House and Senate anticipated deficit reduction of $500 billion over five years, reducing the deficit to around $200 billion in 1998. But to achieve it, taxes would have to go up. The president wanted to raise the top rate from 31 percent to a bit more than 39 percent; 40 percent of families would get a tax cut and another 40 percent suffer a tiny increase. As a package billed as a tax increase, it could have been worse. But getting it passed, even without the BTU business, was a real struggle, with a cliffhanger conclusion worthy of a Hollywood thriller.

We were worried that there might be enough Democrat dissenters to scuttle the legislation, embarrassing Clinton and damaging his infant presidency. D-Day was August 5, 1993. First thing that morning, we targeted people on our side of the aisle who weren't with us but seemed persuadable. I was assigned to Representative Ray Thornton of Arkansas, a former college president from a safe district. I got bad vibes from Ray, and even the president from Thornton's home state couldn't turn around what should have been a slam-dunk vote for us. We lobbied all day. Clinton was working the phones, making promises only a president can to get votes. We were counting heads, but the heads kept turning this way and that. "Oh, we're looking good," I said to one reporter during a break, then grabbed my throat and said "aarrgghhh" in the classic choke sign.

The deciding vote came down, in the end, to a first-term congresswoman from Pennsylvania, Marjorie Margolies-Mezvinsky, who had voted against the bill in May. The House chamber was in an uproar as she stepped forward, then it suddenly quieted. Clearly in tears over this difficult decision, Margolies-Mezvinsky moved toward the speaker, filled out a green card indicating an affirmative vote, and handed it to the clerk. The Republicans went nuts, singing "Goodbye, Marjorie" to the tune of "Goodnight, Ladies," and they were right: After becoming the first Democrat since 1916 to win a seat in her conservative district, she lost her bid for reelection in 1994.

The final bill also included some of the provisions I and other members representing large Native American populations had sought, including tax credits for Indian investment and employment. All things considered, it was a satisfying outcome.

BECAUSE so much time and effort had gone into passage of the Clinton budget plan, we got a slow start on NAFTA, and the heavy political lifting was delayed until fall. NAFTA originally was negotiated by the first President Bush, who joined Canadian prime minister Brian Mulroney and Mexican president Carlos Salinas de Gortari in signing the agreement on December 17, 1992. But the agreement was subject to the approval of the legislative branch of each government, which meant that further negotiation by a new administration and a new Congress in the United States would be necessary.

NAFTA, in my view, was critically important, and not only for the reasons commonly cited by its supporters. Yes, the treaty would create the world's largest free-trade region, a market of 360 million people in the United States, Canada, and Mexico in which tariffs and nontariff barriers to free trade would fall over a fifteen-year period. Estimates of NAFTA's economic impact varied, but based on what I had read from analysts without an ideological ax to grind, the treaty promised to be win–win–win for all three countries. That didn't mean the absence of dislocations: while NAFTA figured to create more jobs in the United States, some jobs would be lost. A key part of the final bill presented to

Congress needed to include worker-adjustment programs and other so-called side agreements addressing such issues as labor standards and the environment.

I felt the treaty was crucial to Mexico. The country had been dominated by one political party, the Partido Revolucionario Institucional (the Institutional Revolutionary Party, or PRI), since 1929. Desperately needed political change was beginning to take root in Mexico, but I worried about its future without accompanying economic reform. I thought NAFTA would create positive economic change and help to stimulate a broader political debate. I thought it also had the potential to affect the immigration issue that was increasingly upsetting many Americans, especially those in Texas, New Mexico, Arizona, and California—the states along the 2,000-mile border with Mexico. The vast majority of Mexicans emigrants headed north for one reason: to find work. If Mexico's economy boomed, it would create jobs, and also better-paying jobs, providing Mexicans an incentive to stay home. If NAFTA went down to defeat, I feared, the United States would lose credibility with Mexico and have even less leverage on immigration issues.

The slow start on NAFTA in 1993 meant that advocates for the treaty had to play catch-up. Ross Perot was out there talking about "that giant sucking sound" of American jobs vacuumed into Mexico, and his arguments were gaining traction. Organized labor opposed NAFTA, as did most African-American lawmakers in Congress, and the president wasn't very aggressive in support of it until fairly late in the game. Republicans were considered the party of free trade, but they weren't about to carry Clinton's water unless Democrats in the House and Senate—a decent number of them, anyway—got behind the legislation.

Those of us backing NAFTA tried to be proactive. Concerns

about air and water pollution along the U.S.-Mexican border, for example, had become a sticking point for environmental groups and their backers in Congress. In February, I introduced legislation to set up a bilateral commission to resolve environmental disputes between Mexico and United States, funded by a Border Environmental Guaranty Fund capitalized with seed money by the two countries and private revenue raised in financial markets. While this did not become law, it was a precursor for the environmental side agreements that were negotiated as part of NAFTA.

Ross Perot really got on my nerves. On June 10, I took to the floor of the House to criticize him for his Mexico-bashing, following it up with a statement that condemned the "hateful stereotypes" and the "racially offensive rhetoric" used in his effort to kill the treaty. "Ross Perot has the audacity to come before Congress and testify that in Mexico, *'if and where there is a strike, they send in the state police, shoot twenty or thirty workers, clear the place out, get rid of the union, cut the wages, put everybody to work.'* These are Perot's own words, and they were outrageous and an insult to Mexico and an insult to Hispanic Americans. And these comments are part of a larger strategy to portray Mexico as a country that (1) is inferior, (2) is run by a bunch of thieves and cheats, (3) cannot be trusted . . . The message from the Hispanic American community today is that we will not sit back and let Ross Perot get away with his racist rhetoric anymore."

On August 13, 1993, negotiators for the United States, Mexico, and Canada completed their work on the side agreements covering labor standards and environmental issues, and less than a week later, President Clinton named Bill Daley as chairman of the administration's Task Force on NAFTA. Given my job as a chief deputy whip, that meant two of the three guys left standing in the Clinton cabinet shuffle would play pivotal roles in getting Congress to approve the treaty.

It wasn't a cakewalk. The Democratic Party leadership, for one thing, was sharply split. The speaker, Tom Foley of Washington, supported the treaty, but Missouri's Dick Gephardt, the majority leader, and Michigan's David Bonior, the majority whip, opposed it. Gephardt, to his credit, didn't twist arms or get involved in heavy lobbying against NAFTA. Bonior, however, was the lead opponent among Democrats and even used the whip's office in his fight, which was technically against the rules, since it's a party office and the party didn't have an official position on NAFTA. But by the second week in September, Bonior wisely relented; he and I jointly announced on September 9 that the whip's office would service both the opposing and supporting factions among Democrats. In my experience this was a first.

I became the guy in the House leadership holding the whip for the pro-NAFTA forces. I was paired with Robert Matsui, a Californian and an ardent support of the treaty. We were both hyphenated Americans but otherwise a very odd couple. Matsui, a Japanese-American first elected to the House in 1978, was a fastidious, perfectly tailored gentleman with an aversion to raw language and back-slapping bonhomie and a penchant for quiet persuasion.

I was, in many ways, his opposite number. I did slap backs, squeeze shoulders, bear-hug, and sometimes use the expressive idiom to underscore a point. Rumpled was the way some colleagues described me—an unmade bed, as a New Mexico reporter once wrote. There was a woman who operated an elevator at the Capitol for many years, and on more than one morning, she'd reach up and swipe away a bit of shaving cream I'd missed before leaving home.

Another trait of mine is to play games with people's names. It's meant in fun, to relieve tension. If someone tells me they don't like it, it only encourages me. I used to yell "Matsu-EEEEE!"

whenever I spotted Bob Matsui, and of course he hated it. I called House Majority Leader Dick Gephardt "Geppy," for example, and drove a fellow chief deputy whip to exasperation by rapid transposition of his given name and surname: "Butler Derrick, Derrick Butler, we've got to talk."

Isabelle Watkins, who worked for me for many years in a variety of jobs, including chief of staff, was "Izzie." She hadn't been called that since she was five years old. The first time I did it she said, "No one ever calls me that. I like to be called Isabelle." And I said, "Thanks, Izzie." I was the only person who could get away with that. I called David Gillette Joseph for some reason and have called all my male chiefs of staff Joseph ever since. John Kerry I called "Johnny," and I could tell he didn't like it. I called Al Gore "Albert" and he didn't like that. He said, "Bill, call me Al." Of course, I said, "Okay, Albert."

For all our differences, Bob Matsui and I respected each other and worked well together, each playing to his own strength. He died on New Year's Day, 2005, and his wife, Doris, won his seat in a special election a couple of months later. Bob Matsui was a classy guy.

We figured we needed at least 100 Democratic votes for the treaty. I worked hard on my side, and also on Republicans. I organized a congressional delegation of mainly Republicans to visit Mexico. We met officials, including President Carlos Salinas de Gortari, and toured factories and the Mexican interior, where poverty might be rampant but American blue jeans and New York Yankees baseball hats were extremely popular. When it was over, we at least had moved some of the uncommitteds to leaners in our direction.

On Wednesday, November 3, with the side agreements already signed by representatives of the three countries, Clinton sent the final treaty, all five volumes of it, to Capitol Hill for a vote. There would be no floor amendments: The president had "fast-track" authority on this, which mandated a straight up-or-down vote on the whole treaty.

Early the following week, we thought we were still well short of what we needed to pull it off. A *Washington Post* piece said we were about 30 votes short, but it actually might have been a bit worse than that. Then the sea parted. On Tuesday, November 9, Vice President Al Gore squared off against Ross Perot on *Larry King Live* in a high-stakes debate on NAFTA. Gore wiped the floor with Perot and made him look foolish, ill-informed, and out of step with leaders of both parties, in and out of government. The veep noted that all five living ex-presidents supported the treaty, as did "distinguished Americans from Colin Powell to Tip O'Neill to Rush Limbaugh."

After the debate, we started to gain ground, and I went from fourteen-hour days to sixteen-hour days. Members on the fence were asking for projects in their districts as the price for saying "yea"—the kind of bartering so common in Congress before a big vote. I remember being part of deals with the White House where million-dollar grants and projects were doled out, including some that had little chance for creating a single job.

In the final week, we made history, or at least history as far as anyone could recall, when we went to a joint whipping operation with the Republicans. Some Republicans had good relationships with Democrats on the fence, ones from their home states; the reverse was true as well. Matsui and I were working closely with the minority whip, a flamethrower from Georgia named Newton Leroy Gingrich. We also called upon our friends in the Senate who were supporting the treaty—Democrats like Bill Bradley of New Jersey and Chris Dodd of Connecticut—to lean on

House members from their states who still claimed to be uncommitted.

November 17, the day of the vote, finally arrived. Unlike the vote on Clinton's budget, this one went quickly, and it was clear in less than ten minutes that we were going to win. Some Democrats, figuratively holding their noses, voted for NAFTA because they wanted to support their president. Some Republicans, figuratively holding their noses, voted for NAFTA because the first President Bush had originally negotiated it and because they knew it was the right thing to do even though Clinton would get most of the credit. Their leader, Bob Michel of Illinois, a strong supporter of NAFTA, reminded the reluctant among his flock of who was on the other side: "Think of the three most famous nonelected opponents of NAFTA: Ross Perot, Pat Buchanan, and Ralph Nader—the Groucho, Chico, and Harpo of the opposition." It was a great line that got a well-deserved laugh, although it was a bit unkind to the Marx brothers.

We'd aimed for at least 100 Democrats; we wound up with 102. Of the Republicans, 132 also said aye, providing a comfortable margin of victory: 234 ayes, 200 opposed. The Senate approved NAFTA on November 20. Six weeks later, on January 1, 1994, the North American Free Trade Agreement took effect.

ON MARCH 14, 1994, I was in Mexico City for a very special occasion. At noon that day, at Los Pinos, the president's residence, Mexican president Carlos Salinas de Gortari presented me with the Aztec Eagle Award, the highest honor his country can bestow on a foreigner. I was born in America but had been raised in this very city, and I was both moved and humbled by this recognition by the Mexican government, and said so in my acceptance speech, delivered in Spanish. My father had told me I should help Mexico, and his words were echoing with me that day.

My mother was invited, of course, and she wouldn't have missed this ceremony for the world. It was, she said, the proudest moment of her life.

Eight

B Y THE TIME NAFTA became law, I had been in the Congress for eleven years, long enough to register some genuine accomplishments on behalf of my constituents and also, I felt, in the interests of the country as a whole. A measure of power had come my way with my elevation to a leadership position in the House's majority party, and I believed in using it.

Some politicians say they feel uncomfortable talking about power, as if it's the nasty relation a family wants to keep hidden from public view. I don't believe Lord Acton, the nineteenth-century historian, was right when he said power corrupts. Politics in a democracy is a competition over ideas, and it is inevitable there will be winners and losers. Any freely elected politician who says he doesn't crave power to get the laws and programs he thinks best for his city, state, or nation is either dissembling or belongs in a different business.

Helping navigate NAFTA through the House was a proud moment for me, but it was far from the only thing I did in the 103rd Congress. Over the two-year period of 1993 and 1994, I introduced fifty-six bills, seventeen of which became law. That represented about 7 percent of all the House bills that became public law in that Congress, not bad for one guy out of a body of 435 members.

Still, my interests were growing beyond the confines of my congressional district. The seat on the House Select Committee on Intelligence gave me the authority to travel abroad. And partly by accident, partly by design, a new phase was beginning to unfold for me. Starting in early 1994, and continuing through 1996, I would make a dozen foreign trips, acting as a fact-finding member of the Intelligence Committee or a requested negotiator or an unofficial representative of the Clinton administration. Sometimes, I was all three. Most of my negotiating partners were not democrats with a small "d." Far from it. Many of them had killed innocents or ordered others to do so and almost all were serial human-rights abusers. I was, during that period, the informal undersecretary for thugs.

IN AUGUST 1993, while I was traveling through Asia with Representative Charles Rangel and former representative Lester Wolff, both of New York, I got a visa to Burma and paid a visit to Lieutenant General Khin Nyunt, the strongman du jour among the country's military rulers. Burma had won its independence from Britain in 1948 and had been a democracy until a military coup in 1962. The generals were now calling the country Myanmar and the capital of Rangoon, Yangon. I was less concerned with what we called the country than with one Burmese citizen: the remarkable Daw Aung San Suu Kyi.

Aung San Suu Kyi's father, Aung San, had been the prime mover behind Burma's independence and was a national hero. He was murdered by a Burmese political rival on July 19, 1947, less than six months before independence. His daughter went to Oxford University and married Michael Aris, an English academic. She stayed in the U.K. until 1988, when she returned alone to her homeland to look after her dying mother. Almost immediately, she got deeply involved in Burmese politics; a year later, Aung San Suu Kyi was placed under house arrest for her prodemocracy activities. A free election was held in 1990 and her party, the National League for Democracy, won 80 percent of the seats. Instead of becoming prime minister, Aung San Suu Kyi was confined to her family compound in Rangoon by the military. In 1991 she was awarded in absentia the Nobel Peace Prize for her heroic work.

I wanted to speak to Khin Nyunt on her behalf. That he agreed to see me at all, I thought, was a hopeful sign. I told the general that letting me see Aung San Suu Kyi would improve the image of the State Law and Order Restoration Council, the military group that ruled the country. The generals were causing us plenty of grief, and not just because of their atrocious human-rights record; at that time, most of the heroin coming into the United States originated in Burmese poppy fields and Burmese processing laboratories, the heart of the so-called Golden Triangle. The United States had imposed economic and military sanctions on Burma, and there seemed little chance they'd be lifted without some political reforms by the military. I contended that we had to engage Burma, not continue to isolate it, and seeing Aung San Suu Kyi was part of the process. If we could do that, perhaps we could then convince the generals to turn her loose.

Khin Nyunt was encouraging: he told me that if I came back early the following year, I might get to see her. I had learned through an interpreter that Khin Nyunt had liked my brashness and candor. He also had heard that I was close to President Clinton, and he wanted the president to think that he was "a reasonable man ready to dialogue," as the interpreter put it.

On February 14, 1994, I became the first nonfamily member permitted to visit Aung San Suu Kyi since her house arrest in 1989. I paid two calls on her that day and talked twice with Khin Nyunt. But it wasn't easy. I'd been to see her husband in the U.K. to get some background and to ask what she needed. But she insisted that I be accompanied by Philip Shenon, a reporter from the *New York Times,* and Jehan Raheem of the United Nations Development Program. They were her insurance: she didn't know me and couldn't be sure that I was there to further her interests. Why had the junta let me see her when hundreds of other Western politicians and parliamentarians had been turned down?

"Where do you stand, Mr. Richardson?" she asked me in perfect Oxbridge English.

"On your side," I said. Aung San Suu Kyi insisted that she would happily discuss and negotiate anything with Burma's military rulers, except one thing: her presence in the country. They had long said that she could go free, provided she left Burma. "That is never going to happen," she told me. I realized this woman was made of steel.

I urged Khin Nyunt to open a dialogue with her and volunteered to mediate if he thought I could be useful. She is the key to Burma's reputation in the international community, I said, particularly in the United States. I cannot speak for President Clinton or the entire Congress, I told him, but it is my belief that sanctions will not be lifted until the Aung San Suu Kyi situation is resolved.

Two days later, at a press conference in Bangkok, I spoke of her "passion and commitment" to the best ideals of democracy and raised the bar: "U.S. policy on Burma will improve only if

Aung San Suu Kyi is released without condition, as well as other political prisoners, and a genuine democratization effort takes place."

I also covered another base: "Let me stress that I also believe that Lieutenant General Khin Nyunt is a pragmatic individual who is sincere about wanting to resolve the divisions in his country." That was intended as a measure of respect, and apparently it was received that way in Rangoon, because a complete transcript of the press conference was published in the main government newspaper, *The New Light of Myanmar,* in both Burmese- and English-language editions.

The next month, however, Khin Nyunt played down the idea of talks. At the same time, his government kept finding excuses to reject my requests to visit Aung San Suu Kyi again. Still, I thought my February trip had had a softening effect on the regime. On Tuesday, September 20, 1994, Aung San Suu Kyi, whom the generals usually called "the troublemaker" or "that woman," met with Khin Nyunt at a state guesthouse. Nothing of substance was discussed, according to news accounts, but this had to mean something; it would only be a matter of time, I believed, before they would set her free.

I returned to Burma in May 1995 and was allowed to make visits to the infamous Insein Prison, where I spoke to several Burmese political prisoners. One of them told me they all knew at the prison that I was coming because they had been well fed for a week before my arrival. After I left, it must have been back to rice and water. Following a prison visit, I would plead with the Burmese generals to release some prisoners: "You'd get some points with the international community," I argued. Periodically, there would be a release. Mostly, though, there was silence.

The generals flatly refused to let me see Aung San Suu Kyi this time. Her detention order was scheduled to expire in early July, six years after her house arrest. The generals were nothing if not unpredictable. On July 10, 1995, the day before the expiration of the detention order, the generals announced that the order to restrict Daw Aung San Suu Kyi to her compound had been revoked.

I felt my work must have had something to do with her release, but the good news wasn't to last. Over the years since then, Aung San Suu Kyi has been in and out of house arrest—mostly in. When her husband learned he had terminal cancer, the authorities refused to let him make a last visit to his wife. He died in 1999. Nor have Burma's generals relaxed their stranglehold on the country. In October 2004, Khin Nyunt, once thought to be among the hard-liners, was himself dismissed as prime minister and perhaps placed under house arrest. His sin? He apparently had advocated some reconciliation with the democratic opposition. In an experiment he pushed, Aung San Suu Kyi was released in May 2002 and permitted to reorganize her party. Predictably, she got enormous support; a year later, the generals cracked down and cracked heads and Aung San Suu Kyi was back in her family compound.

My work in Burma got me a lot of good press among human-rights groups and other advocates. First Lady Hillary Clinton would ask me almost every time I saw her whether I'd heard from Aung San Suu Kyi. And United Nations Ambassador Madeleine Albright invited me to a luncheon at the ambassador's Waldorf Towers residence to talk to a handful of Asian ambassadors about Burma.

Aung San Suu Kyi is the Nelson Mandela of the Burmese people, and one day, like Mandela, she will walk out of the house that is her prison and lead a new democracy movement in her country. That, at any rate, should be everyone's fervent hope for Burma and for its true leader.

. . .

IN EARLY July 1994, a few months after my meeting with Aung San Suu Kyi, I got a phone call from Robert McCandless, a Washington attorney who had been Hubert Humphrey's campaign manager when Humphrey ran for president against Nixon in 1968. He wanted to know if I was interested in going back to Haiti.

The Caribbean nation had been much in the news over the previous decade. The last dictator of the former French colony, Jean-Claude "Baby Doc" Duvalier, had been overthrown in 1986. In 1990, a priest, Jean-Bertrand Aristide, became the first freely elected president of Haiti. He was inaugurated in February 1991 and bounced seven months later in a military coup. The United States imposed economic sanctions on Haiti. From exile, Aristide agitated to get himself reinstated. In July 1993, Aristide and General Raoul Cedras, head of the Haitian military, signed an agreement on Governors Island in New York, mandating Cedras's early retirement and Aristide's return by October 30 of that year. The date came and went and the military remained in power, accusing Aristide of committing a string of transgressions while he was in office.

Aristide certainly was no boy scout, but he had been chosen in what was regarded as a fair election. By early 1994, plenty of others were joining his chorus to give Haiti's military rulers an ultimatum, and they were getting a sympathetic hearing from President Clinton. Through all the tumult over the last half of the twentieth century, there was one constant in Haiti, the crushing poverty that made it the poorest country in the Western Hemisphere.

Two months before McCandless's call, I had traveled to Haiti as a member of a congressional delegation with two other Democrats, Jack Reed of Rhode Island and Julian Dixon of California. We met with human-rights officials, Aristide supporters, and various political and business leaders. Raoul Cedras refused to see us, although one of his representatives told me that a future meeting might be possible.

By July, President Clinton had positioned fourteen Navy warships and 3,000 marines off the coast of Port-au-Prince, the Haitian capital, and was seriously considering using them to remove Haiti's military leaders. Now McCandless, who had connections to the Haitian rulers, was telling me that a peaceful resolution was possible. He arranged for a formal invitation from Cedras, which came in the form of a faxed message to my office on July 15, and left me this guidance: "Allow Cedras to save face and you'll persuade him to leave."

My mission wasn't very popular in official Washington. Deputy Secretary of State Strobe Talbott, a classmate of Clinton's from Oxford days, didn't want me to go. Neither did William Gray, a friend of mine who was a former Democratic congressman from Philadelphia and who was serving as the president's point man on Haiti. They both argued that an independent actor playing a role in the Haiti drama could send mixed signals to Cedras and undermine the tough line recently taken by President Clinton. The U.S. ambassador to Haiti, William Swing, explained the do's and don'ts, but I would be going without the blessing of my own government.

Calvin Humphrey, the Intelligence Committee staffer who had become my running mate on foreign missions, was with me again when we got to Haiti on July 18. Our trip from the airport to Port-au-Prince seemed uneventful until our three-car caravan stopped for no apparent reason and an extremely tall and muscular military bodyguard got out of the lead vehicle and walked toward us with his pistol drawn. I don't scare easily, but on this desolate stretch of road, I was plenty nervous. I grabbed Calvin's hand and squeezed hard. The bodyguard looked in, saw our frightened faces, paused for an extra moment of direct eye contact, then returned to his car. He'd made his point. Even with U.S. Marines and warships off the coast, the Haitian military was not going to be intimidated by Americans, including a high-ranking congressman from Washington.

That evening, it was dinner for seven at Cedras's home. The guest list included Cedras's wife, Yannick, who fully participated in the conversation, and General Philippe Biamby, the Army chief of staff. The meeting lasted five hours, which probably included two hours of ranting about Aristide's many shortcomings and outright violations of laws he was supposed to uphold. My message to Cedras was simple: There was tremendous pressure in the United States for an invasion and the ball was now in Cedras's court. The Congress was not of one mind on the issue, but if President Clinton decided to invade, Congress, including Bill Richardson of New Mexico, would support him.

Cedras was soft-spoken and dignified, and it may be that he and Biamby were playing good cop, bad cop. At one point, Biamby pounded the table with both hands, rose to his feet, and shouted, "We are not goons. We are not thugs." Biamby's eruption was in reaction to comments made by some State Department officials and members of the administration, even Clinton himself, that characterized the Haitian military leaders as border-line monsters. Cedras told Biamby to sit down. "No, he's okay," I said. "Let him express himself." Biamby did, at some length. Biamby acted as though an invasion was inevitable. "Congressman, did you notice that we all ate faster than you tonight? It's because we know the end is near and it might be our last meal." He said he expected to be executed by U.S. Marines and that his last wish was "to smoke this cigar from Congressman Richardson. The last good cigar I smoked was from Fidel." Haiti's people, he insisted, would fight the Americans with whatever they had: "poisons, AIDS, voodoo, and small slingshots and sticks."

In the end, Cedras was noncommittal, but I came away with the sense that he was prepared to negotiate the departure of the military leadership, providing the process left him his dignity and self-respect.

Richardson's Rules

> · **Don't be intimidated.**
> · **If you are negotiating an endgame, allow a dignified way out.**

The next day, we went to lunch with a group of pro-Cedras legislators, one of whom told me that I had an appointment to see Haitian provisional president Émile Jonassaint. Administration officials told me he was a figurehead. Don't meet with him, the U.S. ambassador had warned. You'll just legitimize him. After a brief huddle with Calvin, I told the Haitian legislators that it wouldn't be possible for me to meet with the president. They complained, but I was firm. Lunch was served and the issue was never raised again.

Before we left Haiti, I left a departing statement with the U.S. Embassy to distribute to the press. Embassy spokesman Stanley Schrager embellished my remarks with comments of his own. He left the impression that I had pounded Cedras and warned him of an imminent invasion if he didn't budge immediately. I angrily corrected Schrager's characterization of my meeting and said that Cedras had seemed willing to negotiate. "He was not totally intransigent," I said. "I found Cedras to be a realistic individual." That prompted a note from Cedras, faxed to my office in Washington on July 27, inviting me back for more talks at my earliest convenience. But it got me in hot water with the Haiti hawks, who were anxious to invade. The truth was that I didn't think an invasion was necessary quite yet. The sanctions were working, and I thought we might be able to pull this off without firing a shot. Why cause further grief for the millions of innocent Haitians if we could get what we sought through diplomacy?

Less than two weeks after my visit, on July 31, 1994, the United Nations Security Council unanimously approved Resolution 940, authorizing member states "to use all necessary means" to remove the military regime and restore Aristide to office. With that, Clinton got the protective cover he wanted to send in the Marines. The clock was ticking.

I never did return to Haiti. Some administration officials in the White House and State Department, who opposed my first trip to meet Cedras, opposed a second even more vehemently, prompting me to decline the Haitian general's invitation. The administration was clearly divided between hawks like Talbott and more dovish figures like Defense Secretary William Perry. Clinton himself was keeping the option of force on the table, he said at a press conference the next day, but he wouldn't go into any detail. He also addressed the Richardson issue. A reporter said that I had found Cedras not to be intransigent and that he had asked me back to Haiti. The president replied that it was difficult to conclude Cedras wasn't intransigent. He'd broken his word about stepping down, and he knew what he had to do to end his people's problems.

I had briefed Clinton in a telephone conversation, but the question of a return visit to Haiti wasn't discussed. At his press conference, however, the president was sending a clear signal:

Without saying so directly, he was telling me that my negotiating work in Haiti was finished.

A little more than a month later, Clinton authorized a high-powered delegation to go to Haiti to convince Cedras and his generals to step down. Former president Jimmy Carter headed the group, which included retired general Colin Powell, former chairman of the Joint Chiefs of Staff, and tough-minded Sam Nunn, the Georgia Democrat who chaired the Senate Armed Services Committee. I sent Carter all my notes and briefed the delegation staff before they departed.

By September 20, it was all over, but not without some last-minute high-wire acts. Cedras only capitulated once the invasion force was set in train. The agreement reached between Carter and Cedras parsed strangely against the strong rhetoric of Clinton and members of his administration. There would be a general amnesty for Haitian military officers and an "early retirement" for top leaders. Cedras did not have to leave the country immediately, and for a while there was some question whether he would leave at all. He did, finally, before October 15, when Aristide returned to power as president of Haiti.

Later, President Clinton called me from a vacation on Martha's Vineyard to thank me for my work on Haiti. Whatever I did, though, wasn't enough to help that troubled island. Aristide's rule also was marked by chaos and corruption. And efforts by other countries and international organizations like the United Nations to make Haiti a better place have come up empty, or close to it. I wish I had an easy answer or explanation. I don't. But that's no reason for us to stop trying to improve conditions there.

Nine

THE COLLAPSE of the Soviet Union and the end of the Cold War at the beginning of the last decade of the twentieth century brought profound and welcome changes to much of the world. Moscow's Eastern European empire imploded, giving way to proud democracies throughout the region and the reunification of Germany after four decades. Democracies blossomed throughout Latin America, and in Asia. The United States and a slowly reforming Vietnam reestablished ties in 1995, leading to the exchange of ambassadors and full diplomatic relations.

Conspicuously absent from this movement toward political pluralism was the Korean peninsula, or more precisely, the northern part of it. South Korea, of course, was an extraordinary success story: its economy was booming, in no small part because of its growing exports of quality products to the United States, and its government was transforming from an episodic autocracy run by the military to a liberal democracy. North Korea, on the other hand, seemed a fossil frozen in a bizarre prehistory, its politics imprisoned in a Stalinist cult of personality, its economy a stagnant relic isolated from the market forces and high productivity driving prosperity elsewhere.

North Korea did have one claim to modernity that earned it the enmity of the United States and other Western countries: It had a fairly sophisticated uranium-enrichment program dating back to the 1980s that was not limited to uses permitted under the Nuclear Non-Proliferation Treaty. By the early 1990s, in fact, it was clear that North Korea was prepared to produce nuclear weapons and might even have made a couple of them.

Shortly after Bill Clinton was inaugurated as president, his administration engaged the North in a long and arduous set of negotiations aimed at ending its nuclear-weapons program. To get from here to there, Clinton's negotiators were using more carrots than sticks, tactics they felt were necessary to blunt North Korea's paranoia about U.S. motives. It took nearly eighteen months of work, but on October 21, 1994, in Geneva, the two countries signed an agreement to freeze and eventually unplug those North Korean nuclear facilities that were capable of making atomic weapons.

The agreement, to be phased in over a decade, included loosened trade restrictions; oil, food, and other aid for the North; and two "light-water" nuclear reactors worth $4 billion to generate electricity. In return, North Korea had to permit inspectors from the International Atomic Energy Agency to examine the prohibited nuclear facilities, where work was supposed to end within a month's time. But much of North Korea's compliance was pushed well into the future, from five to nine years out, which meant that Washington had to take it largely on faith that the North would live up to its commitments. Still, for all the uncertainty, the so-called framework agreement was regarded as a historic breakthrough. It was a pact, Clinton said at the time, that "will make the United States, the Korean peninsula, and the world safer."

Less than two months later, on December 15, 1994, I was flying to Los Angeles to make a connection for a nonstop flight to
Beijing. It was the start of one of those congressional delegation
trips—a CODEL, in the bureaucratic shorthand—but this time, I
was the only member of Congress along for the ride. I had asked
for and received a visa to North Korea and was on my way there
to discuss the framework agreement, the possibilities for a genuine dialogue between the two Koreas, human rights, and other
issues. There were four of us, including my able foreign-policy
aide, Miguel Marquez, now an ABC network reporter; Dick
Christianson, a State Department Korea expert; and a Defense
Department logistics officer. We had an eight-day itinerary, with
stops in China, both Koreas, Indonesia, and Taiwan, but the main
chance was thirty-six hours on the ground in North Korea. It was
a fact-finding mission to this isolated and secretive nation. I
learned plenty, but in ways no one could have anticipated.

We were to fly into Pyongyang, the North Korean capital,
from Beijing. The agent at Air Koryo, the national carrier of the
Democratic People's Republic of Korea, the North's formal
name, was a model of efficiency, as if he wanted to get us up and
away as quickly as possible. Miguel informed me as we were
boarding the flight that Air Koryo had one of the highest accident rates in the world, a comforting thought. I found myself
seated next to a North Korean who was a ringer for Mao Ze-
dong. So far so strange. I managed to concentrate on my mission
during the ninety-minute flight.

The North Koreans had not provided a list of appointments or
indicated where we would be staying, which was typical, according to my embassy briefers in Beijing. My Korean handlers would
fill in the blanks when we arrived, I was told. I was briefed ex-
tensively before all my trips by the State Department, and I paid
close attention. I also read up on the person I was meeting. The

briefings were very thorough. Before I met Saddam, I'd been told not to cross my legs and show the sole of my foot. I was just so tired, I didn't stop myself.

Richardson's Rules

· **Learn as much as possible about your adversary.**

We landed in Pyongyang in darkness at 6:17 in the evening. Our flight had been uneventful; what happened next was not. Barely into the terminal, we were besieged by a gaggle of reporters and cameramen. The homegrown news people were focused on the purpose of my visit, but a reporter from Xinhua, the official Chinese news agency, asked me to comment on the downing of a U.S. military helicopter in North Korea.

What? I didn't know anything about it. Before I could respond, my hosts from the North Korean Foreign Ministry got between me and the reporter and, through a blaze of blinding television lights, whisked me a waiting car. Later, I was told the TV footage made me look extremely tired, not surprising after more than thirty hours of nonstop travel. Barbara put it more bluntly. "You looked awful," she told me.

As we sped away from the airport in a Mercedes–Benz, Vice Foreign Minister Song Ho-Gyong started to outline a schedule jammed with high-level meetings. I cut him off: What's this about an American helicopter? Song explained that a U.S. Army helicopter had in fact been shot down at approximately 10:40 that morning after it was tracked more than three miles inside North Korean airspace. I asked after the crew. Song told me the helicopter had a crew of two, but he said he could not comment on their condition. With that, my mission in North Korea was utterly transformed. "It is critically important to turn over these pilots to U.S. authorities," I told Song. Not possible, he said: This was a military matter, and nothing would be done until the Korean People's Army completed its investigation of the incident.

For the rest of the forty-minute drive to our complex of guesthouses outside Pyongyang, I pressed and Song gave me the party line. He said the same thing, but developed an edge in his voice and an increasingly dour expression on his face. Preparing to leave us with our North Korean handlers, he muttered harshly that a dinner in my honor was scheduled in thirty minutes. It might have to wait, I told him, because I had to speak to officials of my government in Washington. This did not improve Song's mood, and he left in a huff.

We had crossed the international dateline, so it was now early evening, December 17, in Pyongyang, which meant it was sixteen hours earlier in Washington, the wee hours of the morning of the same day. The phone service wasn't terrific, but I managed to get through to Stu Nagurka, my press secretary, at home. It was 4 A.M. in Washington. Before I could finish my first sentence, Stu interrupted breathlessly: "The secretary of state is urgently trying to reach you." We rang off and I got through to Warren Christopher. Chris got right to the point: "The president and I want you to stop all your other activities and stay in North Korea until you get our people out." I verbally saluted and went to work.

My handlers swept me off to the small dinner in my honor. I was an hour late, which probably wouldn't have mattered much if I had dropped the issue of our guys and enjoyed their hospitality. But I didn't, and the dinner was a disaster. There were no toasts, and the North Koreans seemed rattled when I told them that I would be discussing only one subject during my stay in their country—the safe return of the two helicopter pilots, Chief Warrant Officers Bobby Hall and David Hilemon. The North Koreans, stone-faced, kept repeating their mantra: The matter was under investigation and couldn't be discussed until the investigation was completed.

We got back to our guest quarters close to midnight and immediately got on the phone to Washington for three hours of strategizing with Christopher, other State Department officials, Defense Secretary William Perry, and Samuel R. "Sandy" Berger, chief deputy to Tony Lake, Clinton's national security adviser. My new mission was clear: Gather as much information as I could on the incident, the whereabouts of the pilots, and their condition; inform the North Koreans that a failure to resolve this issue properly could harm relations between our countries; and bring Hall and Hilemon back to South Korea. I was specifically instructed not to link the incident's resolution to the framework agreement signed in October, but I could suggest that the atmosphere surrounding its implementation could be adversely affected.

Sunday, December 18: Early in the morning, we headed off for our appointed rounds as if nothing had happened. My schedule included meetings with the chairman of the North Korean Congress, the economics minister, the chairman of the Socialist Workers Party, and finally, Foreign Minister Kim Yong Nam. I was struck by the absence of traffic. The only vehicles on the road seemed to be military trucks and what I was told were coal-fired buses spewing huge amounts of fumes. There were, however, plenty of pedestrians walking on a broad asphalt strip alongside the road. We passed through no identifiable towns on our trip to Pyongyang, and side roads seemed to snake off to a gauzy, ethereal horizon. It was eerie.

We entered Pyongyang, greeted by colorful billboards advertising the North's revolutionary spirit and singing the praises of Kim Il Sung, the founder and "the Great Leader" of the DPRK, who had died less than six months earlier, on July 8. His son, Kim Jong Il, known as "the Dear Leader," either was or was not in charge now. Countless trees had died for the papers and reports produced by Western intelligence officials and think tanks on North Korea's leadership, but no one knew for sure whether the son had risen, because he had been practically invisible since his father's death.

Unlike his son, Kim Il Sung was everywhere in evidence—on posters and at the Korean Revolution Museum, where an immense bronze statue of the Great Leader towered over the city. Across the Taedong River stood the Juche Tower, a white granite obelisk 492 feet high. (The Washington Monument is 555 feet.) Juche is the North Korean philosophy of self-reliance cooked up by Kim Il Sung. But its tenets apparently do not translate well from Korean to English. Despite repeated attempts by our hosts to educate us, we were more confused than enlightened. I figured it was some special hybrid of Buddhism and Communism and left it at that.

We met for eight hours and got precisely nowhere, or so it seemed to me. I carefully explained at every opportunity the importance of dealing with the helicopter incident in a timely and constructive manner. Failure to do so risked a serious breach in U.S.–North Korean relations. They just didn't get it. I came to discover that it's difficult to negotiate with the North Koreans. They speak from prepared texts. If anything comes up that requires them to go off the text, they have to consult and come back to you.

This day, the North Korean officials bashed South Korea again and again and again, reiterating after every pummeling their desire to improve relations with the United States and develop a security arrangement between our two countries that, of course, excluded our ally to the South. Their line on the helicopter intrusion was consistent: The Korean People's Army was investigating the incident, and no external pressure would affect the timing of its report.

As the day dragged on, I began to sense the nature of the problem. In my judgment, there was a rift between the Foreign Ministry and the Korean People's Army. The Army representatives asked what the two guys were trying to find out and why they had flown into North Korea. While the Army was talking about spies who couldn't be released, the Foreign Ministry seemed keen to deal. We were left in no-man's-land. It was clear to me that the fate of our pilots needed to be raised at a higher level. I made repeated requests for an audience with Kim Jong Il. On the chance that I might see him, I'd brought along a tape of the movie *Maverick,* knowing Kim was a big fan of American film, especially westerns.

I was told there was no chance of a meeting. The Dear Leader was seeing no visitors because he was still in mourning for his father. We were assured that he was firmly in control, that he possessed outstanding leadership skills, and that I could see him if I returned to North Korea in a few months' time. It might have been true. Or it might have been true, as many analysts in the West believed, that the young Kim had a serious liver ailment and was in no condition to receive visitors. As I said, no one knew for sure, because no one in the West had laid eyes on Kim Jong Il since his father's death.

My final formal meeting with Foreign Minister Kim was as desultory and useless as the rest. In some ways, it was worse: The minister was talking conspiracy, a linkage between my arrival and the helicopter affair, all of it orchestrated by the government in Seoul that wanted to drive a wedge between Washington and

Pyongyang. The meeting ended and I asked to be taken back to my guesthouse to see if things looked any better from Washington's vantage point. Instead, the North Koreans drove us to a scheduled cultural event in my honor where children were to sing and dance. In disbelief, I said it was inappropriate to attend this event while American servicemen were in captivity. I wheeled around and headed for the car. Vice Foreign Minister Song was offended. The North Koreans huddled separately before we departed and I thought they were getting ready to ask me to leave the country.

Sure enough, Song pitched up at the guesthouse that night to assure me that I was expected to leave in the morning as scheduled and that if I did, North Korea's office at the United Nations would keep me informed about the pilots. I suppose they could have forced me to board a plane to Beijing, but that seemed unlikely given their interest in better relations with the United States. I told Song that I couldn't leave until the two Americans were released. The North Koreans could get a little hostile if things didn't go their way, and Song was steamed on this occasion, telling me in a parting shot that I'd better be prepared to stay in Pyongyang for at least two weeks.

I tried to call Christopher and Defense Secretary Bill Perry, but the phones were down. We had no information about the pilots or about anything else. Later, I asked whether it would be okay to call Hall's and Hilemon's families. Sure, they said. I called Bobby Hall's wife Donna, trying to be as upbeat as I could without lying. But I felt even worse when she told me that folks in their hometown of Brooksville, Florida, about forty miles from Tampa, were holding candlelight vigils for Bobby's safe return. That night, I wrote a note to Hall, telling him what his friends back home were doing, and gave it to our handler in the hope that it eventually would find its way to our imprisoned pilot. I wasn't able to reach the Hilemon family.

After the acrimony of Sunday, I thought a brief cooling-off period was in order. I don't know what our North Korean opposite numbers did, but on Monday, December 19, we went sightseeing in Pyongyang. We toured the historic sites, rode the subway, and visited a department store and an archaeological museum. My North Korean handler suggested I lay a flower at the immense bronze feet of Kim Il Sung and got visibly angry when I declined. But how could I take such a step when they wouldn't tell us where our pilots were or even whether they were still alive?

We lunched at a hotel and drove around a clean, well-designed city swarming with military people, a reminder of the North's million-man army. We returned to the guesthouse in the afternoon and learned that our failure to check in with Christopher and Perry earlier had caused a near panic in Washington. At State's behest, the German and Indonesian embassies in Pyongyang were trying to find me to put me in touch with the secretary. Sure enough, Christopher was irate, worried that we had been kidnapped, or worse.

After everyone settled down, we replotted strategy, in a fashion: We requested a meeting with Vice Foreign Minister Song, the only person who would see us. He arrived at the guesthouse late that evening. It was clear he'd been talking to the military and there had been some movement. He explained that he and other Foreign Ministry officials had been in long discussions with top officers of the Korean People's Army and that there appeared to be a new appreciation of the seriousness of the issue. A resolution now seemed possible, Song said; he suggested that he was looking for a pragmatic way out.

The North's "new appreciation" also included a sense that the situation was spinning out of its control. My mission was big news in America and around the world—the story of a relatively obscure congressman from New Mexico trying to defuse a crisis and bring the two helicopter pilots home. Every day without fresh news developments left a vacuum filled by rumors, including one that former president Jimmy Carter or the Reverend Jesse Jackson would be dispatched to North Korea to break the impasse. When my foreign-policy guy, Marquez, suggested that Carter's presence probably would be needed, I about took his head off. I'd been in tough negotiations before, and I was convinced I could do the job here.

Song, the deputy foreign minister, conveyed some sad news. Bobby Hall was fine, but David Hilemon had perished in the downing of their helicopter. I told Christopher about Hilemon's death that night; he said he'd make a public announcement after President Clinton talked to Hilemon's family, and I reiterated to my hosts that I wouldn't leave North Korea until my mission was completed.

We hit another wall of North Korean intransigence; nothing seemed to be happening. My original Asian agenda, which was to include visits to Indonesia and East Timor, was now ancient history, and Christopher was suggesting that I come home. I was deeply frustrated, but I kept insisting that he give me a bit more time. All I wanted was to be home by Christmas—with the two pilots.

Then, on Wednesday night, December 21, Song made his play. If I left Pyongyang the next morning, he said, I could escort Hilemon's remains across the Demilitarized Zone (DMZ) into South Korea and Hall would be released "very soon." I said "very soon" should mean before Christmas, which was an important date for Americans—a point I had made several times before. Hall's return on or before December 24 would be a suitable outcome. Song said he understood and suggested that Hall would be in the United States by Christmas, but it wasn't a promise or even a commitment.

I consulted with our U.S. State Department adviser, Dick Christianson, an invaluable resource as translator and a walking, talking encyclopedia on all things Korean. Dick said he would put me in touch with Colonel Ray Miller in Seoul. "Would I be leaving one of our men behind?" I asked Miller, a decorated Vietnam veteran. "Was this deal acceptable to our military?" Absolutely, he said. I had done my best and it was fine to take the deal. The U.S. military people in Seoul, Ray said, were proud of what I had done.

On Thursday morning, December 22, I was driven to the DMZ for the transfer of Hilemon's remains. But first, I had to settle up. The North Koreans had informed us a day earlier that while we were their houseguests, we made the long-distance calls on our own nickel. The bill was $10,000, payable on departure. The cash, in U.S. dollars, mysteriously moved from South Korea to North Korea, and only then did the solemn military ceremony proceed. The late David Hilemon, at least, was in friendly hands.

Later that day, in the VIP lounge of the airport in Seoul, I got a congratulatory call from President Clinton, who wanted to know how I did it, what the North Koreans were like, and whether they wanted a broader relationship with us. An American soldier saluted me, and the military command in Seoul treated me like royalty. The president and foreign minister of South Korea wanted to see me, as did Kim Dae-jung, the opposition leader, who later was elected president.

But Bobby Hall was still in captivity. Christmas came and went and Hall wasn't released. North Korea was now claiming publicly that the helicopter flight was intentional and therefore an act of espionage; according to the Korean Central News Agency, the United States had to "admit its responsibility as the offender," presumably before Hall would be released.

The day after Christmas, Clinton dispatched Thomas Hubbard, a deputy assistant secretary of state and a Korea expert, to meet with North Korean officials in Pyongyang. Hubbard crossed the DMZ into North Korea on December 28, a day after the North's news agency reported the results of the military's investigation. The conclusion, predictably, was that Hall and Hilemon were "criminals" and had engaged in espionage, and that the United States now had to "admit its responsibility as the offender" if it hoped to set things straight. The American side continued to insist that the two pilots got off course during a routine training mission limited to the South Korean side of the border. But the next day, the North's state news agency reported that Hall had confessed: "I admit that this criminal action is inexcusable and unpardonable," the pilot was quoted as saying. He apologized, the news agency said, for his "flagrant violation of international law."

If the North Koreans were angling for some sort of formal apology as the price of Hall's release, they came up short. On December 30, 1994, Hall was released to U.S. officials at the DMZ after Hubbard signed a document in which the United States government expressed "sincere regret for this incident." It also agreed to meetings "in an appropriate forum designed to prevent such incidents in the future." It was a fairly routine statement for what was, in fact, nothing more than a mistake. The official U.S. Army investigation of the incident described a series of minor factors that had caused the two pilots to overfly the border. The investigations recommended that "no administrative, nonjudicial, or judicial action be taken against any individual," and none was.

Hall got home for New Year's Eve with his family and I caught up with him, courtesy of a U.S. Air Force jet, on January 3, 1995, at MacDill Air Force Base in Tampa. Bobby Hall told me what I already knew—that the North Koreans had dictated the confession he signed. He also said he had no idea what was happening during his time in captivity until the North Koreans handed him the note I had written to him. Unfortunately, they didn't give it to him until the day he was released. Hall was generous in his comments about the work I had done on his behalf; he told me and several news organizations that he believed the reason he was not tortured, beaten, or denied decent food had to be my presence in North Korea at the time of his capture and the pressures I brought to bear during my days there.

I did have something to do with it; it would be false modesty to say otherwise. But my success also had to do with the bigger picture. There is no doubt in my mind that the North Koreans, at least then, were aware that a bad outcome could hurt or even destroy the better relationship they sought with the United States, a relationship that included tangible aid they desperately needed.

Several weeks later, I got a call from David Hilemon's mother, thanking me for all I had done to get her son's remains back home. It turned out she was a former constituent from Gallup, New Mexico. Later, I met David's sister at a town meeting and she thanked me in front of one hundred people. You never know; it really is a small world.

I VISITED North Korea three other times in the mid–1990s. In 1995, it was to make good on my promise to come back after the helicopter incident. I wanted to talk to military people about the framework agreement and about continuing efforts to resolve questions about U.S. servicemen missing in action—presumably killed—during the Korean War. Calvin Humphrey, the Intelligence Committee staffer with me on some previous trips, was aboard on this one, which led to momentary confusion when we met with a senior military officer. Our translator wasn't too precise about the rendering of Calvin's title—senior Democratic counsel. Somehow it came through as "undercover operative." The military guy heard it as "spy" and had a fit until another translator came to the rescue.

We left with no great accomplishments to speak of, except that I got a sense that the North Koreans were beginning to trust me, or at least trust that I would treat them with dignity and respect even during tough negotiations. They invited me back for a visit in late May 1996. North Korea had suffered through the worst floods in a century and urgently needed emergency food assistance if its people were to avoid widespread famine. I consulted with Clinton administration officials, but I did not travel as a special envoy of the president or carry a message from him to Kim Jong Il. My main objective was to urge the North Koreans to respond positively to a proposal for multilateral talks on a formal peace treaty ending the Korean War once and for all. The MIA issue also was on my agenda. The North Koreans said they would continue to move forward on MIA issues—we even visited an MIA site—and I sensed at least some modest give on the peace-treaty question. We discussed food aid, and I told them that while I couldn't speak for the administration, I would convey my opinion that severe shortages existed and that international assistance was badly needed. In fact, the administration later said it would donate a few million dollars in food aid, but unfortunately, North Korea never responded in kind by agreeing to the multilateral peace talks.

.   .   .

In August 1996, a twenty-six-year-old American, Evan C. Hunziker, got drunk and naked, climbed into the Yalu River, and swam across it from China to North Korea. Hunziker was a troubled missionary from Alaska whose mother was South Korean and whose father was a Korean War veteran. He might have thought this was one way to get in touch with his roots. Or he may have done it on a dare, as his father later suggested. Or he may have wanted to proselytize the atheists in North Korea. Whatever the explanation, the North Koreans tended to frown on unannounced visits to their country. After some farmers found him and turned him in, Hunziker was charged as a spy for South Korea. But the authorities soon realized that he was simply a confused young man. They signaled me that a visa application would be promptly processed and that I would be welcomed as a negotiator on Hunziker's behalf. On this one, I was an official envoy of the Clinton administration.

I arrived in Pyongyang in late November and got to the table immediately, but our talks didn't seem to be getting us very far. I wanted to free him and they wanted him out of their hair, but there were certain protocols to be observed first. The North Koreans don't much like give-and-take in negotiations; they believe you should give and they should take. They knew where we would wind up, I suspected, but first I had to jump through some hoops. Still, it was frustrating that they wouldn't even tell me whether Hunziker's health was good or bad. So I dusted off a line I had used before: "Can you at least tell me whether he still has his fingernails?" I said it with a straight face, and there was the predictable intake of breath after the translator finished. Then they all began to laugh and we got down to business.

They initially wanted Hunziker to pay a $100,000 fine for illegal entry into North Korea. It smelled like ransom money to me, and the United States doesn't pay ransom to free prisoners held abroad. We settled for a "hotel fee" of $5,000 to cover the cost of Hunziker's house arrest. On November 28, 1996, the North Koreans released Hunziker to my care. In the United States, it was the day before Thanksgiving.

On our flight to Tokyo, I had a chance to talk to Hunziker, a big, handsome kid who seemed largely incoherent and unfocused. I knew there would be reporters and cameras at Yokota Air Base, where our military transport was headed, but I felt this young man was in no condition to face them. We got off the plane, gestured to the crowd, then moved toward a waiting car.

It was a happy ending, except it wasn't. Evan Hunziker had gotten into trouble in Alaska, and there were three outstanding arrest warrants for him for drunken driving and assault. He wanted to go home, but he couldn't, his father said, because he feared jail. Drugs and booze were parts of his life, too, and he had trouble shaking them. In North Korea, he apparently tried to commit suicide, which may have been one reason the authorities there were eager to see him leave. In a hotel room in Tacoma, Washington, six days before Christmas 1996, less than a month after his release, Evan Hunziker put a gun to his head and killed himself.

Ten

By MARCH 1995, nearly four years after the Persian Gulf War ended, the United Nations Security Council had approved four resolutions demanding the identification and destruction of Iraq's weapons of mass destruction. The job of monitoring compliance was given to a United Nations Special Commission—UNSCOM for short. There would be an additional eight UN resolutions related to Iraq's weapons over the next four years. On December 17, 1999, UNSCOM was replaced with UNMOVIC, or the United Nations Monitoring, Verification, and Inspection Commission. The United States government likes alphabet-soup agencies, but it's an amateur compared with the bewildering bureaucracies of the United Nations.

Additional resolutions would follow, culminating in United Nations Resolution 1441—the one unanimously approved by the fifteen-member Security Council on November 8, 2002, that recalled all the other resolutions before and after the Persian Gulf War, determined that Iraq was in "material breach" of them, and gave Iraq one last chance to comply. Otherwise, the resolution said, Iraq would face serious consequences. Resolution 1441 passed a month after both houses of Congress gave President George W. Bush the authority to wage war, which he did on March 19, 2003. The consequences of those decisions are with us to this day.

But in 1995, despite tensions between Iraq and the United States, few people would have prophesied a second war in less than a decade. Despite worries about Saddam Hussein's unconventional weapons, Iraq in the mid-1990s was generally not regarded as the "gathering threat" to America described by President Bush in the run-up to the Iraq war and reinforced by Secretary of State Colin Powell's compelling presentation to the UN Security Council six weeks before the invasion. By most accounts, Iraq's military had suffered a devastating blow in the Gulf War, and punishing sanctions had sharply circumscribed Saddam's freedom of movement. Still, Saddam was capable of making mischief, where and when he could, and of seizing an opportunity when one landed in his lap. On March 13, 1995, one did.

This was when William Barloon of Hampton, Iowa, then thirty-nine, and David Daliberti of Jacksonville, Florida, then forty-one, oil mechanics working in Kuwait for U.S. defense contractors, got to a fork in the road, took the wrong turn, and found themselves in Iraq and under arrest by Saddam's border guards. There were hints in Iraq's state-controlled press of spying and potential sabotage. Not true: These guys had a couple of beers, set off in search of their buddies, and lost their bearings. For that, they were sentenced to eight years in Abu Ghraib Prison, where Saddam had locked up and tortured his real and imagined enemies over the decades—and where, less than a decade later, some American troops and intelligence officers abused and humiliated Iraqi prisoners. The Clinton administration, not contesting the charge of entering the country illegally, said it would press for the release of Barloon and Daliberti as a humanitarian gesture, but would make no concessions to Iraq. There would be no quid pro quo.

About a month later, I got my call from Peter Bourne. The Iraqis had called him, he said, to express their unhappiness with the state of negotiations over the fate of Barloon and Daliberti. As he told it, both Carter and the Reverend Jesse Jackson had talked to Iraq's representatives, but there was no movement and no prospect of it in the foreseeable future.

The Iraqis clearly were seeking a way out of what was an embarrassing episode at a particularly sensitive time. Saddam's people wanted to talk to someone they thought they could trust. That someone, Bourne insisted, was me. The Iraqis knew of my connections to the Clinton White House and the work I had done in North Korea and other hot spots, he said, and they considered me an honest broker. This was something of a backhanded compliment, considering the source. I was leery about getting involved with the Iraqis on any level, not least as a freelance diplomat. But in the end, I figured there was nothing lost in taking a first step. I contacted Clinton's national security adviser, Tony Lake, to let him know about the overture and to seek guidance.

Bourne arranged for me to meet in New York with Nizar Hamdoon, Iraq's ambassador to the United Nations. Over the next three months, Hamdoon and I met ten times at his official residence in New York, usually over a sumptuous Iraqi lunch. I briefed Lake's Middle East adviser, Mark Parris, after every session, but not many others in the administration were aware of my visits to New York. You need to keep things like this very quiet. United Nations Ambassador Madeleine Albright, for one, was kept out of the loop. Madeleine was a friend, embarked at the time on a campaign to depose UN Secretary-General Boutros Boutros-Ghali, who was considered unfriendly to U.S. interests.

My problem was that I kept running into her at the airport shuttle gates in New York and Washington, which required some creative invention on my part. One day, it would be a fictitious speech I had to deliver to a Hispanic group in New York, another day a visit to drum up business investment in New Mexico. So it went.

Hamdoon, an elegant rail of a man with a black mustache and a seemingly permanent smile, made plain what we already knew—the Iraqis wanted to free Barloon and Daliberti. By this time, the oil workers' wives were waging an effective international media campaign for the release of their husbands, who had become mute witnesses against the regime in the court of public opinion. Even the Clinton administration was feeling a little heat.

Still, in our first nine meetings, Nizar had asked for everything from the end of economic sanctions to medical equipment to be delivered by a third country. Not a chance, said Parris, Tony Lake's guy. Hamdoon's master in Baghdad also wanted something else, a letter from Clinton, expressing the American president's appreciation for the Iraqi dictator's gesture and a formal thank-you from the United States government for turning over the oil workers. No way, I kept telling Hamdoon. Nearing the end of the ninth meeting, Hamdoon insisted, one more time, on the Clinton letter and the public thank-you from the government. "Nizar, this just is not going to happen, and I'm out of here," I told him. This is sometimes a useful technique in negotiations with autocrats or their minions, because if talks are to be broken off, they want to be the ones to do it. Sure enough, Hamdoon called a week later and said I had to come back to talk.

"Screw you, Nizar, we're done."

His grasp of the English vernacular was excellent. "Really, Bill, we can do this. Let's meet one more time." We did and he tried, yet again, to play his losing hand. I said no. But I did say

I would make an appropriate statement, as a United States congressman, if the oil workers were released to me. We agreed, finally, that there would be no Clinton letter and no U.S. government thank-you note, but that any communiqué or statement by me would have to be negotiated with Iraqi Foreign Minister Tariq Aziz. The decision on whether to release the prisoners ultimately would fall to Saddam. "It will depend on how he feels when he meets you in Baghdad," Hamdoon said.

It took us a week to organize the logistics, get briefed by the State Department, and discuss how we would think about the upcoming trip to Baghdad. Once again, my chief aide was Calvin Humphrey, who had supported my efforts so well on previous trips to Africa and North Korea. On July 13, we flew from Dulles to Heathrow in London. We phoned Linda Barloon and Kathy Daliberti, to tell them that we were headed to Iraq and that we hoped to bring their husbands home. Then, we jumped a connecting flight to Amman, Jordan. We got to Amman in the early evening of July 14, a Friday, and were met by U.S. ambassador Wes Egan. His news wasn't comforting. Egan told us that there had been a clandestine radio broadcast at 2 P.M. the previous day, allegedly by opposition groups inside Baghdad; they claimed that Iraqi authorities had foiled an attempted escape by the two American prisoners. Egan's people thought this was disinformation, but the timing was weird. What was the point of putting out this stuff now? Was the regime fabricating a reason *not* to release Barloon and Daliberti? And if so, why? The embassy was concerned.

Egan also said that he had been in touch with Marwan Muasher, the chief of staff at the Jordanian royal palace—in effect, King Hussein's top aide—who was under the impression that I was carrying a message from President Clinton and was authorized to speak on behalf of the United States government. The ambassador disabused the Jordanians of these ideas, telling them I spoke only for myself as a United States congressman. "This is disturbing news," Egan quoted the palace chief of staff as saying.

I found it disturbing, too. Under American law, private citizens cannot talk to foreign governments "with the intent to influence the measures or conduct of any foreign government . . . in relation to any disputes or controversies with the United States" unless they are officially authorized by the president or his designee in the executive branch. The Logan Act, passed in 1799, came about after a Philadelphia Quaker named George Logan went to France carrying documents from Thomas Jefferson in an effort to avert a war with the young United States. Logan was never prosecuted, and I couldn't think of anyone who had ever been convicted of violating the Logan Act. But Logan had been raised as a potential sword against several people in recent years, dating back to the Vietnam War. There could always be a first time. I was feeling pretty lonely on this one.

I was a friend of the president, I told Egan and the Jordanians, but I was not his official envoy or in any way authorized to negotiate policy disputes between America and Iraq. King Hussein, when we met with him that evening, said he understood the distinction. He also said something that stuck with me. He said that Iraq is to Jordan what Mexico is to the United States. By that, he meant that Jordan and other Arab countries couldn't solve the problems in the greater Middle East without dealing with Iraq and its military and economic impact on the region. His point about Mexico, of course, was that the United States had to come to grips with the interconnected problems of immigration and poverty if it wanted a truly stable country on its southern border.

King Hussein was an imposing man despite his physically small stature, an articulate leader with a rich baritone voice that had become familiar to Americans from his many appearances on television news programs. Even more impressive was his wife, the American-born Queen Noor; with her regal bearing and deep convictions, she often dominated the conversation.

Next morning at first light, we set off by car for the Jordanian-Iraqi border, a distance of 210 miles or so. We had a U.S. Embassy driver and Jordanian security in two other vehicles. It took us nearly four hours to reach the border, because the closer we got, the heavier the traffic became. Merchants had erected sheds that lined the road for dozens of miles, and they were selling everything imaginable—clothing, electronic products, food, appliances, rugs, even cars. It amounted to a makeshift bazaar for Iraqis who could get across and made me wonder how effective the sanctions were after all.

At the border, we moved from an immigration center on the Jordanian side to an immigration center on the Iraqi side. I worked on our Iraqi escorts, who were almost certainly spies. I tried to establish a rapport that might be useful later, especially if we got into trouble. Maybe it worked, maybe it didn't. But I sensed that the Iraqis, deeply distrustful and hostile at first, started to warm up. One Iraqi guard said I looked like an Arab. I took it as a compliment, and told him so.

Then, an Iraqi driver and a guy riding shotgun took over. We piled into the back seat of a black Mercedes and took off, almost literally, followed by a fleet of lesser vehicles. At one point, I glanced at the speedometer and saw the needle tick past the 200-kilometer mark; we were doing nearly 130 miles an hour. High speeds don't bother me much, but I could see Calvin, on my right, sinking lower and lower in the seat. At that instant, I thought of Butch Cassidy telling the Sundance Kid in that unforgettable scene from the movie that the fall and not the swirling rapids probably would kill them. "You know, we'll probably crash before we get there and Saddam won't have to kill us," I deadpanned. The look on Calvin's face and a somber nod of agreement told me that he saw imminent death as a real possibility.

At this rate, with Baghdad a mere three hundred miles away, I figured we'd reach our hotel in the Iraqi capital within four or five hours, even with stops for gas and city traffic. What I didn't calculate was the impact of 125-degree temperatures on our vehicle. We would travel at top speed for, say, forty miles, and then stop because our Iraqi drivers needed to let the car cool down. Soon we also were forced to slow not by the condition of the road, which was reasonably good, but by what was strewn alongside it. The remnants of war were everywhere. Shards of glass and shell casings. Canisters of every size and shape. Burned-out military vehicles and even bits of uniforms. We didn't arrive at the Sheraton Hotel in Baghdad until early evening.

The hotel was plush but run-down. To get through the lobby, you had to step over a rug with the image of President George Bush the elder on it. I danced around it, drawing a frown from the hotel manager. We were met by the Polish chargé d'affaires, whose embassy represented United States interests in Iraq. He told us that he had no information on when we would see Saddam Hussein or even Foreign Minister Tariq Aziz, who would be my negotiating partner on the language of any communiqué. As far as I was concerned, it was just as well. I was dog-tired: I wanted food, then a bed.

The Sheraton was the best hotel in town, and its dining room produced a decent meal. The kitchen wasn't pressed, because there were only ten or fifteen other people in the room. It was a strange scene. The Iraqi dinar, the official currency, was maybe a dime short of worthless, which meant that some dinner guests were toting around bags of money to pay for their meals. Either our dinners were part of a Full American Plan or the Polish ambassador took care of it, but I don't recall us dipping into our wallets to pay the bill. Then it was time for sleep. We had a huge two-bedroom suite with a balcony that looked out on Baghdad. The skyline looked amazingly normal, given the beating Baghdad had taken barely four years earlier in the Persian Gulf War. Later, we learned that this was Saddam's version of a Potemkin Village: The Iraqis had rebuilt many of the façades of Baghdad's modern buildings, but inside they were unoccupied shells.

Sleep, it turned out, would have to wait. We had barely dumped our bags in our rooms when the Iraqis assigned to us said it was time to meet Tariq Aziz. "It's 10 P.M.," I said. "At this hour?" Yes, one of them said, right now.

They drove us to the Foreign Ministry, a modern building that wasn't a shell. Tariq Aziz, decked out in green military fatigues, was in a spacious air-conditioned office with nice American-style furniture and an adjacent conference room. This was the guy, I remembered, who refused to budge when Secretary of State James A. Baker III met with him in Geneva on January 9, 1991, in Baker's last-ditch effort to find a diplomatic solution before the war.

Aziz was cordial enough, but he staked out positions that were impossible for me to satisfy. As if my conversations with Nizar Hamdoon meant nothing, he said the Iraqis expected a letter from Clinton acknowledging the humane act of setting convicted criminals free. And he wanted a commitment to a follow-up visit—in writing. He had drafts of the documents already prepared and asked us to examine them. We moved into the conference room, and Calvin told me I couldn't sign either piece of paper. He was right.

Over the next hour, we fiddled with language, went back to Aziz, then back to the conference room. In the end, we never signed either document. "I'm a congressman, not part of the executive branch of government," I finally said to Aziz, getting a little excited. "You know the difference, don't you?" He did, he

said with a tight smile, he knew of the Logan Act and he respected United States law. He also said that a top aide to King
Hussein, Marwan Qassem, had called him to report a conversation with Wes Egan, the American ambassador in Amman. The
ambassador told Qassem, the head of the king's royal court, that
Richardson was not an official envoy. I'd never said I was, but I
also thought, Shit, they're already disowning me.

We moved on to other matters, and Aziz did most of the talking. UNSCOM inspectors were about to pay another visit to
Iraq, specifically to investigate the issue of Iraq's biological
weapons. He insisted that Iraq had satisfied all the requirements of
United Nations Resolution 687, Section C, requiring Iraq to destroy weapons of mass destruction and related production facilities under international supervision. But he argued that nothing
would satisfy the U.S. government, which kept moving the goal-
posts. Calvin was taking contemporaneous notes and wrote the
following in his green notebook:

"Tariq Aziz: This is a position that truly means the U.S. government will not support lifting of sanctions until the current
government is removed. The last two administrations have done
their best to ensure that sanctions are not removed and that the
government is toppled." He added that Iraq was approaching a
crossroads. "Iraq seriously wants to normalize relations with the
United Nations Security Council. That is why Iraq is agreeing to
Bill Richardson's demands. It is a difficult sacrifice, but Iraq is
willing to do it to normalize. But if there is no prospect of normalization, then why should Iraq continue to implement sanctions? Only two reasons: Iraq is made up of fools, which we are
not. Iraq is afraid of being bombed, which we are not."

Aziz dismissed Madeleine Albright's insistence that the main
concern was democracy and human rights in Iraq. "There are
other more important reasons in formulating policy," Aziz said.

"Saudi Arabia has a terrible record [on human rights], yet you have normal relations with them." He also cited China and Russia. "All we need is an honest dialogue," he went on. "It should not be difficult to achieve a reasonable level of understanding—not one hundred percent, but reasonable and possibly more reasonable than U.S. relations with other countries." Toward the end of a long soliloquy, he said, "When we get into another crisis, everybody will suffer—not just Iraq, but everybody."

I interrupted only a couple of times, to tell him that complying with the sanctions was important to eventual normalization and to reiterate that I could not speak for the United States government either on Iraqi-American bilateral relations or on the U.S. role in multilateral organizations such as the United Nations.

He understood. He obviously wanted to get a lot off his chest that night. He told us to be ready to meet Saddam the following morning—and that while the release of the prisoners was possible, it was by no means guaranteed, especially if Saddam got angry during our audience with him. He also insisted that a statement by President Clinton showing his gratitude for the release of Barloon and Daliberti was crucial and that its absence posed a possible roadblock. The president would make no such statement, I told him.

Tariq Aziz, which means "glorious past" in Arabic, was a member of the Chaldean Catholic Church, the "Church of the East," which traces its beginning to the preaching of Jesus Christ's disciples in ancient Mesopotamia between A.D. 37 and 65. A half-million Chaldeans lived in Iraq. What mattered most to Aziz was his religion, his wife and family, and Saddam Hussein, though not necessarily in that order. He also liked good cigars, a passion we shared. Nizar Hamdoon had briefed me on Tariq, and I had made a mental note to try to establish a connection with him based on our common religious background. The tension between us eased when I told him that I was a Catholic and that I wanted to attend services. Maybe my wife will take you, he said.

Around noon the next day, we headed for our meeting with Saddam. Our Iraqi drivers took us into a compound of palaces, outbuildings, ponds, and gardens. We went through several checkpoints, manned by uniformed armed guards and buttressed by sandbags, and pulled up to the entrance of one particularly impressive palace. Amazingly, there was no security at the gate at all. But as we drove through, we looked directly at an armored personnel carrier, its gun lined up perfectly with the front entrance. The building itself was huge, with what seemed to be dozens of ornate and empty rooms. Where was everybody? This was when we were taken into the room with the men hiding behind the curtains that I've already mentioned.

Calvin Humphrey's notes provide more details of my meeting with Saddam Hussein. After he came back into the room after my gaffe with the shoe, I launched into something of a speech.

"On behalf of the American people and President Clinton, I would like to request the release of the two Americans in your custody. The release would be viewed as an important humanitarian gesture. I am just one politician in a government with many pockets of power. Congress has a lot of power and influence in the international relations field. We do not always agree with the president; in fact, I did not vote for the war, because I believed further diplomatic activity should have been pursued. And I hoped the meeting between Tariq Aziz and Jim Baker would have been the start of that activity." (Later, when I became United Nations ambassador and had to deal with Saddam again, I realized that my congressional vote on the war had been a mistake.)

"I am a close friend of President Clinton," I went on. "I have taken a number of diplomatic initiatives such as this. . . . I am not an official envoy. I don't work for President Clinton and I cannot negotiate for him or for the United States. But the president, Vice President Al Gore, and Secretary of State Warren Christopher are all aware of my visit. I spoke with them in the last week and advised them in detail of my mission and my intentions. Mark Parris of Tony Lake's staff has been my contact in the administration. But I want to make it clear, abundantly clear, that I do not work for the president. He cannot fire me and I am not his envoy.

"If this effort is to succeed, you must begin to trust me. Additionally, there must be complete trust and confidence among the four of us." By that, I meant the two of us, Calvin and Tariq Aziz.

"I have come to Iraq to try to resolve this humanitarian problem. We treated this as completely confidential, except for people in the Clinton administration. The current relationship is not helpful for Iraqi citizens or the United States, and it has potentially drastic implications for the entire region, including the Israeli–Palestinian problem. Should you release the two Americans, I believe the American people would appreciate this humanitarian gesture."

I'd made my case. The meeting was now into the second hour, and Tariq Aziz was sitting in the back, motionless. Now what? There was a silence of about two minutes, with Saddam staring at me with his small eyes; then he spoke.

Saddam said he appreciated my comments and gave us his word that the entire matter would be treated confidentially. Then he got to the point: "Based on the principles that you have appealed to me, and on the respect that you have shown me, and the request of Bill Clinton, and the long journey you have taken without any reassurances, I will use the constitutional powers vested in me in the Iraqi constitution and release the two individuals to your custody. You will be able to take them with you." I immediately said that he was doing the right thing and instinctively put a hand on his arm in a gesture of goodwill. Saddam started, the only emotion he'd shown the entire time except for his bolting over the display of my heel, and along the wall, eight hands suddenly touched sidearms. But Saddam composed himself, the Republican Guard relaxed, and Iraq's dictator in chief continued.

"I hope this humanitarian gesture will be noted by the leadership in the administration, by the Congress, and by the international community. And that I and Tariq Aziz can call on you for further dialogue in an effort to avoid further confrontation, which can and should be avoided.

"However, I want to be certain, in regard to the two individuals, that the Iraqi courts have acted in a just and honorable manner. The court has issued harsher sentences for non-Americans accused of illegally crossing the border. And this includes Arabs as well. In accordance with the law, courts pass sentences, but I can't deny that the courts, when considering a case involving Americans, [may] be influenced by the state of relations between Iraq and the United States. But I am not accusing them of that. The courts acted appropriately." This homage to Iraqi justice and the rule of law was touching, but I knew it was bullshit, and somehow I sensed that he knew I knew it was bullshit. We both knew the only law that mattered in Iraq was Saddam's law.

Saddam went into a monologue about U.S.-Iraqi relations, essentially arguing that Washington was entirely to blame for the breach. "Until August 2, 1990, our relations were generally good with the West and the East. We had good, balanced relations with Britain, France, Germany, and the United States. We don't want to discuss what happened on August 2 [the day Iraq invaded Kuwait], because that will be a long talk, and it gives us heartburn."

He maintained that Iraq was never a threat to America. I didn't interrupt him, because I didn't want to take a chance he'd have second thoughts about our guys. Still, I was tempted to note that seizing a neighboring country, which happened to be a major oil exporter, and threatening Saudi Arabia, a U.S. ally and the nation with the world's largest oil reserves, added up to a threat to the United States in my book. And that didn't even take account of the unconventional weapons programs he had started.

I kept my counsel and we made it out of the palace to the Polish Embassy, where we picked up the two Americans. The Iraqis insisted on trying to spin the meeting. While we were waiting for Barloon and Daliberti, the Iraqi News Agency was breaking the story the way its boss wanted it broken: "President Saddam Hussein told Richardson that he accepts the plea by President Bill Clinton, the Congress, and the American people. His excellency issued an order . . . to pardon the two detainees and set them free immediately." The Iraqis, in other words, wanted to make it sound as if I was an official envoy after all. I set the record straight in my statement to the international press: "I undertook this mission as a member of Congress and not as a presidential envoy. There was no quid pro quo or concessions. President Clinton's quiet but firm diplomacy on the prisoners' behalf was effective. I commend the Iraqi government for taking this positive humanitarian action."

Eleven

I WAS ELEVEN YEARS OLD when Fidel Castro seized power in Cuba. For people of my generation, for people of every living generation in America, Castro has proved an enduring, familiar, and irritating presence in our lives. Is there any foreign leader with greater name recognition in the United States? Saddam Hussein, I suppose, if he were still the dictator of Iraq, and maybe Queen Elizabeth. But Castro may top the list because of his remarkable staying power and outsized role in our political life. He played bait-and-switch at the beginning—first suggesting he was a democrat at heart, then coming out of the closet as a dedicated Marxist and Communist. For three decades, his Cuba was the Soviet Union's proxy puppet in our neck of the woods, no farther away from our shores than Philadelphia is from New York City. He played his hand with skill, frustrating U.S. presidents from Eisenhower forward, and occasionally menacing us, to which anyone with memories of the Cuban Missile Crisis can attest.

In the middle 1990s, even given the end of the Cold War, anti-Cuban sentiment in the U.S. Congress still ran high, stimulated in part by the Cuban American National Foundation, the powerful lobby of anti-Castro exiles founded in 1981 and based in Miami. By 1995, there was a bill before Congress that actually proposed to stiffen the trade embargo. Its sponsors, Republican senator Jesse Helms of North Carolina and Republican representative Dan Burton of Indiana, were taking aim at foreign companies that invested in properties confiscated without compensation from United States firms by Castro's Communist government. Under the proposed law, executives and majority shareholders of such foreign companies could be denied U.S. visas. U.S. companies also could sue these foreigners in American courts if they could demonstrate that the foreign firm profited from seized U.S. property in Cuba.

President Clinton opposed Helms–Burton as an infringement on his foreign-policy powers; many prominent American businessmen opposed it as well. But the Republicans now controlled both houses of Congress, having swept to victory in the off-year elections of 1994, and they were exercising their political muscle with considerable skill.

Over the years, particularly after the end of the Cold War, the Cubans had sent signals that they would welcome a visit by me to Havana. But my first trip didn't come until mid-January 1996, when Cuban-American relations were becoming increasingly difficult. One source of the tension was Helms–Burton. Another was the growing number of flights close to, and occasionally in, Cuban airspace by a Cuban exile group in Florida called Hermanos al Rescate, or Brothers to the Rescue, which dropped leaflets, engaged in search-and-rescue operations for people fleeing Cuba, and otherwise badgered the Castro government.

As usual, I was not traveling to Cuba as an envoy of President Clinton; I was going as a member of the House Intelligence Committee, once again with Calvin Humphrey of the committee staff to assist me. Tony Lake, Clinton's national security adviser, was aware of my upcoming visit and curious about the outcome. He asked me to coordinate with Peter Tarnoff, undersecretary of state for political affairs, if anything interesting developed.

Cuban–U.S. relations had fascinated me ever since my first experiences with the issue as a staffer for the Wednesday Group on Capitol Hill. Later, members of the Cuban American National Foundation, eager to influence the views of a Hispanic congressman, had sponsored several Miami fundraisers for me over the years. I had struck up a friendship with Jorge Mas Canosa, the rabid anti-Castro business tycoon who had started the foundation and who harbored ambitions to be Cuba's first post-Castro president. (Mas Canosa died in 1997 at the age of fifty-eight.)

My views on the Cuban issue were conflicted. On the one hand, I felt the embargo was not working and was wasting precious political capital in Latin America. After all, the end of the Cold War had undermined the larger geopolitical rationale for the embargo and the logic of those who insisted on the status quo. On the other hand, I found Castro's human-rights record, his treatment of political dissidents, and his antipathy toward free elections downright abhorrent. One thing was certain: I desperately wanted to visit Cuba to see for myself.

Back in New Mexico there was another solid reason to travel to Cuba. In 1971, three men—Michael Robert Finney, Charles Hill, and Ralph Lawrence Goodwin—allegedly shot and killed Robert Rosenbloom, a New Mexico state trooper, during a routine stop on Interstate 40. They got away and, days later, hijacked a TWA jet in Albuquerque and ordered the pilot to fly to Havana, where they were given asylum by the Cuban government. I had been in touch with Rosenbloom's wife, Linda, and had a list of several dozen American fugitives, including Finney and Hill, who were thought to be in Cuba. Goodwin had died in the intervening years. Castro, meanwhile, was publicly floating the idea that the general issue of criminal exiles like Finney and Hill could be discussed in the context of improving U.S.-Cuban relations.

Castro is a notorious night owl. In those days, his routine was to get up at eleven in the morning, read newspapers and brief himself for his day's work, and hold his first appointment mid-afternoon. He was famous for scheduling meetings with foreign officials at all hours of the night and early morning, and I figured my treatment would be no different. It wasn't: I met with him twice, once during the day, and once late at night in a session that didn't end until past three the next morning and included dinner in a banquet room adjacent to the conference room.

Richardson's Rules

- It helps to be in good shape. You never know when you're going to be called to the negotiating table.

I found Castro a very personable guy, engaging and humorous. He had more dandruff than I'd ever seen on anyone. He was extremely well informed, especially about American politics. Castro showed me a towering pile of paper that was his day's reading. He said he liked Clinton and that he'd never do anything to hurt him, like praise him publicly. We spoke in Spanish, with someone translating for Calvin, and covered a wide range of issues, including human rights, the release of jailed dissidents, and the fees Castro's government charged any Cuban who wanted to emigrate to the United States.

At the time, Cuba charged anyone who sought to emigrate to the United States $600 for exit documents. This was a ridiculously high figure, prohibitive to thousands who wanted to leave the island. The "Richardson Agreement" with Castro cut that figure in half for up to a thousand Cubans per year who could demonstrate financial hardship. Castro suggested, without making a promise, that we could build on this agreement, perhaps leading to the relaxation of restrictions in other areas.

I was in Havana for three nights on this trip and decided to use one of them to check out the local baseball talent. Cuba is a baseball-crazy country, but the game I saw was all offense and no defense. The score was something like 17–12. Later, Castro and I got to talking baseball. He had been a pretty good player in his younger days and was still a baseball nut, and he knew that I'd played quite a bit myself. I couldn't resist needling him: "Mr. President, I went to a game and the hitting was great, but Cuban baseball needs better pitching."

"No, no," he said, "you must have gone to the wrong game." But I'd done my homework and learned that the lowest earned run average in the Cuban league was 4.20, which would bench a lot of pitchers in major-league baseball. Castro got a little testy when I told him that, but it wasn't serious; he respected me because I knew my baseball.

I left Havana with no concrete promises on human rights or the fate of the political prisoners whose release I'd sought, but there were enough hints that I thought we might get some movement in a couple of months.

Richardson's Rules

· **Find common ground and establish a personal connection.**

It came sooner than that. I had given Castro's ambassador to the United Nations, Fernando Remirez, a list of ten dissidents that I wanted released, names I received from Frank Calzon of Human Rights Watch in Washington. I was traveling in my car to Pecos, New Mexico, when the Cuban ambassador called. Fidel probably would give me four or five people, he said, but I had to come to Cuba to get them. So in early February, I went back to Havana with the expectation, if not the explicit promise, that some political prisoners would be turned over to me.

This time, it was to be a quick trip, less than twenty-four hours, and I desperately wanted Isabelle Watkins, my chief of staff, to join me. One of the people I thought Castro might free was Carmen Arias Iglesias, an activist who was locked up in 1992 because she spoke out in favor a stronger trade embargo on Cuba. Her "home" for the four years since then had been a notorious prison outside Havana known for its overpopulation, windowless cells, and terrible health care. I had no idea what kind of physical and especially psychological condition Arias would be in, and I thought Isabelle—with her kind heart and great common sense—might provide critical emotional support.

There was only one problem, Isabelle explained to me: Since I was going in my capacity as a member of the Intelligence Committee, I would need approval from the speaker of the House for a staff member to tag along. The new Republican speaker was Newt Gingrich. We had worked closely together to get NAFTA through the House in late 1993, but I had no idea how he would react to this request from a Democrat, and one who might have some laurels tossed his way if he managed to pull off a prisoner release. Newt was terrific, essentially saying that if Bill Richardson insisted his chief of staff was necessary on this trip, it was good enough for him.

Castro and I spent more than two hours Friday night, February 9, 1996, talking about the political prisoners he said he would release to me. Arias, then thirty-one, was among them, and she was in better shape than we had any reason to expect. The others were Luis Grave de Peralta, who had publicly backed Arias when she advocated a tightened embargo, and Eduardo Ramón Prida, a physicist by training whose crime was nothing more than vocal support for a free-market economy in Cuba. I tried to convince Castro to release others on my original list, at one point telling him, "Look, you released more than forty to Jesse Jackson, and all I'm asking for is ten. Do you favor blacks over Hispanics? Do something here for your fellow Hispanics." In 1984, as part of what he called a "moral offensive," the Reverend Jesse Jackson had gotten Castro to release forty-nine prisoners. Castro laughed and laughed at my appeal, but he would go no further than the three.

With the released dissidents in tow, we flew from Havana to Miami in a U.S. Air Force jet, thanks to the intervention of State's Peter Tarnoff. I had pressed Castro to release the families of the three people he was turning over to my care, and he left me with the impression that he would in the near future. Under the circumstances, I told Arias, Prida, and Grave on the flight back, it would be wise to watch what you say to the press, at least until your relatives join you in the States. Arias and Prida understood that bashing Castro immediately after their release could cause the Cuban dictator to reverse course and keep their relatives in Cuba. But Grave couldn't resist the temptation to unload on Castro when reporters met with us in Miami. It's my understanding that Arias and Prida got some of their relatives out, but so far as I know, Grave's relatives remain in Cuba to this day.

Castro was keenly interested in American politics. He loved to show off how much he knew. But he knew what he didn't know, and he wasn't shy about asking questions to fill in the blanks. It was a presidential election year, and he knew a lot about Clinton and liked what he'd seen and read. But he was less informed about the Republican side, and during our visits, he pressed me hard on the primaries. Senate Majority Leader Bob Dole of Kansas was expected to be the nominee, mainly by virtue of his many years of distinguished service in Congress. But there was a long cast of characters lined up to challenge him that included two other heavyweight senators (Richard Lugar of Indiana and Phil Gramm of Texas) and an eclectic bunch of mavericks such as conservative columnist Pat Buchanan and magazine publisher Steve Forbes. Castro seemed particularly intrigued by Forbes, who represented new economic thinking, he believed, even though he didn't agree with any of it.

I am no fan of Castro's politics and the repression he has visited upon the Cuban people for the past forty-six years. But all in all, he probably was the best-informed foreign leader I met during that period in the mid-1990s. He could talk with knowledge and authority about geopolitical issues—the crisis in the Balkans, the Israeli-Palestinian situation, the United States as the only remaining superpower, and Russia's struggling economy—as well as the wide range of domestic challenges facing the president and Congress in Washington.

In late February, a couple of weeks after my second Havana trip, I was in Bangladesh trying to negotiate the release of Eliadah "Lia" McCord, a young Houston woman who had made a dumb mistake four years earlier when she agreed to carry a few pounds of heroin for a new acquaintance and got busted. She received a life sentence, but Lia had been a model prisoner, and even our own Drug Enforcement Administration thought she deserved clemency because of the help she had provided both the Bangladeshis and the DEA in busting some drug dealers. I learned about Lia when I went to Bangladesh to monitor elections, and although it took a couple of trips to plead her case, she finally was released to me in late July 1996 and I brought her home.

So I was a long way from Washington or Havana on February 24, 1996, when two Cuban MiG fighter jets shot down two Cessna Skymaster twin-engine planes piloted by members of Brothers to the Rescue. The Cuban government claimed the planes had violated its airspace and had even ignored a warning from air traffic control in Havana. Cuban exiles in Miami said the planes were still well beyond Cuba's twelve-mile territorial limit and over international waters at the time they were shot down. There was no question, however, that Cuba had violated international agreements that outlawing military attacks on civilian aircraft.

Clinton said the right things about what had happened, condemning the attack as "an appalling reminder of the nature of the Cuban regime" and taking some steps to respond, such as suspending all air charters between the United States and Cuba. He also signaled that he would work with members of Congress who favored Helms-Burton, which by that time was in a conference committee whose members were trying to reconcile differences between the House and Senate versions of the bill. A few weeks later, in March, Clinton signed the Cuban Liberty and Democratic Solidarity Act of 1996—the formal name for Helms-Burton—into law, with relatives of the dead pilots in attendance at the White House ceremony.

Postscript: There was some speculation in the media that my meetings with Castro contained an explicit or implicit quid pro quo—that in exchange for the release of political prisoners, the United States would put the brakes on flights in and around Cuban airspace by Brothers to the Rescue. This was categorically false. First, I had no authority to make such a pledge. Second, I said nothing to Castro suggesting that I would try to persuade President Clinton to do something about the flights. Anyone who said otherwise then was either misinformed or was moved to speak by considerations that had nothing to do with the truth.

Twelve

WHEN I WAS ABOUT to leave on a foreign negotiating adventure, my mother usually asked the question any mother would ask if she sensed a child moving toward potential danger: "Why do you have to go, Billy? Can't they find someone else?" I always tried to assure her that the risks were minor, even if they were somewhat more than that, and she grudgingly accepted that these trips had become a part of my life—a part she knew I loved. She was concerned, but she never panicked at the prospect of her son going off to Africa or Iraq or North Korea. My mother was not then, and isn't now, a woman easily given to panic.

So I was surprised on the morning of Friday, April 19, 1996, when Barbara came into our bathroom in Washington and interrupted my shower with an announcement: "Your mother's on the phone and she's hysterical." In the next breath, she told me why: "Vesta's been kidnapped." It was half past seven in Washington, an hour earlier in Mexico City, where my mother lived at the time.

My sister Vesta is a clinical pediatrician. Her life had gone in a different direction from mine in that she has remained more attached to Mexico. She had gone to school in Mexico—my mother put her foot down and told my father she wasn't going to have her second child taken away from her, too. More recently, following a divorce, she had moved to Cuernavaca from Boston to open and become director of the city's first children's hospital. Around midnight the previous evening, Vesta called our mother using her cell phone. She was okay, she said, but she'd been kidnapped.

The people who'd taken her wanted to talk to Mother, whom Vesta had identified as her closest family member. One of the kidnappers got on and told Mother to go to Cuernavaca and await further instructions from them. It occurred to me that my mother had waited six and a half hours before she called me; she obviously had been up all night with this, but she didn't want to alarm me with a call in the wee hours. That's the way she was, always thinking of others, never herself.

Having been so brave through the night, she was now letting her emotions take over. She wanted me to call the president of Mexico. She talked about getting the U.S. Embassy involved and perhaps the CIA. She was being a mother, and she wanted to go all out. No, I said, let me think about what to do. I told Mother that I wanted to ask Willie Lombera to go to Cuernavaca to manage this for us. Willie, a banker in Mexico City, was a first cousin who had a good friend working for the governor of the state of Morelos, Jorge Carrillo Olea. He could make the initial contact with the local and state authorities.

This was my sister, the kid sister who idolized her big brother when we were growing up, who always seemed to be around when my friends were over, who gamely volunteered to play catch with me once and ended up with a broken nose because she had no idea how to handle even a softly thrown baseball. I still called her *bebe,* even though she was a talented adult.

Yet at that moment I reverted to form and became a prisoner of process. I asked myself, Is this just a random kidnapping or is this a political kidnapping tied to me? Willie could get a reading from the local authorities. Then I thought, What if the local authorities are involved? Kidnapping prominent people or their relatives—people who could pay big ransoms—had become a chronic problem in Mexico. Too often, police and politicians *were* involved. I needed a reality check. Luis Telles was then chief of staff to Ernesto Zedillo, the president of Mexico; we'd gotten to know each other over the years, and I knew I could trust him. I explained the situation to him and asked for his guidance. He said he would call back that night and that I'd probably hear from Zedillo as well.

Later, they called on a conference line. Our best information, they said, was that this was a random thing, strictly local. The worst thing you could do, they added, was to get engaged in it yourself and call in the Marines. Telles said that they needed to let the Cuernavaca police and Carrillo take the first crack at the case. You should know, Zedillo chimed in, that we'll have some of our people, federal investigators, undercover in Morelos to make sure the police are playing it straight. It sounded right.

What had happened the previous night was an example of the law of unintended consequences. Vesta had attended an evening meeting of a women doctors' group at the Hostería Las Quintas, a hotel on the edge of Cuernavaca. After a light supper with other doctors, she headed home around half past ten. But instead of taking big, brightly lit roads, she wanted to get home as fast as she could to see her two sons, ages ten and eight, before they went to sleep. The shortcut went through one of Cuernavaca's best neighborhoods, a quiet area of big, walled-off houses and not very good lighting. She was still playing by Boston rules, where vigilance about the possibility of kidnapping wasn't second nature among confident professional women. Vesta spotted a parked car, thought nothing of it, then suddenly found its headlights in her rearview mirror. Before she knew it, the car was around and in front of her, forcing her to stop. Three guys with guns got out and started banging on her window. She thought it was a mugging—that they wanted the van and her purse—so she opened the door and offered the keys and her bag. But the leader told the others to get her into their car, and one of them split her lip slapping her with the barrel of his gun. That's when it dawned on Vesta that she was being abducted.

The kidnappers stuffed Vesta into their car and headed for Yautepec, an old Aztec city about ninety minutes' drive away. They arrived at a house and locked her in one of its bedrooms. But she could hear their conversation in the adjacent room. In response to their earlier questions, she said she worked at a hospital and that her family included her mother, three cousins, and a brother, who lived in the States. Now they were going through Vesta's purse for the first time and discovering that there was more to her story. She had a card from Carrillo, who had hired her to run the children's hospital, that included her title. And she had a card that identified me as a U.S. congressman, complete with my phone numbers. "Oh, we've got a big fish here," she heard one of them say. Vesta recalled being frightened, but it was only at that moment she realized the situation could get dangerous.

The men asked her questions about how close she was to the governor and how important her brother was. Vesta was scared, but she wasn't suddenly struck stupid. To the contrary, she understood intuitively that it was important to minimize everything. They'd been to the States and knew what a congressman was, but they didn't have much grasp of the details. Oh, he works in a small town in New Mexico, she told them, and represents his people. He doesn't get very involved in anything but local affairs. They dropped it and focused on Carrillo, the Morelos governor. Well, she said, I hardly know him; there must be thousands of people who have this card from him. They dropped him, too. But they had her watch and her earrings, and they started to question her about her jewelry. Well, yes, she had been given some jewelry by our mother, but not much.

The sleeping arrangements at the house were simple: A single king-size bed accommodated Vesta on one side and one of the kidnappers on the other; the other two slept on the floor. What these guys wanted was money. Sexual violence, thank God, was not part of their agenda. But Vesta knew she was still in peril, so she did another smart thing that first night. She figured that if these guys didn't think she was dangerous or very bright, they might not harm her. She feigned a deep yawn, then said, "I'm really tired. It's been dark and I haven't really seen you guys and I don't want to see you again. I want you to be sure I won't be able to recognize you, so please give me something to cover my eyes." They thought this was a great idea and gave her a scarf to cover her eyes and tie in the back. It obscured her vision until she could hear all three of them snoring; at that point, she edged the scarf up just enough to get a good look at her captors.

In the early evening of Friday, April 19, the leader of the kidnappers, who we later learned was a nineteen-year-old named José Luis Ponce, called Vesta's house in Cuernavaca, expecting our mother to answer the phone per his earlier instructions. Instead, Willie Lombera picked up. Ponce was furious and started to scream at Vesta: You told me you had no family? Who is this man who answers the phone? He sounds like he's crying when he talks. Willie had a tremulous voice that got worse when he was nervous. That has to be Willie, one of my three cousins, she said. You can trust him.

Ponce made a ransom demand—half a million pesos, about 50,000 U.S. dollars. By then, of course, a unit of local and state police had moved into Vesta's house for security and to coach Willie on negotiating. He told Ponce that he was new at this and that given the amount of money, he would need time to consult with our mother. They agreed to talk the next day. Willie called me. The Cuernavaca police were recommending that we pay them 200,000 pesos, or $20,000, and suggesting that we could get my sister out safely, apprehend the bad guys, and get our money back, too. This sounded strange to me, so I got back to Telles and asked him to check with their undercover people. He got back to me within an hour: Don't do anything yet, he said. We think there's something dirty here.

That night, it so happened we were giving an engagement party for Barbara's brother John and his fiancée Lisa. We got the call that morning and didn't say anything all day to John or Lisa. As you can imagine, it was excruciating, knowing this was the first day of Vesta's capture, but we did it.

I told Willie to say no when the kidnappers called on Saturday. I was thinking to myself, I want my sister's safety, but I was also thinking, You're not supposed to negotiate for ransom. I was still convinced that it was an inside, local thing, because there was no press. It wasn't about me or that they were trying to get some money from the gringos. Meanwhile, my mother was desperate, urging me to give them whatever they wanted. I said, just wait, Mother. I know how to do these things. I won't do anything to jeopardize Vesta's safety.

On Saturday, they called and let Willie talk to Vesta. She said she was fine, was being fed, and wasn't hurt, although we learned later that she was nursing her split lip. She urged Willie to do what they were asking. The Cuernavaca police were now saying they thought a deal could be done for 100,000 pesos, or $10,000. But Telles had urged me to keep the negotiation going, so I told Willie to tell them no, with a new wrinkle: Maybe we should give them some of Vesta's jewelry. Willie doubted they'd bite, but I told him to try and to make it convincing. When Ponce called again, Willie offered Vesta's jewelry, saying her collection was worth at least a half-million pesos and probably much more. Ponce wasn't dumb; he told Willie, Look, your cousin has described these jewels perfectly to me, so make sure you put all of them in the bag for us. Vesta hadn't done any such thing, and the jewelry combined wasn't worth that much; it was mainly sentimental heirlooms.

The deal went down late Sunday night, with a male cousin of Vesta's maid handing over the bag to the kidnappers on a pedestrian walkway over a highway. By one o'clock Monday morning, the men were back at their safe house, and Vesta could hear them dividing her jewelry into three parts. Five hours later, they said they would release her. But they thought it would look a bit strange for a woman to be sitting in the back seat of a car with a scarf covering her eyes so they took back their blindfold and gave her dark sunglasses and a magazine instead. Her instructions were to wear the glasses, close her eyes, and keep the magazine close to her face. She followed orders except for the part about keeping her eyes shut. Vesta saw everything.

Two of the three kidnappers—José Luis Ponce and his seventeen-year-old brother Carlos—took Vesta to a main road in Cuernavaca, stopped the car, and told her to get out, with a final warning: Don't report this to the police or do anything else about it if you know what's good for you and your kids. Then they were gone. Vesta hailed a taxi. She rang her front doorbell, gave

Willie a big hug when he answered, and told him to pay the driver. Then she called her mother and her brother to tell us she was fine, and headed for a hot bath.

Her two boys, Blaine and Jorge, had been deposited at a cousin's house and told that their mother had a hospital-related crisis that required nearly nonstop work through a long weekend. Jorge, my godson, accepted the explanation, but his older brother Blaine was suspicious. Still, even Blaine didn't pay much mind when she showed up after her ordeal. Oh, hi, Mom, he said, then went back to play with our cousin's kids.

After I contacted Telles, the Mexican feds had put out the word to the Cuernavaca police that they shouldn't screw around with this. There clearly was some dirty business going on, with certain locals getting cuts from kidnappers. It was important that I'd touched base with the president of Mexico. The local and state cops knew who I was and that there would be consequences if something happened to my sister.

Vesta was after the kidnappers almost immediately. One Cuernavaca investigator involved in her case told her to take a week or so before she came back to help track down the bad guys. She was in his office two days later. She described in minute detail how to get to the house where she had been held, including fairly accurate time estimates from spot to spot. That surprised the cops, because the kidnappers had taken her watch. How do you know these distances? Well, she said, five Hail Marys would take this long and seven Our Fathers would take that long. Really, that's how she was able to give them estimates.

Still, they seemed to be having trouble finding it. She spent two successive nights with small commando units, scary guys dressed entirely in black and armed with assault rifles, who went from little town to little town in search of the house. Frustrated, she finally talked to their boss and described the house and where she thought it was. He said he knew exactly which *colonia,* or district, she was talking about. On April 30, eight days after her release, Carlos Ponce, the ringleader's younger brother, walked into the house to pick up some things he'd left behind. The police called Vesta at midnight to tell her the news; she identified him the next morning. He was tried and convicted, but given a light sentence for kidnapping—a mere ten years—because he was said not to be a threat to society. Not a threat? My sister is tough. She knew he could be out in five years and come after her, so she appealed the sentence and won. Carlos Ponce's sentence for kidnapping was increased to twenty-five years, plus another ten for theft: Having forced Vesta to give them her personal identification number, the kidnappers had ripped off her bank account through an ATM.

José Luis Ponce, the older brother, got picked up by police in Delaware last year and is now in custody in Mexico. The third kidnapper, the eldest, at twenty-four, was never found.

And Vesta? A new Morelos governor fired her a couple years ago after she raised a ruckus over a ridiculously large budget cut at her hospital. She now practices in Mexico City and drives with considerable attention to the details of her surroundings. Chronic kidnappings throughout Mexico continue, and regrettably, too many of them involve the local police.

Thirteen

O N NOVEMBER 1, 1996, John Early, a fifty-year-old Canadian-born pilot who had become an American citizen, touched down on a dirt landing strip at Wunroc, in a remote part of southern Sudan. With him were his copilot, a Kenyan named Mohsin Raza, and an Australian nurse, Maree Worthington. Early worked for a Swiss company that contracted air services to the International Committee of the Red Cross, the organization that, among many other things, does such admirable and necessary work nursing the sick and wounded in war zones around the world.

Sudan had been a war zone since independence from Britain in 1956, with the exception of an eleven-year period in the 1970s and early 1980s, and the death toll—abetted by disease and famine—was estimated by the mid-nineties at more than one million people. Sudan's civil war pitted the government in Khartoum and northern Sudan against the Sudanese People's Liberation Army in the south. The government side was mainly Arab and Muslim; the non-Arab rebels in the south represented indigenous cultures and were mainly animist, although some of them were Christian.

Complicating matters, the SPLA had splintered into factions by the mid-nineties. One was led by an SPLA founder, an American-schooled and -trained Sudanese military officer, John Garang (he attended Grinnell College in Iowa and underwent training at Fort Benning, Georgia); another was headed by a largely uneducated rebel commander, Kerubino Kwanyin Bol, who also was one of SPLA's founding fathers. Early and his ICRC crew were returning five rebel Sudanese soldiers—fighters in Garang's faction—who had been treated at a Red Cross hospital in Kenya, which borders part of southern Sudan.

The United States had a dog in this fight partly because the Sudanese government had played host since 1991 to an exiled Saudi Arabian who was making an infamous name for himself. Osama bin Laden had set up shop in Sudan to train terrorists at camps underwritten by some of his commercial ventures, and he already had executed some attacks in neighboring countries and elsewhere. By the time Early landed in southern Sudan, however, bin Laden was gone. Under pressure from the United States and Saudi Arabia, among others, Sudan had booted bin Laden in May 1996; he had taken up residence in Afghanistan, an honored guest of the ruling Taliban extremists. But Sudan's government was still in Washington's doghouse for its alleged complicity in several terrorist plots, and the United States Embassy in Khartoum had essentially been shuttered and temporarily moved to Kenya.

The Red Cross is studiously neutral in its work, and Early had received security assurances from the Sudanese government and Garang's SPLA before he took off. But by the time he arrived, his landing site in southern Sudan had been seized by Kerubino's rebel group. Suddenly, the ICRC crew and its human cargo of five were in custody. Kerubino was claiming that the crew was transporting weapons of war: not only Garang's five soldiers, but twenty boxes of ammunition as well. The Red Cross, which denied the charge, had a crisis on its hands.

Early, I learned when the story broke, had New Mexico ties. He had been an Army Special Forces guy during the Vietnam War and done more than his share of thrill seeking. He got to my state in 1984, started a business, then left to become a flight instructor in Arkansas. He returned to Albuquerque in the early nineties and went to work for the Swiss company Zimex Aviation, which contracted pilots and planes to the Red Cross. But he was overseas so often, mainly in Africa, that he and his wife decided in 1994 to move to Nairobi so they could spend more time together. I contacted the State Department, Red Cross officials, and Sudan's ambassador to Washington, Mahdi Ibrahim Mohamed, to let them know of my interest in helping with negotiations if they thought it useful and appropriate. I also heard from the U.S. pilot's wife, Sherry Thomas Early, who had read about my offer, thanking me for my support and interest in her husband's situation.

At first, the ICRC, working in part through the Sudanese government, which was thought to have some influence with Kerubino, felt its people could negotiate a prompt release of the plane's crew and Garang's soldiers. By mid-November, a breakthrough seemed imminent, and Red Cross officials counseled the United States and its representatives to steer clear of the situation. But Kerubino twice promised to free his prisoners and reneged. He was asking for money, first $100 million, then $50 million, then $2.5 million. The Red Cross wasn't in the ransom business, but it had made good on some promised humanitarian aid, including food, medicine, and five electrical generators. By late November, however, the ICRC was still coming up empty;

negotiations to spring the prisoners, held at Kerubino's bush camp about sixty miles from the town of Gogrial, seemed to be going nowhere.

Through these mood swings, I had remained in touch with my sources at State, the Red Cross, and the Sudanese government. In early December, the ICRC finally conceded with considerable reluctance that the time was ripe for outside intervention. As usual, the rules had to be understood by one and all. I was a United States congressman, not a negotiator for or employee of the Red Cross. And I was not an official envoy of the State Department or the Clinton administration. Officially, my trip was a congressional delegation to Switzerland and Sudan, but I still needed something—a request for help from someone representing the families of the prisoners. We got in touch with Sherry Thomas Early and she quickly provided the protective cover in a faxed letter to my Washington office on December 2, 1996:

Dear Mr. Richardson,

I request your assistance in a matter of great importance: obtaining the release of my husband John Early and his two crew members, Mohsin and Maree, along with the 5 Sudanese patients which were detained in South Sudan on November 1st, 1996.

They have been held for one month now.

Please assist us in anyway you see necessary.

Thank you.

Once again, I packed my navy blue Brooks Brothers blazer for good luck. I had worn it during every rescue mission, and although it was getting ragged from all the times it had been repaired, I couldn't leave home without it. Superstition? Why take a chance, I figured. To this day, that blazer hangs in my closet, too tattered to be worn, too valuable a talisman to be discarded.

My traveling party—including Calvin Humphrey, Colonel Dan Fleming, a military aide, and Stu Symington, a nephew of the great Missouri statesman and senator, on loan to my congressional office from the State Department—left Thursday, December 5, 1996, on an overnight flight to Geneva, where we spent a good part of the next day meeting with ICRC staff. The visit also gave me a chance to catch up with Daniel Spiegel over lunch. Spiegel was an old friend from my days as a staffer on Capitol Hill, a top aide to Hubert Humphrey and the husband of Mary Ann Spiegel, who was on the long trip to Africa I took with Senator Dick Clark of Iowa. Dan was in Geneva as United States ambassador to the United Nations offices there, and had helped to keep me apprised of ICRC efforts since Kerubino seized Early and his crew.

The ICRC briefings that afternoon were useful, although the Red Cross people were clearly annoyed that one American congressman might be successful after their entire organization was not. I met with Jean de Courten, ICRC director of operations; his chief deputy, Paul Grossrieder, and Christophe Hannisch, head of the ICRC's Africa Bureau. They wanted me to make clear to Kerubino and Sudanese government officials that my negotiations were completely separate from previous ICRC talks and that I was there on behalf of the hostages' families. They also suggested that I try to negotiate a package deal—that is, not talk just about Early's release but about the release of Raza and Worthington as well. Finally, they said I ought to give Kerubino and the government people a deadline, eliminating any attempt to stretch out my stay for unrelated political purposes.

Grossrieder had been the ICRC's principal negotiator, having spent a total of six days over the previous month in Sudan, and he had assembled a brief assessment and personality profile of Kerubino based on his many hours with the rebel leader. According to Grossrieder, Kerubino considered himself a Christian, although he also claimed to have eleven wives. He came from rural southern Sudan, had little formal education, although he spoke tolerable English, and said he had been fighting in the bush since the age of sixteen. He was by this time close to fifty years old. Grossrieder said that Kerubino divided the world into three groups— his camp of simple people from the Sudanese bush, the Arabs from northern Sudan, and the educated people of the world, who clearly were the bad guys. The educated people included SPLA founder John Garang, the ICRC, the United Nations, the United States and the rest of the West, the press, and, presumably, the representative of the Third Congressional District of New Mexico.

In conversation, Grossrieder continued, Kerubino often was unfocused and easily distracted, rarely staying on subject for more than a few minutes. He didn't close deals and preferred to raise an issue again even if he previously said the issue was resolved. He sought to project independence from the government of Sudan, but Grossrieder believed he depended on the government at least for some arms and other support. Some of his forces apparently were intermingled with government troops, and Grossrieder sensed that he became somewhat more conciliatory when he was within the orbit of Sudanese government officials. All in all, one hell of a briefing. At a minimum, I thought, my conversations with the unpredictable Kerubino figured to enrich my diplomatic experience.

The next twenty-four hours included a tale of two aircraft. On Saturday, December 7, we left at eight in the morning on a five-hour, twenty-minute flight from Geneva to Khartoum, accommodated comfortably in a sleek United States Air Force C-20.

That night in Khartoum, the Australian and Kenyan ambassadors to Sudan asked to join me, noting their responsibilities to their captured citizens. I said no: The fewer big shots, the better. They were not happy campers. The next morning, we boarded our transport for the flight from Khartoum to the south Sudanese bush.

In its day, the DC-3, manufactured by the old Douglas Aircraft Company, was the king of the skies: It went into service in the 1930s and quickly became the principal airliner of most commercial carriers. If you were of a certain age and flew commercially, you probably remembered boarding a DC-3, which required passengers to walk up an angle to their seats because of the different set of its front and rear wheels. Still, it was quite the thrill for anyone riding in it for the first time.

But that was then. Our DC-3 wasn't exactly government-issue, at least not U.S. government. It was a decrepit old thing that should have been retired years earlier. It had no air conditioning, except for the natural kind blowing through empty window ports. DC-3s supposedly had a cruising speed of two hundred miles an hour at an elevation somewhat above 20,000 feet, but we seemed to be moving so slow and so low that you had to wonder whether we were traveling fast enough to stay aloft. This is it, I thought. My last day on Earth is at hand.

Geographically, Sudan is the largest nation in Africa, slightly more than 25 percent the size of the United States, including Alaska. Vast parts of it are barren and seemingly uninhabited, which more or less described the areas below us as we flew toward our destination dozens of miles from the nearest paved road. Kerubino was expecting us, but we buzzed the dirt landing strip once before setting down so the rebel leader could see we were friendlies and the pilot could take note of the potholes.

It was a surreal scene. Here was this guerrilla camp in the middle of nowhere, housing about 35,000 Dinka in crude

thatched-roof huts with no way to communicate with the outside world. Food and medicine, we knew, were in short supply.
What apparently wasn't in short supply were boys, ten- and
eleven- and twelve-year-old boys armed with AK-47 assault rifles
and other semi-automatic weapons. These kids were everywhere,
and they weren't shy about taking a look at the strange visitors to
their camp. We were there as negotiators on a humanitarian mission; we just hoped all the children knew it.

The Dinka men and women of southern Sudan are a tall
people, and Kerubino probably was at least my height, six-one or
six-two, maybe taller. He was wearing a gun in a holster. We sat
down at our outdoor negotiating table, with armed boys circling
us and vultures observing the scene from nearby rooftops. The
United States ambassador to Sudan, Timothy Carney, also was
there, as were two representatives of the Sudanese government,
Lieutenant General Mohamed Ahmed Mustafa el-Dabi, deputy
chief of staff for operations of Sudan's armed forces, and Mahdi
Ibrahim Mohamed, the Sudanese ambassador to the United
States, who had flown over from Washington.

We started to talk and it became clear very quickly that
Grossrieder's take on Kerubino was on target. He wasn't entirely
coherent, moving from point to point without much rational
connection, and he had this habit of switching back and forth between two pairs of glasses, one of which was missing a lens, the
other of which was missing an arm. But I was getting the message
nonetheless. Kerubino was insisting that he had been promised
$2.5 million in addition to the humanitarian aid he already had
received, and he wanted his money. He also knew he had a cap-
tive audience, including reporter Tim Weiner of the *New York
Times,* and he unloaded on U.S. policy toward Sudan. We had
imposed sanctions on Sudan when we labeled it a state supporting terrorism, but Kerubino wanted me to understand that it

wasn't the government in Khartoum that bore the brunt of our embargo. The people who suffered most, he said with a sweep of his hand, were the rural people of the south.

It's important in negotiations to show respect for your adversary, to listen to what he has to say. But I also explained that the Red Cross did not pay ransom money; neither, I said, did the United States. If we did, Americans serving or traveling abroad would be targets not only of terrorists but also of anyone eager to make a quick buck. I acknowledged that an embargo could sometimes be a blunt instrument, but the United States felt it had little choice under the circumstances. We talked for four hours and made no progress: He kept insisting on the money and I kept saying no. He kept attacking the U.S. sanctions and I kept listening. Finally, I suggested a break. I briefly visited the three prisoners in what amounted to thatched-roof prison cells; all of them looked haggard and depressed. I'm trying to get you out, I told them, but right now, it doesn't look good. Early grabbed my arm and said that if anyone could get them out, I could. As a military man, he knew I had helped military guys like Bobby Hall back home. The nurse, Maree Worthington, told me not to worry. They all knew I had done my best.

"No," I said, "you don't understand. I'm not leaving here without you."

During the plane trip from Geneva to Khartoum, I had read the CIA profile of Kerubino and learned that he had children, twenty-six of them. When we got back to the negotiating table, I asked about his children. Kids had been dying of measles, cholera, and other diseases by the thousands in southern Sudan. The second I mentioned his children, Kerubino seemed to soften. He told me that a two-year-old daughter had died just a couple of days before I arrived and another child, a four-year-old son, was near death.

Then I asked whether I could see his son. He stood up immediately and so did all his security. He looked over to them,
gestured at me, and said, "Me and him." He led me to a crude
hospital tent nearby. The boy was on a cot, emaciated and clearly
very ill. I reached down, stroked his cheek, and touched his fore-
head, which seemed feverish. Kerubino was the leader, I said,
why couldn't he take care of his son? He said he didn't want pref-
erential treatment. It was a clarifying moment for me and, I
thought, for Kerubino as well. I took a risk. He might have thought
I was trying to manipulate him, but he realized I really cared.

We returned to the negotiating table and got serious. "You
want weapons and fuel, but you have children dying all around
you here," I said. In this camp alone, I pointed out, there are 415
coffins for the children who have died recently. "Your number
two told me he lost four children to disease." I said we needed to
know what medicines and food to bring. He'd kidnapped people
from the Red Cross, for God's sake. They could help improve conditions around here. He should stop asking for money, because he
wasn't going to get it. I didn't have much time, and if we didn't
focus on the humanitarian aspect of this, I would leave.

Richardson's Rules

· **You can walk out, but only if you're prepared to walk**
back in later.

That threat, coming after the appeal to his humanity, did the
trick. Kerubino dropped his ransom demand and agreed to a
package of aid that Tim Carney typed up and printed out on his

laptop. The package included five tons of rice, four Toyota Land Cruisers, and nine new radios. Critically, it also included some-thing that I suggested near the end of our talks, what the agree-ment described as "a water and sanitation survey team to examine the needs of the community with a view to improving both wa-ter quality and hygiene." The Red Cross did this kind of thing all over the world. With that, Kerubino and I signed the agreement, witnessed by Carney and the two Sudanese government officials, Mohamed, the diplomat, and Mustafa el-Dabi, the military offi-cer. Unfortunately, Kerubino wouldn't agree to free Garang's five soldiers. Later, I learned they did get released.

Someone brought Early, Raza, and Worthington from their thatched-roof hut about 100 yards away. They still looked ragged, but they brightened when they saw our little group, because they seemed to know that after thirty-eight days, their captivity finally was over. They told us that they had been roughed up immedi-ately after they were captured, but not harmed after that. They were fed—not well, but enough—and passed the time playing cards and reading books that the Red Cross left before it pulled out of Sudan. When aircraft flew overhead, they would run out-side and wave to attract attention, which eventually got them the equivalent of house arrest: they were confined to their hut around the clock.

Kerubino insisted on a small celebration. He was sick of the hostage issue and wanted the ordeal to end, too. We shared an elaborate meal that included grilled goat meat, which had little hairs stringing out of it, and exchanged gifts: He gave me an elephant-hair bracelet, and I gave him and a few of his lieutenants pairs of congressional cufflinks. Then it was time to go. On the trip back to Khartoum, I spent some time talking with Mohsin Raza, the Kenyan copilot, who said he would like nothing more than to emigrate to the United States. I liked him enormously and told him that I would do what I could. Four days later, I wrote Prudence Bushnell, our ambassador in Kenya, on Raza's behalf, scribbling in longhand in the lower-left corner, "He's a first-rate guy. Please try to help him." According to a friend at the State Department, Raza tried and tried to make it to the States, and finally did.

The Sudanese general and ambassador, trying to take a little credit for what had just happened, suggested that I call on their president, Omar Hassan Ahmad al-Bashir, in Khartoum before returning to Geneva. At the meeting, al-Bashir said he wanted a dialogue with the United States. First, you must stop the massive human-rights violations and enter into peace talks with John Garang of the SPLA, I told him. He scowled and committed himself to nothing, but at the end of the meeting, he gave me a hearty hug.

On the plane ride back to Geneva, the Australian nurse, Maree Worthington, said through tears that it felt as if "the Yanks had rescued Australia again." The ordeal in Sudan had turned her into an instant celebrity in her own country. We landed in Switzerland to a small army of reporters and assorted dignitaries, including Ambassador Dan Spiegel and Red Cross president Cornelio Sommaruga. The ICRC people were extremely gracious, but Sommaruga grimaced a little when I told him to make sure his representatives turned over the Land Cruisers to Kerubino as soon as possible.

On the flight to Geneva, I also got a congratulatory call from President Clinton. A month after his reelection, there was plenty of speculation in the press and in political Washington about changes in the cabinet, and once again I was getting prominent attention. United Nations ambassador was one possible spot listed under my name in the news accounts, but it wasn't mentioned as often as Commerce or Energy Secretary. Clinton didn't say so directly, but he strongly suggested that my time for a cabinet position had arrived and it seemed to me he was leaning toward Energy.

Later, I talked it over with Barbara, who agreed that the United Nations was the place I wanted to be. It was cabinet level, foreign affairs, and the diplomatic troubleshooting I found so addicting. What's more, I knew and liked Madeleine Albright, the new secretary of state, and Sandy Berger, who had succeeded Tony Lake as Clinton's national security adviser. If I had a choice, I told White House Chief of Staff Leon Panetta when he called to follow up, I wanted the United Nations.

He passed the word to Clinton; the next time Panetta called, around eight-thirty in the evening of December 12, he asked whether I was prepared to accept the UN job should Clinton offer it to me. I said yes.

"Well, he'll call you tonight," Panetta said.

"What does that mean?" We both laughed, knowing that "tonight" for this president could mean almost any hour of the evening or very early the next day.

"Figure sometime between midnight and six in the morning," Panetta said with a chuckle before he rang off.

The call from the White House operator came a bit past one in the morning, rousing me from a sound sleep. "The president wishes to speak with you," she said.

"Give me a chance to wake up first." A minute later, the president of the United States was on, offering me the job of ambassador to the United Nations. I accepted immediately, but said there were some details I wanted to discuss. Fine, fine, Clinton said, we can discuss them later on, but I want to announce this later today. He did, at a morning press conference that included several other nominations, among them Bill Daley, another one of the losers in the musical chairs of 1992, as commerce secretary; Daley became the inadvertent focus of the press conference when he fainted and took a frightening tumble from the podium. Fortunately, he was fine. Later, he told me my acceptance speech was so boring he fell asleep.

Clinton hit the right note when he introduced me: A few days ago, Bill Richardson was eating goat meat in Sudan with a Sudanese rebel and securing the release of three Red Cross workers, the president said. "Today, I'm nominating him to be our United Nations ambassador."

It was Friday the thirteenth, and I considered it one of the luckiest days of my life. When I got to my congressional office, two security agents informed me that as of that day forward, they would never leave my side. I knew our lives were about to change.

POSTSCRIPT: On January 9, 2005, with United States Secretary of State Colin Powell in attendance, representatives of the Sudanese government and the Sudan People's Liberation Army signed a peace agreement in Nairobi, Kenya. By then, the toll from civil war had topped 2 million dead and an estimated 4 million homeless. The two sides agreed to a period of interim self-rule for the south, followed by a vote to determine whether its people wanted to secede or stay within the Sudanese government. During the six-year interim period, John Garang, who signed the agreement for the SPLA, would become first vice president of Sudan. Garang was sworn in to his new post as al-Bashir's deputy in July but died in a helicopter crash a few weeks later. As for Kerubino: In September 1999, he died of wounds suffered in factional fighting. According to some accounts, he was thought to have fired the first shot in the civil war that began in 1983.

Powell, who also signed the treaty as a witness, could count the Sudanese negotiations among his finest hours as secretary of state. And one of my successors as United Nations ambassador, former senator John Danforth of Missouri, also played a key role as a special envoy to the peace talks. In praising the agreement, Powell urged the two sides to turn their attention immediately to western Sudan "to end the violence and atrocities that continue to occur in Darfur—not next month, or in the interim period, but right away, starting today."

As of this writing, the peace agreement seems to be holding, but the predations by a government-backed militia upon the people of Darfur continue. By some estimates, as many as 200,000 have died since the conflict broke out in 2003, with entire villages "ethnically cleansed" and burned to the ground. For the most part, the Sudanese government has ignored Powell's plea for an end to what he has called genocide, and neither the Bush administration nor NATO nor the European Union has provided much help to supplement an undermanned African Union intervention force.

Fourteen

THE UNITED STATES SENATE confirmed my nomination as ambassador to the United Nations on February 13, 1997. The confirmation had one interesting moment. Senator Jesse Helms liked to use hearings for UN ambassadors to discuss the failings of the institution. Barbara and I attended President Clinton's second inaugural, and at the lunch, following the ceremony, the Richardsons and the Helmses were seated at the same table. Barbara asked me what she should say to the senator, but he was a perfect Southern gentleman. He charmed her, and it helped my confirmation, since he chaired the Senate Foreign Relations Committee, which conducted my hearings.

On the day I was confirmed—by a Senate vote of 100–0—I officially resigned from the House of Representatives in identical letters to House Speaker Newt Gingrich and New Mexico secretary of state Stephanie Gonzales. They were short and heartfelt:

"I hereby resign my congressional seat effective immediately so that I can assume my post in the President's Cabinet as Ambassador to the United Nations.

"It has been an honor to serve in the United States Congress as New Mexico's Third District representative for the past 14 years. I have been especially proud to represent the people of New Mexico, whose kindnesses toward me and my family have been equaled only by the unmatched beauty of the state itself."

What I said about New Mexico was the God's honest truth: The people in my adopted home state had been wonderful to Barbara and me since we moved there in 1978, and I wanted everyone to know how deeply thankful we were for their graciousness and, when I needed to hear it, their straight talk. I hoped New Mexicans wouldn't forget me, because I knew I wouldn't forget them.

Even before I started at the United Nations, I was getting some straight talk from another quarter. It was inevitable, given my international missions, that I'd gotten to know Madeleine Albright over the years she served as United Nations ambassador. I liked her and found her to be tough-minded, engaged in her work, and knowledgeable, especially about Eastern and Central Europe. Now that Clinton had promoted her to secretary of state, she was my new boss, and she had some marching orders for me in the couple of months between my nomination and my confirmation. I had to shut down any contacts or negotiations that amounted to independent diplomacy, she said. She reminded me that Andy Young got fired as UN ambassador during the Carter administration when he met with an official of the Palestine Liberation Organization. "You've got to be careful, Bill," Albright said. I couldn't go off freelancing the way I used to. I couldn't be Red Adair anymore.

In my last couple of years in Congress, I'd become a diplomatic go-to guy for anyone who had a delicate negotiation in need of attention. An American was among a group kidnapped in the disputed territory of the Kashmir, and I went out there to see what I could do. I talked to the Pakistanis and the Indians to no avail. Alas, we later found out that the hostages had probably been killed months before I got there.

I met Yugoslav leader Slobodan Milosevic, a wily and charming individual, despite his brutal nature, at his dacha in Yugoslavia. I went to Nigeria as an advance man and envoy for Tony Lake to meet with the repressive dictator Sani Abacha. We wanted to find out if Abacha was receptive to negotiation about some of his regime's human-rights practices, but after meeting with him, I reported back that in my opinion, he wasn't. Needless to say, I haven't responded each and every time someone has called on me. I quite frequently get feelers. Milosevic had tried to reach out to me before he was bombed by the coalition. Recently, President Hugo Chávez of Venezuela has been dumping on the United States in general and, shamefully, on Condoleezza Rice in particular. In a recent speech, Chávez said there was an American he could really deal with—Bill Richardson. So there's another one that likes me. His foreign-policy team has been trying to contact me consistently since I became governor. As I have said, a personal connection can transcend even the deepest ideological differences.

At the end of my time in Congress, another venture involved contact with Iran. The Israelis had approached me about helping them secure the release of Ron Arad, an Israeli pilot. I got in touch with their UN ambassador, Kamal Kharrazi, about the fate of Arad, an Israeli lieutenant colonel who had had to bail out of his plane over southern Lebanon when it developed mechanical difficulties in October 1986. Arad, the plane's navigator, was seized by Lebanese terrorists and imprisoned. The word was that he was passed along from bad guy to bad guy—from Hezbollah to the Syrians to Iran—like some sort of trophy.

I was go-between for Kharrazi and an Israeli Mossad agent whose name I probably shouldn't mention here. The Israelis, the

Mossad agent said, still believed Arad was alive and in Iranian hands. The idea was a prisoner exchange: Arad for Hezbollah prisoners held in Israel. As usual, I alerted the White House to my activities and, once again, was told to stay in touch with Mark Parris, the Middle East adviser on the National Security Council staff.

Within days after my nomination as UN ambassador, Kharrazi called me at my house in Washington with congratulations and a suggestion that we use my appointment as an opportunity to open a broad dialogue between our two countries. I was diplomatically noncommittal and called Albright immediately. I told her about my Arad-related activities and about Kharrazi's latest overture. I was still a little green about this business of formal diplomacy, I suppose. She couldn't have been nicer, but she didn't mince words: "You've got to end all contact with the Iranians, Bill. We have no diplomatic relations with them; in many ways, we're at war with them." With that, my talks with Kharrazi and the Iranians came to an abrupt end.

About a year later, I was at the annual meeting of the World Economic Forum in Davos, Switzerland, and found myself face to face with Kharrazi in a small study group. I suppose we could have ignored each other, but that might have called even greater attention to the episode. Instead, I stuck out my hand and said hello, in what was the highest-level encounter between the United States and Iran in two decades. Uncomfortably, without looking at me, my old ex-friend Kharrazi reciprocated.

I'd also been negotiating with the Peruvians for the release of Lori Berenson, an American woman in her mid-twenties who had gone to Peru and fallen in with members of the Tupac Amaru Revolutionary Movement, a Marxist group. Berenson and some of her new friends were arrested on charges of treason in November 1995; she was tried, found guilty, and sentenced to life in prison. Her crime, the prosecutors said, was participation in a planned assault on Peru's Congress in an effort to take members hostage and trade them for Tupac Amaru prisoners in Peruvian jails. Berenson's family in New York asked me to see if there was anything I could do. Talks with Peruvian officials had yielded the rough outlines of a deal: Berenson would plead guilty, but she would be released in exchange for a Peruvian being held in a Texas prison.

One problem, however, was that members of her family were dead set against an admission of guilt. That made it tougher when I went to Lima in late August 1996 and sat down with Peruvian president Alberto Fujimori. I told him that I didn't want to get into the merits of the case, but that releasing her would be a good thing for him, a humanitarian gesture that would improve his image in the United States. At the time, Fujimori was under some fire in Washington, not only for the Berenson situation but also for lax prosecution of drug traffickers and for increasingly authoritarian behavior in office.

I had been warned not to press Fujimori too aggressively, since he was known to be short-tempered. From his gaze, I could tell he liked me, but he wasn't responsive to my message. He shook his head. Maybe if we can work an exchange where she admitted her culpability, he said. After all, he went on, we have her confession. On tape.

Maybe they did, maybe they didn't. In the end, it didn't matter, because the family, on the advice of Ramsey Clark, a former attorney general under President Lyndon Johnson who had become an international celebrity for his defense of leftist causes, was adamant: She wouldn't admit guilt to a crime she said she didn't commit. I admired the Berensons for backing their daughter unconditionally. But it was nuts, in my view, for the family to reject the deal, given that Lori was in poor health and serving time in a harsh mountain prison 10,000 feet above sea level. With a little more time, I believe, I could have gotten her out.

As of this writing, Lori Berenson remains in jail, her sentence reduced in 2001 to twenty years.

THE UNITED NATIONS has a reputation of being somewhat stuffy and hidebound, and in some respects, it lives up to its billing. What else would you expect of an organization whose mission is to meld nearly two hundred countries with different cultures and customs into an international body that is supposed to work for the common good? Rough edges get sanded away, diplomatic niceties are observed, traditions are maintained. It all helps to keep the place reasonably civil and functional, but in that tower of babble on New York's First Avenue, something gets lost in translation. There just isn't much room for spontaneity or retail politics.

My own spontaneity sometimes got me into trouble. Shortly after I arrived in New York, there was a big dinner held in my honor attended by United Nations delegates, the local political and media establishment, and plenty of celebrities. One of them was Paul Newman. As the guest of honor, I spoke at one point, thanking everyone, saying how much I looked forward to the work ahead and generally how thrilled Barbara and I were to be in New York. Apparently, my use of the royal "we," a reference to the Clinton administration I served, sounded uppity to Newman. He rose to offer a toast, but wound up gently chastising me for what he perceived as my absence of humility as the United Nations ambassador representing the world's only superpower. You're a regular guy, he seemed to be saying; you've got to act like one.

I probably do some of my best thinking late in the evening, when I'm watching an old movie where I know the outcome.

Butch Cassidy and the Sundance Kid is among my favorites: I've seen it at least two dozen times, and huge chunks of the dialogue seem hard-wired in my memory. As I mentioned earlier, the script even came to mind during that high-speed ride from the Jordanian-Iraqi border to Baghdad.

Anyway, when Newman stepped down, I immediately walked up to respond to his toast. It just popped into my head. I raised my glass, pointed it at Newman, smiled, and said, "You just keep thinking, Butch. That's what you're good at." The audience roared, but Paul Newman was not amused; he was clearly angry. Later, he came over and said he was only trying to help me. "Yeah, I know," I said. "But I had to connect with those people and you kind of set it up with that dig. The movie line really helped me." Newman's a good guy. I'd wisecracked at his expense, but it wasn't a serious hit and he understood the difference. I think we parted as friends.

My arrival wasn't about to transform either the U.S. mission to the United Nations or the UN itself. But my operating style was, if not a shock to the system, at least a bracing change for my American colleagues and the institution. My deputy at the UN, Edward "Skip" Gnehm, was baffled when I told him I wanted to shake every hand at the United Nations Secretariat the first day. They talked me out of trying to meet everyone in the whole building. I'm not one for tight bows or formal handshakes when a bear hug or a gentle fist to the shoulder is an available option. Sure, I owned a couple of chalk-stripe suits, but I usually preferred my old Brooks Brothers blazer, khakis, and cowboy boots even at Security Council meetings. Diplomats can be very stuffy, and I think people responded well to my style.

The Council most often met from 10:30 in the morning until one in the afternoon, after which members would break for lunch. Most members headed for the delegates' dining room. I usually headed for the cafeteria, because it gave me the opportunity to visit with the UN's regular employees—New Yorkers who spoke Spanish and many other languages in addition to English and who didn't pull their punches just because the guy across the table was America's UN ambassador.

When it came time for me to leave the UN, the *New York Times* said I was "about the most relaxed and genial envoy this diplomatic hothouse has seen in a generation" and that I had a style that was "zany by U.N. standards." I may have called a distinguished diplomat "what's his name," as the *Times* reported, but I must have done something right, because when I said I was leaving, twenty-eight countries wanted to give me a farewell dinner.

THE UNITED NATIONS sits on international ground, but it's also a part of the New York community. I thought it was important to spread the gospel, which is why we hosted town hall meetings at Columbia University in Manhattan and Fordham University in the Bronx, among other places. They usually went well, but not always. One town meeting with the Russian ambassador, Sergei Lavrov, in the Russian section of Brooklyn turned testy when Lavrov got mad at a question about Chechnya.

Barbara and I also tried to use New York's social whirl—there is nothing like it anywhere else—as an extension of the UN ambassador's job. We got wined, dined, and toasted by New York celebrities in the arts, finance, and media, and we entertained at the grand apartment maintained for the ambassador at the Waldorf Towers on Park Avenue. We had the most fun we ever had in a job, no question, but it was work, too, as we helped get the administration's message out to important and influential groups in the city. We also wanted to show the UN in a positive light. I wasn't only ambassador to the UN, I was an ambassador for the UN, too.

Situated on the forty-second floor of the hotel, the residence overlooks St. Patrick's Cathedral on Fifth Avenue and the Chrysler Building in the distance. The apartment itself was across from the Royal Suite, so named because the Duke and Duchess of Windsor would stay there during their visits to the United States. In the early 1960s, the Houghton family, which controlled Corning Glass, offered to donate their elegant house on Sutton Place as the official residence of the U.S. ambassador to the United Nations. Adlai Stevenson rejected the offer, apparently preferring room service at the Towers instead. The Houghtons then offered their house to the UN, which quickly accepted. It is now the residence of the UN secretary-general.

Kofi Annan, in fact, became a pretty good friend. Barbara and I had met Kofi and his Swedish wife, Nane, at an international conference some years earlier, when he was assistant secretary-general at the UN and I was in Congress. He was named UN secretary-general the same day Clinton nominated me to be U.S. ambassador, so we were both new to our jobs. Barbara remembers the paper that day had two pictures on the front page: mine and Kofi Annan's.

I ended up talking to him nearly every evening on some issue or other. On occasion I would go to his house about eleven at night and we'd smoke a cigar and get our business done. That way it wouldn't get reported that I was paying him a visit. He was under a lot of pressure during the situation with Iraq: from us, from the French and the Germans, and from everyone else.

We'd also get together socially quite often—with our wives for the movies, without them when we went to the fights. Kofi Annan used to box himself, and we would talk about the great tradition of Ghanaian boxers. Barbara and Nane became tight, making afternoon forays to New York art galleries to plead for loans of works that might hang at their residences. When we arrived at the residence, there was nothing on the walls, just great big hooks to hang pictures from.

The Annans hosted the last of a bunch of farewell dinners for us when we left; it was a spectacular night, and wandering through the garden overlooking the East River, you couldn't help but question Adlai Stevenson's judgment thirty-seven years earlier.

It also made sense to me to encourage members to get out of the United Nations cocoon and mix it up with the locals, or at least taste the local scene. When I arrived in the early months of 1997, relations between the UN and its host city were downright frosty. The issue went back a half-century, to the UN's earliest days, and it involved a treasured commodity for New Yorkers—a place on the street to park an automobile. UN diplomats parked pretty much where they liked and racked up huge numbers of unpaid parking tickets. The Russians were the biggest violators. In practice, their diplomats—and many diplomats from other countries—shredded the tickets, and the city groused. But despite episodic flare-ups, New York City rarely played hardball.

Then, in December 1996, diplomats from Russia and Belarus, a former Soviet republic and another big parking scofflaw, tried to interfere with New York City police officers who were ticketing their illegally parked car. There was some pushing and shoving, and suddenly diplomatic parking became an international incident, a new Cold War along the East River of midtown Manhattan. Mayor Rudolph Giuliani was furious, threatening to send the United Nations packing or at least urging it to find another home. UN ambassadors and lesser lights were getting huffy, and the State Department in Washington found itself somewhere in the mushy middle.

I got involved in helping to broker a deal, which I announced with Giuliani at New York City Hall in March. Under the new arrangement, State could and would suspend the special license plates given to diplomats for their personal cars if they accumulated unpaid parking tickets going back one year. Giuliani loved it: Here was red meat for New Yorkers resentful of abused diplomatic privilege. But the deal came unstuck when United Nations and State Department lawyers said the plan violated the tradition of diplomatic immunity and even commitments made by the United States in the UN's founding documents. A fallback position was developed; it wasn't as tough, but it cooled things off, and Giuliani grudgingly went along.

I also had a very good relationship with Cardinal O'Connor in New York when I was at the UN. I sought out a meeting with him, and we spoke very frankly with each other. Like the mayor, Cardinal O'Connor was a very important figure in New York. I felt that as UN ambassador, I also was ambassador to the city.

Going to church is still an important part of my life. It affects a lot of what I do. I made sure to call on the representative from the Vatican when I was UN ambassador, and not everyone does that. Politically, the Church and I have clashed on abortion, as you would expect with any Catholic politician who is pro-choice, but not acrimoniously. I know the Church has its precepts, and although I am personally opposed, I don't think abortion should be any kind of litmus test. I respect the Church greatly. I believe that the Church has an important role in modern life. In New Mexico, my administration has formed a coalition with the Church in areas like the eradication of poverty, eliminating the tax on food, health care access, preschool education, and fighting predatory lending.

ALL IN ALL, given the tensions at the UN, we needed to work to reduce the grumpiness wherever we could. What better time and place for that than a late-spring afternoon at Yankee Stadium? In June 1997, a little more than four months after my arrival at the UN, we took the Security Council ambassadors out to the ball game—specifically, the rubber game in a subway series between the New York Yankees and the New York Mets. This wasn't our only social: I also arranged a screening of the latest James Bond movie, which everyone enjoyed greatly.

I organized the trip to Yankee Stadium in part so delegates could say goodbye to two of my valuable colleagues: Skip Gnehm, my deputy and a foreign service officer who later capped his career as our ambassador to Jordan, and Karl F. "Rick" Inderfurth, who was leaving the UN to become assistant secretary of state for South Asian affairs. We could have done the honors over a formal dinner, the United Nations way, but I figured the Richardson way was better.

I made sure the delegates had briefing books with the rules of the game and its history, and I bought Yankees and Mets caps for our guests to divvy up. New Yorkers sitting nearby seemed puzzled at first, then caught on. There were a few jeers, but most people seemed to embrace the foreign big shots in their midst. The reaction of the delegates, who dined on ballpark cuisine (hot dogs, peanuts, beer, and soft drinks), varied according to their knowledge of and interest in baseball. A few, such as Japanese ambassador Hisashi Owada, knew their baseball and hung in until the end of an extra-inning win by the home team. But most of these guys were at sea and bailed out in the middle innings.

Two of them, Russian ambassador Lavrov, later Vladimir Putin's foreign minister, and the Chinese ambassador, never could figure out what was going on. Lavrov and I developed a solid friendship, but we were foes on the issue that dominated my time at the United States: Iraq and its refusal to cooperate with United Nations weapons inspectors.

Fifteen

I FELT GOING IN as ambassador that I had a terrible handicap, in that the United States was not paying its dues to the United Nations. Congress felt the institution wasn't reforming itself adequately and stopped payment on our contributions to the UN budget. By some estimates, we owed about a $1.5 billion when a deal was made on the arrears in 1999. This was after my time. When I was ambassador, our refusal to pay caused the United States to be viewed with skepticism, especially by our friends. It made my job much harder when we went around looking for support on issues of the day. The Canadians were always saying, "When are you paying your dues?"

I quickly generated even more antagonism. Even before I started work at the UN, Madeleine Albright told me we should try to limit U.S. vetoes on the Security Council to one a year; otherwise, we'd risk even greater resentment on the international stage. Just my luck, I ended up vetoing two anti-Israel resolutions in my first three weeks.

Needless to say, this didn't endear me to Arab ambassadors

in New York. The Egyptian representative, Nabil Elaraby, was pretty frank about it: He said he'd never seen a U.S. ambassador get off to such a bad start with Arab countries. But he also said he wanted to give me a dinner at his residence, no wives included, with all the other Arab ambassadors in attendance. He thought it would help, and it did. I didn't make excuses for our policy in the Middle East, and I didn't apologize for my vetoes. But I told the ambassadors I'd always be open to discussion if peaceful relations were the objective. I think they liked the fact that I was dark-skinned and that I was from a minority group in the United States. Maybe I charmed them, I don't know, but it seemed to me that the bad vibrations disappeared afterward. At the end of the dinner, I got a big hug from the Palestinian permanent observer at the UN, Nasser Al-Kidwa, who is now foreign minister for the Palestinian Authority.

Albright had said from the beginning that Iraq was the single biggest issue for the administration. My job, she said, included two critical tasks. First and foremost, I needed to make sure that United Nations Secretary-General Kofi Annan worked with us and remained aligned with us when it came to Iraq-related matters. Second, I had to keep an eye on and even babysit, if necessary, Richard Butler, executive chairman of the United Nations Special Commission—UNSCOM—the weapons inspectorate established after the Persian Gulf War. Butler was a smart, mercurial Australian who had been his country's ambassador to the UN before he was named to head UNSCOM in 1997. In short, he was a very important guy for us. Butler turned out to be a real team player as far as I was concerned, although the anchor for us was Charles Duelfer, an American who was Butler's deputy.

Iraq had been frustrating UN efforts to get it to comply with Security Council resolutions from the first. I can't recall who said it, but there's a line that in many ways summed up Iraq's behavior over the years after the Gulf War: Agree enthusiastically, report progress, then gradually introduce obstacles. Iraq accepted Resolution 687 three days after it was passed in 1991. Given that hundreds of thousands of U.S. military personnel were on his doorstep, Saddam Hussein had little choice. At first, the inspections process seemed to go according to plan, and with Iraqi cooperation, UNSCOM began its first inspections in June. But by August 1991, Iraq already was throwing up roadblocks. It failed to make full disclosure of its proscribed weapons and programs, which was a requirement of 687. It blocked the use of helicopters by UNSCOM inspectors. New resolutions were passed, their demands either ignored or compromised by Saddam's government. Along the way, UNSCOM managed to destroy significant quantities of chemical warfare agents and what appeared to be the infrastructure for a nuclear-weapons program.

Iraq's missile and biological-weapons programs were another matter. Iraq would provide its third "full, final, and complete disclosure" of prohibited biological weapons. UN experts would find the declaration "incomplete, inadequate, and technically flawed." A fourth and fifth declaration would be forthcoming, with a predictably identical result. By the time I got to New York, Iraq was interfering with UNSCOM operations and even roughing up the occasional inspector. Then, in the fall of 1997, UNSCOM teams were stopped because they wanted to see three places, previously approved for inspection, that the Iraqis were now labeling "presidential sites" and therefore off-limits.

On one of these occasions, I called Kofi Annan in the evening to express our displeasure and to urge him to call Saddam Hussein directly. He did, and Saddam relented, permitting a team headed by Duelfer to conduct its inspection the next day. (Duelfer later became head of the Iraq Survey Group, replacing David

Kay—the group that looked for weapons of mass destruction after the U.S. military took down Saddam's regime in the spring of 2003; like Kay, Duelfer found none, and so reported to the Congress in 2004.)

Later, Iraq's presidential palaces again were ruled off-limits. Then, on October 29, 1997, Iraqi deputy prime minister Tariq Aziz, the Chaldean Catholic I had joined at church in Baghdad more than two years earlier, sent a letter to the Security Council saying that his government had decided not to deal with any UNSCOM personnel who were United States nationals. The Council rejected this decision the same day and warned of "serious consequences" if Iraq failed to comply with its obligations under what at that point were eight unanimous resolutions. In the wonderful acronym of the U.S. military, Iraq had become one giant SNAFU: situation normal all fucked up. But I'm not sure many Americans were paying much attention at the time, not with the vigorous economy, the Internet boom in its early stages, and a stock market that had doubled over the previous three years. Yet these were important developments for long-term U.S. foreign policy.

On November 12, 1997, we managed to push through yet another resolution—Security Council Resolution 1137—which condemned Iraq's continued violation of previous resolutions and imposed travel restrictions on Iraqi officials who did not cooperate with UNSCOM. Tariq Aziz held a press conference in Baghdad to denounce what we did, and the Iraqi foreign minister, Mohammed Said al-Sahaf, said we had pressured Council members to vote with us and even resorted to threats of blackmail. That was just pure bullshit. It was true that we had certain advance intelligence on what delegates might be saying in Security Council sessions, but we weren't in the blackmail business.

If we had been, the Council probably would have been more united than it was. The resolution was supported unanimously, but that didn't mean everyone interpreted it the same way. I said publicly after the vote that Iraq had to comply or face the consequences: "We are not precluding any option, including the military option." We and the British believed that previous UN resolutions on Iraq essentially authorized the use of force to make Iraq comply. Russia, China, and France—the other permanent representatives on the Council—thought otherwise and insisted that a separate use-of-force resolution would need to be approved. If that has a familiar ring, it should. The divide then was not unlike the one in February and March 2003, when the Bush administration said that Resolution 1441 and all the Iraq resolutions that preceded it justified military action to force compliance.

Our resolution represented the will of the international community, as the diplomats like to say, but frankly, it didn't mean a hell of a lot if we weren't prepared to back it up. The United Nations had imposed a sanctions regime on Iraq, and Saddam regularly said he would be more forthcoming on inspections if the UN was more flexible on sanctions. There were efforts to weaken the sanctions, by the Russians and the French in particular, but we always felt it was a ruse by Saddam to exploit what he perceived as weakness in a supposedly united front. In our view, it wasn't a subject to be bargained in the bazaar: he was in violation of multiple Security Council resolutions and had to comply. As we would learn much later, Saddam already was ripping off the one "flexible" element of the sanctions—a program that allowed Iraq to sell a certain quantity of oil in exchange for food and medicine.

Little changed over the next seven months. The day after Resolution 1137 passed, Iraq said all U.S. personnel with UNSCOM had to leave Iraq immediately. That action was condemned by the Council. The Americans were allowed back a week later after Russia intervened diplomatically with Iraq. There were other episodes: Iraq barred access to "presidential sites," then allowed them, then barred them again.

Clinton and British prime minister Tony Blair had just about had their fill of Saddam's delays and violations, and were beginning to work the phones to get international support for air strikes on Iraq. Our meetings in the Special Operations Room at the White House were not debates about *whether* we should use military force; they were about when we would act and what kinds of air strikes we would use.

Then, on February 20, 1998, Kofi Annan went to Baghdad to talk to the Iraqis about renewed cooperation with UNSCOM. Annan was a skilled political operative, maybe the best I'd seen except for Clinton, and he was effective at selling his "triumphs." But this trip to Baghdad was not a good idea, in our view, because we felt it would undermine our military options. Unsuccessfully, we tried to stop the trip.

Annan came away on February 23 with a "memorandum of understanding" that supposedly put the inspections process back on track. In fact, it wasn't worth the paper it was printed on. I delivered a speech to the Security Council, criticizing Annan's visit as a fruitless exercise that yielded a memo the terms of which Saddam would almost certainly violate. My friend Kofi sent me a note afterward that said simply, "Bill, your heart wasn't in it."

Maybe not, because I was not happy to criticize my friend Annan, but my head was. Less than six months later, Iraq said it was quits with UNSCOM—and on October 31, 1998, the Iraqis effectively kicked out all international inspectors. They wouldn't return for four years.

. . .

IN 1960, a huge country in central Africa called the Belgian Congo gained its independence, dropped the colonial adjective in its name, and became enmeshed in an internal struggle for political power. After five years of turmoil, an army general overthrew the existing government and established a one-party state with himself at the top of it. Joseph-Désiré Mobutu Africanized his name to Mobutu Sésé Seko, changed his country's name to Zaire, and ruled for more than three decades, becoming Africa's longest-serving autocrat.

Mobutu was a U.S. administration favorite, supposedly a bulwark against Communism during the Cold War, and he played his hand to the hilt. He backed Jonas Savimbi and his UNITA rebels in their insurrection against the Angolan government, and he got involved in civil wars elsewhere in the region. He also made official corruption an art form, enriching himself, members of his family, and his cronies, and impoverishing a nation the size of Western Europe that was incredibly rich in mineral resources.

The end of the Cold War devalued Mobutu's currency in Washington, and by the mid-1990s, Zaire had its own civil war, fueled in part by the ethnic divisions plaguing other countries in central Africa. The ethnic strife that got the world's attention was between Hutu and Tutsi tribes in Rwanda; in 1994, during a genocidal spasm that lasted only a matter of weeks, Hutu tribesmen murdered hundreds of thousands of Tutsis as well as many moderate Hutus.

By early 1997, Mobutu's regime was finished, even though Mobutu himself didn't understand it. Mobutu was dying himself, from prostate cancer. Laurent-Désiré Kabila, who was involved in failed efforts to oust the Mobutu government in the sixties and seventies, had come out of nowhere to launch a full-scale rebellion. He had the backing of Rwanda's new Tutsi leader, among others, and his forces, many of them Tutsis, were taking city after city in eastern Zaire, and moving west, toward the capital, Kinshasa. There were claims, by the United Nations and international relief organizations, that Kabila's troops were killing Hutu refugees, who had fled to Zaire from neighboring Rwanda, by the thousands. It was a mess, and it wasn't going to get better until Mobutu left and Kabila could be persuaded to end the violence and stage national elections.

In April, President Clinton and Madeleine Albright decided to send me to Zaire. This time, in a departure from my foreign adventures as a congressman, I would be officially representing the president as his special envoy. My job was to bring Mobutu and Kabila together for talks and to try to negotiate a peaceful transfer of power. I arrived in Kinshasa on Monday, April 28, and spent the following day shuttling between Mobutu in the capital and Kabila, who was then in Lubumbashi, a city his forces held in southern Zaire. They agreed to a meeting and little else—not the place, not the agenda.

I have seen the results of the ravages of war in many countries, and among the worst consequences is the plight of the inevitable refugees and displaced persons. This was brought home to me with particularly shocking force on this trip. We visited a UN refugee camp near Kisangani, where I picked up a terribly sick-looking infant. The child died in my arms. Leaders who make decisions to go to war are most responsible when they understand the full implications of their actions.

President Mobutu, during that meeting and subsequent talks, had a quiet dignity and regal manner about him. I gave him a note from the president telling him that it was time to go, yet his advisers were counseling him that his forces still had a chance to beat back Kabila's. He still thought he could survive in Zaire. He didn't, and I told him so in pretty frank terms: "You are living in a fantasy world if you think this will end on your terms. I am speaking for the president of the United States when I say our support for you is finished. You're history in Zaire. You can leave with dignity and your money or you can leave as a carcass, but you're going to leave." Frail as he was from the cancer eating away at him, Mobutu looked as if he wanted to clobber me with his cane.

Richardson's Rules

- Deliver a strong message with dignity and without insults.
- Never lie when negotiating, because lies catch up with you. Be direct.

Kabila was street-smart and, as I was to learn, had no scruples. I told him that it would be wise to slow his advance toward Kinshasa, because we needed time to arrange his meeting with Mobutu and stage-manage Mobutu's exit from the country. In fact, I said, if you want our help, a peaceful occupation of Kinshasa is essential. Kabila said he understood. He also promised that investigators from the United Nations and international relief agencies could have unimpeded access to Hutu areas of Zaire. Kabila insisted he could repair Zaire's shattered economy, boasting that his business experience—he once ran a whorehouse in Tanzania—had helped prepare him for the job ahead. But he wanted a $100 million loan from the administration, and his idea of economic development seemed to be a bunch of projects created by and run by the state.

I was optimistic in public after our first meeting; privately, I was beginning to get the feeling that he might be only marginally better than the man he was about to replace. Kabila talked about elections down the road, but this guy, it seemed to me, was no democrat. It was at this meeting, by the way, that I gave Kabila the Yankees cap I'd brought along. I'd found out he was a baseball fan, improbably. I gave him the cap and called him the Yankee Clipper. He loved it. He wore the cap to the press conference afterward and, as I recall now, looked a bit like burly Boston Red Sox slugger David Ortiz committing heresy.

Richardson's Rules

> · **Find something your adversary likes and use it to your advantage.**

Mobutu was prepared to meet Kabila, but only in Libreville, the capital of Gabon. Kabila insisted on talks aboard a ship that South Africa said it would make available. After two days of scrambling, we thought we had everything set. We were going to meet on May 2 on the ship at Pointe-Noire, a port city on the South Atlantic coast of the Republic of the Congo, the country to the west of Zaire. Mobutu privately had agreed to leave the country, probably using his health as the reason.

We flew into Pointe-Noire, landing only after we circled for an age. We learned later that the tower was giving priority to the heads of state who were coming in: President Pascal Lissouba of the Republic of the Congo, Mobutu himself, and South African president Nelson Mandela, who was Mobutu's escort. We also

learned, when someone read it in *Condé Nast Traveller,* that we'd
been involved in a near miss with one of the VIP planes. We sped
to the port in a makeshift motorcade, a slightly unnecessary precaution in a town that seemed to have no traffic lights and few
vehicles, and boarded the South African vessel the *Outeniqua,* an
icebreaker. Figuratively, an icebreaker could have come in handy
when we met, but there was no ice for many a mile, not even for
our sodas.

We sailed out to international waters, one of Kabila's stipula-
tions for the meeting, and waited for him to arrive by helicopter.
Mandela and I discussed tactics. The issues by now were familiar
to everyone—the timing and nature of Mobutu's departure and
of Kabila's arrival in Kinshasa, access to Hutu refugees, and a
pledge to hold national elections in the near future. The plan we
worked out called for me to start things off, then for Mandela to
jump in and take the lead in the negotiations. I would then retreat
to the sidelines.

At one point, an aide brought a note to Mandela. He read it
and excused himself for a few minutes. The next thing we heard
was his voice in the room next door, elevated, because he was
talking on a satellite phone. What we heard was this seventy-
nine-year-old legend making love talk to his fiancée, Graca
Machel, the widow of Samora Machel, former president of
Mozambique and an old Mandela ally. He wound up marrying
her a couple months later, on his eightieth birthday.

Until that phone call, Mandela and Mobutu had sat in the
same little room with me on the ship, both stone-faced and unwilling to talk to each other. Mobutu was mad at Mandela for appearing to tilt toward Kabila, and Mandela refused to make the
first move. Buoyed by the phone call from his true love, Mandela
turned to Mobutu with his infectious smile and said, "How are

you, Mr. President?" The ice was broken. South African deputy president Thabo Mbeki and I smiled at each other.

We waited all day for Kabila, but he never showed up. Frustrated, we sailed back to port. There was nowhere for us to stay in Pointe-Noire, so our party decamped that night to the American Embassy in Libreville, Gabon. Kabila, it turned out, was in northwestern Angola, where he was making new demands as the price for his appearance. Thabo Mbeki went to Angola to find Kabila. Separately, I also went to Angola in search of Kabila, but he was nowhere to be found. Angolan president Eduardo dos Santos was no help at all. Eventually, Mbeki tracked him down, but Kabila still balked. Then Mandela got on the phone and read him the riot act. That did it; Kabila agreed to go to Pointe-Noire, and he and Mobutu got in the same room at last.

Richardson's Rules

· Give up the locale. Don't insist on neutral ground, but go to his or her turf. It's the substance that counts, not the place where you negotiate.

The talks were now firmly under the auspices of the South Africans and Nelson Mandela. We stepped back and Mandela, the continent's most revered democrat, worked to resolve this crisis in his own neighborhood. On Wednesday, May 7, 1997, President Mobutu Sésé Seko of Zaire left Kinshasa for Libreville, in Gabon, ostensibly for a meeting of French-speaking leaders in the region to discuss the crisis in his own country. He returned briefly. But nine days later, on May 16, Mobutu quit Zaire for good, pitching up in Morocco, where he had a palace and where he died the following September. Kabila's forces took Kinshasa the next day, and Zaire ceased to exist: Kabila renamed it the Democratic Republic of the Congo—Congo for short.

Mobutu was a tyrant—for many years, actively supported by the U.S.—and his departure from the country he had ruled and pillaged for more than three decades was not to be mourned. But I still had reservations about Kabila, and he wasted little time confirming them. I returned to Congo in early June 1997, because Kabila, having installed himself as president, was holding international human-rights investigators at bay, in violation of the promises he had made to me and others. He kept saying that his forces had not deliberately killed Hutu refugees during their seven-month campaign to oust Mobutu, but he refused to permit the United Nations or international relief agencies to prove or disprove it. He wanted aid from the United States, and his country certainly needed it. He wasn't going to get it, I told him, unless he allowed the inspectors to do their work. Kabila again said he understood and pledged to permit the inspection teams to begin their work on July 7, one month after our meeting.

July 7 arrived and so did the inspection team. It got nowhere: Kabila's government effectively blocked the inspectors from meaningful work by restricting them to Kinshasa, and they left five weeks later. Kabila himself, meanwhile, was raising new issues with United Nations Secretary-General Kofi Annan, which only prolonged the process. The United Nations High Commissioner for Refugees listed 200,000 missing people, most of them Hutus once housed in refugee camps that Kabila's rebel forces may have swept through on their way to Kinshasa. I had argued that Kabila should be given time to demonstrate his bona fides, but time was running out: This guy sure behaved as though he had something big to hide.

I gave it one more shot on a third trip to Congo in late October 1997. It was the same merry-go-round. By the time I left, Kabila had promised to allow an inspection team to come back and get to work. But when the three-person team got there, they again were confined to the capital. It went on like that for months, until Annan pulled the inspectors out for good in April 1998 with virtually no serious fieldwork finished. Kabila was utterly incapable of keeping his word. He was murdered less than three years later, reputedly by some of his senior officers, and his son, Joseph Kabila, only thirty years old at the time, replaced him. Kabila the younger is still president, Congo's economy remains a mess, and free elections have yet to be held.

KARL F. "RICK" INDERFURTH, the talented diplomat Albright moved from the United Nations to the State Department in the summer of 1997, had South Asia as his new portfolio and had been pressing me to visit India and Pakistan from my earliest days in New York. Inderfurth felt strongly that we needed to break the logjam between these postcolonial antagonists, now nuclear nations. I agreed and thought we might be able to change the conversation between them if we got engaged in some direct diplomacy. When you have a problem, you deal with it; you don't let it fester.

Separately, but connected with the region, I'd been meeting with assorted Afghans for some months. I hadn't seen anyone in the Islamist Taliban, which now controlled most of the country, including the capital, Kabul, but various representatives of the opposition forces had loosely grouped together as the so-called Northern Alliance. It wasn't difficult to make contact. The Taliban regime was recognized only by three countries—Pakistan, Saudi Arabia, and the United Arab Emirates—and Afghanistan's seat at the United Nations was still held by the alliance that drove out the Soviets in 1989.

Since that time, the United Nations had appointed five mediators, all of whom had failed to engineer an enduring peace among the warring factions. There were questions as to whether the opposition to the Taliban was fraying and in danger of coming completely apart. No cabinet-rank American had visited Afghanistan since 1974, and I was itching to give it my best shot. The Taliban had kicked the UN out in a dispute over women in its Afghanistan workforce, and the nongovernmental organizations were getting the cold shoulder even to offers of humanitarian assistance; both the UN bureaucrats and the NGOs supported my intervention.

After checking with the White House, I told Inderfurth to count me in for a South Asia trip, provided we could include Afghanistan and talk to both the Taliban and the Northern Alliance. The idea was at least to get them to the table to discuss the possibilities for peace. The South Asian leg of the trip was important because President Clinton was considering a visit; we wanted to make sure the Indians and Pakistanis would be receptive.

Another, critical part of the mission wasn't on anyone's public radar screen. We wanted to persuade the Taliban either to expel Osama bin Laden or to extradite him to the United States, where he was under indictment for complicity in the 1993 World Trade Center bombing. Bin Laden was continuing to cause us grief. In February 1998, he effectively declared war on the United States when he decreed in a fatwa that all true Muslims should attack U.S. civilian and military targets everywhere.

The trip launched on April 10, 1998. A week later, we boarded our UN plane and flew at first light from Islamabad to

Kabul for what was to be a fourteen-hour exercise in nonstop diplomacy. With twenty-five or thirty people on our plane, we had a substantial entourage, with perhaps ten of us in the core delegation, plus Pakistan Embassy staff and a press contingent that included *Washington Post* reporter Kenneth Cooper and Andrea Mitchell of NBC News.

We flew into a huge airport with no planes visible on the ground and were met on the tarmac by a group of unsmiling Taliban who seemed uncomfortable or unfamiliar with the role of official greeters. Then, out of the blue, a dozen gleaming black Mercedes-Benzes headed for us. Stunned, we were invited to pile in, three to the back seat, for the ride into Kabul. Along the way, our driver pointed out with some pride two amazing statues, giant figures carved from a wall of stone nearly two thousand years ago, one of them nearly 200 feet tall. These were the famous Bamiyan Buddhas, which the Taliban ordered destroyed in early 2001.

Kabul was a war zone and that's what it looked like. It was stark and desolate, with no building seemingly untouched by the two decades of conflict. There were men on the street, but we saw only one woman, conspicuous in a light purple burka. My boss, Madeleine Albright, had called the Taliban's treatment of women "despicable" during her 1997 visit to Pakistan, and this was a characterization no one in the West disputed. One of the things I wanted to do was to press the Taliban leaders to expand women's rights.

We drove around Kabul for fifteen or twenty minutes, with a guide alongside the driver pointing out the sights: "This is where we hang our enemies," he said at one point, indicating a particular square we were moving through. We made a brief stop at the old U.S. Embassy, which closed shortly before the Soviet invasion in 1979, and I placed flowers on a memorial to Adolph Dubs, our last ambassador to Afghanistan; Dubs was kidnapped and murdered in 1979. Eventually, our caravan pulled up to a somewhat battered building, where the press contingent got siphoned off for a further tour of the city. The official delegation moved on to the presidential palace. We were ushered inside through a cordon of colorful armed guards with swords in the air. It was time to talk business.

This was the Taliban ministers' first contact with a U.S. cabinet member, and they weren't versed in the arts of formal diplomacy. A half-dozen ministers, led by their number-two man, Mohammad Rabbani, faced us across a table, all of them armed with automatic weapons. It was obvious they hadn't had much contact with Westerners. I always was prepared to be casual in international talks if that's what the situation required, but when one of the guys you're negotiating with takes off a sandal, puts his foot on the table, and starts picking at his toenails with a knife, it redefines informality.

None of the Taliban leadership would look at me directly; instead, they looked down, apparently taking their cues from Rabbani. We expected them to begin with an at least perfunctory welcome, but they sat there and said nothing. I started to talk, trying to fill the awkward vacuum. Lakhtar Brahimi, an Algerian who worked for the United Nations, had been in and out of Afghanistan trying to kick-start talks among the warring factions. And Nawaz Sharif, Pakistan's prime minister, had told me in two meetings earlier in the week that he had leaned on the Taliban to cooperate in our attempt to start peace talks with the Northern Alliance. (Pakistan had been the Taliban's original patron.) As I began to lay out what we sought, it was clear that these messages from other Muslims had been heard. *My* message was that there was a chance of U.S. aid to help rebuild Afghanistan and gain broader international recognition, but not unless they made peace with their opposition and took steps to improve the status of women in the country.

Our talks ran slightly over two hours, including translation time, and we got some of what we wanted. The Taliban agreed to talks within ten days and dropped their earlier opposition to the United Nations and the Organization of the Islamic Conference, an umbrella group of Muslim countries, serving as sponsors. They said they would forgo a spring military offensive, an annual ritual after the snow melted, if the Northern Alliance groups did the same.

They also yielded some on women's issues, but not much. We wanted them to relax their blanket prohibition on girls' attending primary and secondary schools. They would not, but they said they would permit Afghan women to work for UN agencies delivering aid. Women could give aid only to other women and to girls; still, it was something for a regime that essentially banned women from working outside the home.

On bin Laden, of course, I struck out. Our ambassador to Pakistan, Thomas W. Simons Jr., who was a career foreign-service officer, had conveyed to the Taliban through Pakistani intermediaries that bin Laden was the key issue on the American agenda. His extradition or expulsion would do wonders for their standing in the international community, I told the Taliban ministers, and I requested an audience with Mullah Mohammad Omar, the Taliban leader and the key to bin Laden and his whereabouts. That would give me the opportunity to convey President Clinton's deep concern about bin Laden's terrorist activities, I said, and his use of Taliban territory as a base of operations. I repeated what we sought—bin Laden either extradited or kicked out of Afghanistan for good.

Meeting Mullah Omar won't be possible, Rabbani said. He also said, Osama is our guest in Afghanistan. He is under our control and poses no threat to the United States while he is here. These guys weren't hearing us, I thought, or they just didn't care. I tried again, getting as forceful as I could under the circumstances. Rabbani gave a bit of ground, saying he would consider our request if he discovered that bin Laden was fomenting terrorism. Later, on the national evening news, Andrea Mitchell of NBC reported that bin Laden, apparently made aware of what I asked of the Taliban, had threatened to kill me.

Barbara had always understood and grudgingly accepted the risks I sometimes took in foreign negotiations. But a public threat on my life by a known international terrorist was different. All of this isn't worth your getting killed, she said to me when I got home.

The business part of our visit concluded, we moved into another room, where our hosts had set up lunch on a big banquet table on which was laid some mystery meat, rice, bread, and a few other dishes. There was one woman in our delegation, Mona Sutphen, a career foreign-service officer I first met in Thailand who so impressed me that I drafted her for the mission in New York when I got the UN job. Mona was dressed appropriately in a *shalwar kameez*—an Indian outfit of long, baggy pants and a loose tunic down to her knees—and her head and face were covered so as not to offend the extremist Taliban. Still, they weren't expecting a woman, and there were moments when we wondered whether they would cause an incident by demanding that she leave. They didn't, but they watched her every move. At lunch, when she took a piece of bread and brought it under her veil to her mouth, the room froze. It was like the old E. F. Hutton commercial: The Taliban stopped talking, we stopped talking, and all eyes turned to Mona. She was cool as ice, a complete professional.

Just past two in the afternoon, we left for Sheberghan, a city in the north where we were to connect with leaders of the alliance groups. Their reception was the polar opposite of the Taliban's. There were military aircraft at the airport where we landed, and we were greeted warmly by a large delegation that included young women in colorful Afghan costumes. We climbed into Land Cruisers, and with people lined up ten deep along the highway to cheer us, we headed, we thought, for our rendezvous with the Taliban's enemies.

But that's not where our drivers were headed. They took us instead to an area set up as a sports stadium, with bench seats and a big playing field. We were wildly applauded here as well, escorted to special seats, given Fanta sodas, and invited to watch the action. In the center of the field, two teams of men on horseback circled what seemed to be the headless carcass of an animal. Then the game began. This was an exhibition of Afghanistan's national sport, *buzkashi,* which literally means "goat grabbing" in Dari, one of the country's two main languages. The idea is to compete for the goat or calf carcass and take it to your scoring area at one of the two ends of the field. Think of football on horseback with no passing, no helmets or pads, and no rules.

Interesting though this spectacle was, it certainly wasn't why we were there. There were other distractions. One of our delegation, Bruce Riedel, the National Security Council's expert on the region, slipped and badly cut his leg, almost to the bone. He tried to wrap something around it to stop the bleeding, but it wasn't working. Fortunately for us, Andrea Mitchell's cameraman was a former British special forces guy who traveled with a good first-aid kit. He knew his stuff and put together a serviceable tourniquet that helped Bruce get through the day.

Just as Rick Inderfurth was about to blow a fuse, our minders swept us up and took us to our meeting, again in a building with visible war damage. We knew we wouldn't have trouble getting the Northern Alliance leaders to go along with the agreement we'd reached with the Taliban; they were the underdogs in this civil war and had nothing to lose in peace talks. The bigger question was whether all the factions would show up. There was no love lost, for example, between Abdul Rashid Dostum, an Uzbek warlord, and Ahmed Shah Massoud, an ethnic Tajik and a legendary figure known as the Lion of the Panjshir because of his ferocious resistance to the Soviet occupation forces. Would they even appear in the same room together? But both men were among this gathering of Afghan fighters.

They welcomed us with gifts—not trinkets but enormous, handmade carpets. I hadn't expected that, not here, so I couldn't respond in kind. But I did have a good stock of pens, in blue and maroon, with the Great Seal of the United States of America and my signature on every one. Our hosts seemed to appreciate the gesture.

Richardson's Rules

> · Carry a bunch of nice pens, but not necessarily of Montblanc quality. When your opponent admires one, give it to him. When your watch is admired, don't give it away. If you do, it's a sign of weakness.

Flying back to Pakistan that night, I thought, Well, this was a good day's work. Peace talks would get started later in the month, and if they went well, we might get bin Laden after all. But it wasn't to be. The agreement held for a while, but we quickly learned that the Taliban had no intention of making peace with the Northern Alliance. By early May, a belated spring offensive had begun and the two sides were at it again.

On August 7, 1998, bin Laden's al Qaeda bombed our embassies in Kenya and Tanzania, killing hundreds. On August 20, a cruise missile strike on bin Laden's training camps in Afghanistan killed a number of his fighters, but not bin Laden himself. On October 12, 2000, al Qaeda terrorists exploded a bomb alongside the USS *Cole,* which had stopped to refuel in Aden, Yemen. Seventeen sailors were killed.

Ahmed Shah Massoud, the Northern Alliance leader, was assassinated by two Algerian agents of bin Laden posing as journalists. The date: September 9, 2001.

Sixteen

WHEN PRESIDENT CLINTON appointed me United Nations ambassador, he suggested that I also could help him on some other matters—domestic issues, Hispanic politics, and an up-coming vote in Congress to give him special powers to sign trade agreements. It was clear that even without my helping him on these things I would be spending a lot of time in Washington. I flew down every Wednesday morning for a weekly foreign-policy breakfast in National Security Adviser Sandy Berger's office that included Madeleine Albright, CIA director George Tenet, Defense Secretary Bill Cohen, and Leon Fuerth, Al Gore's national security adviser. There also were national security decision meetings in the White House Situation Room on everything from Bosnia and Iraq to Mexico and Burma. Sometimes, the president and vice president would attend, too. It was at these meetings that the real power invested in the job lay. I could weigh in on issues that did not directly concern the UN. At the UN itself, the ambassador consults with the secretary of state on how to vote. I worked for Madeleine Albright. I liked her personally and we got on very well.

I remember with some satisfaction teaming up with Albright to convince the foreign-policy team to impose additional sanctions on the Burmese regime. Payback time, I thought; this will drive the generals in Rangoon crazy. In all, I probably was averaging two or three days a week in Washington and quickly became a familiar fixture on the shuttle flights to and from New York.

Besides giving him an assist on fast-track trade legislation, I also told the president that I might prove useful in congressional relations generally. Clinton had been reelected against Kansas senator Bob Dole, but he still faced a Republican-controlled Congress, headed by two guys I'd known from my years on the Hill—Senate Majority Leader Trent Lott, who was in the House when I arrived there in 1983, and House Speaker Newt Gingrich. Clinton wasn't real popular with Republicans in Congress, to say the least, and I thought I could help.

Because I was in Washington so much, we got a special rate at the Watergate Hotel. I had an official office and staff at the State Department, but the Watergate was my home away from home in Washington during my time at the UN, and it was where I often held business meetings. Which was why I found myself in a Watergate suite on October 31, 1997, with a young woman named Monica Lewinsky.

I was there innocently enough. Earlier in the month, I had been part of a large presidential group that took a weeklong swing through Venezuela, Argentina, and Brazil to celebrate Latin American democracy and promote free trade. One day aboard Air Force One, Deputy Chief of Staff John Podesta took me aside and asked whether I would interview someone for a possible job at our mission to the United Nations. Podesta couldn't at first recall her name. A former White House intern and Defense Department employee, Monica Lewinsky, was eager to relocate to

New York; she was a friend of Betty Currie's, the president's secretary, Podesta said, and this would be a favor to her. We had an opening at the time for an assistant in our public-affairs office; the job paid $35,000 a year. Sure, I said, have her send her résumé along. She did, and one of my people set up an appointment for October 31 at 7:30 in the morning.

The thirty-first of October was loaded with appointments on Capitol Hill. As it was, I would be taking a late shuttle back to New York. Seven-thirty was the only hole in my schedule. I was joined by two top aides, Mona Sutphen, my executive assistant, and Rebecca Cooper, my chief of staff and a former CNN producer. The three of us interviewed Lewinsky for perhaps forty-five minutes, with Cooper and Sutphen doing most of the talking because I was busy in another room and kept moving in and out of the conversation. Later, on the way to the Hill, the three of us discussed Lewinsky. We all felt that she was impressive—bright and poised, with a good sense of humor and what seemed to be a genuine interest in work at the UN. We decided to offer her the job. She mulled it over for a couple of months but eventually turned us down.

That should have been the end of my Lewinsky moment, but it wasn't. On the evening of January 20, 1998, I flew to Washington so I wouldn't miss Sandy Berger's regular 7:30 breakfast the next morning. Sometime after midnight, Peter Burleigh, my deputy at the UN mission, called from New York, interrupting a sound sleep. The *Washington Post* was breaking a story in the Wednesday morning newspaper that said the president of the United States had had an affair with Lewinsky. Making matters worse, Burleigh said, the Drudge Report—the online news and gossip site of conservative Matt Drudge—had an item saying that a Clinton cabinet official had offered Lewinsky a United Nations job at the president's request. Drudge didn't mention a name, Burleigh said, but it was fairly clear who he had in mind. Jesus, I said, I didn't know anything about her relationship with the president.

The next morning, I went to the national security breakfast as the Washington press corps went into full feeding frenzy. Dodging reporters, I managed to get back to New York in time for a long-planned luncheon at the ambassador's residence in the Waldorf Towers. One of the guests was Lisa Caputo, a corporate communications vice president at CBS, who had been Hillary Clinton's press secretary during the president's first term. At one point, I took her aside and frankly asked for her advice on how to handle this thing. Caputo strongly urged me to get it all out, to make a straightforward public statement detailing my limited involvement with Lewinsky. She was preaching to the choir: all my instincts shouted the same thing.

Given the subject matter and its sensitivity, I also felt a phone call to the White House was in order. I called Erskine Bowles, the North Carolinian who had taken over as chief of staff a year earlier after Leon Panetta resigned to return to California. I began to tell him what I planned to do, to get it all out, when Bowles interrupted: "I don't give a damn what you do," he said. "Don't you tell me about this. I have nothing to do with it. I'm not touching it." Then he hung up. Oh, great, the chief of staff to the president was above it all, unwilling to participate with a bunch of seedy bastards like me.

We issued the public statement, saying that I had interviewed Lewinsky at Podesta's request and that we did offer her a junior position in our public-affairs office appropriate to her previous experience at the Pentagon and the White House. "There was no pressure by any individual to hire her and nothing improper occurred," said my spokesman, Calvin Mitchell, in the statement. Furthermore, the statement said, I was unaware of any relationship Lewinsky might have had with President Clinton. It helped to clear the air, but we still made headlines the next day. Suddenly, I was part of the nightly cable fodder. Was I ordered to hire Lewinsky? (Answer: No.) Did I interview anyone else for the job? (Answer: Yes.)

On Friday, January 23, Clinton sat down with his cabinet in what had been a regularly scheduled meeting. Full-dress cabinet meetings were rare in those days, mainly because this president didn't much like them. This one, though, was only four days before Clinton's State of the Union Address. International and domestic public-policy issues dominated the agenda, and I started to think that Topic A, which was dominating front pages and TV news broadcasts at home and abroad, would go unmentioned.

I was wrong: Clinton waited until we were near the end of the allotted time, then took on the Lewinsky flap directly. He said, in effect, that the story was complete bullshit—that he hadn't had an affair with that woman, Miss Lewinsky. This was slime spread by the right wing, which had been after him, he insisted, and the lapdog press was wallowing in it. Commerce Secretary Bill Daley broke in and said he'd defend the president. So did Albright, and suddenly there was a kind of competition to speak up on Clinton's behalf. I was ready to do so: At the time, despite the tales about liaisons with Gennifer Flowers, Paula Jones, and others, I really believed him. It was eerie: the camaraderie in the room at that moment was the greatest I can remember during my years in Clinton's cabinet.

Given the spontaneous rallying behind the president, the White House press people thought that cabinet members ought to take their expressions of support public and that Albright and Daley should lead the way. They did, in a rump press conference outside the White House:

Albright: "I believe that the allegations are completely untrue."

Daley: "I'll second that, definitely."

Education Secretary Richard Riley and Health and Human Services Secretary Donna Shalala also spoke of their support for the president and their conviction that the Lewinsky story was phony. All in all, it was a strong performance by the cabinet, but you had to be wearing earplugs and blinders to think the sound and fury would dissipate anytime soon.

The brief of Kenneth W. Starr, the independent counsel named in August 1994 to investigate the Clintons' involvement in the so-called Whitewater land deal in Arkansas, had grown substantially to include other areas of possible malfeasance, such as the firing of longtime employees in the White House travel office. Now Starr had his teeth into the Lewinsky thing, because Clinton had apparently denied that he had a fling with Lewinsky when he testified under oath in the Paula Jones sexual-harassment case.

Starr got around to me soon enough, subpoenaing my phone logs and meeting schedule. One of his deputies wound up deposing me for ninety minutes on April 30, 1998—not at the federal courthouse, where many of these depositions were taken, but in a private office. The interview lasted about an hour and a half. Starr's people were interested in two things. First, of course, was the Watergate interview. Mona Sutphen and Rebecca Cooper were deposed separately, and our accounts differed from Lewinsky's testimony in some of the details. But the overall thrust was identical: Mona and Rebecca described the job and its responsibilities and asked Lewinsky some questions, and that was it. We said we'd get back to her within a week or so. We didn't check out her work experience at the White House or the Pentagon because I figured Podesta wouldn't have agreed to send her name to us if he thought she couldn't do the job. I told Mona to offer her the position, which she did on Tuesday, November 3.

About that time, Barbara and I had to cancel a trip we'd planned to celebrate my fiftieth birthday on November 15. But being grounded in New York was the next best thing, and Barbara asked where I'd like to have my birthday dinner. I said I wanted to go to "21," a restaurant with a great tradition where I'd never been. We walked in that evening and I scanned the tables. There was Monica Lewinsky with two other people. While Barbara checked her coat, I wandered over to say hello to Lewinsky and her parents, then returned to escort my wife to our table.

"Who was that?" Barbara asked.

"Remember that girl the White House asked me to interview?"

Nine days later, on November 24, Lewinsky called Mona to beg more time because she also was looking at opportunities in the private sector. Mona asked how I wanted to handle it, and I said giving her the extra time was fine. We weren't in a great hurry to fill the position. On January 5, 1998, Lewinsky called to turn down the job. What a godsend. We moved Paul Aronsohn, a young and experienced State Department hand, into the open spot, and he did a terrific job.

The second thing Starr's people sought were details from a breakfast I had with Vernon Jordan while Lewinsky was still looking for a job in New York. Jordan told me he wanted to get together to discuss my future. I wasn't about to brush it off—Jordan was a major player. He ran the Voter Education Project in the South during the height of the civil rights movement in the 1960s, was president of the National Urban League in the 1970s, and had become one of Washington's most powerful lawyer lobbyists. He also was one of Clinton's best friends and had hosted a big dinner party for the president-elect in late 1992 that I attended. I invited him to the ambassador's residence at the Waldorf Towers and we traded political gossip. Vernon wanted to ask me about the speculation that I might be Al Gore's running mate in 2000. It was just a friendly conversation between friends. We traded cigars and said our goodbyes, and that was it.

None of this held any interest for Starr and his investigators. What they wanted to know was whether we had discussed Lewinsky. Jordan, it was revealed later, had acted at the president's request to help her get a job in New York. Among others, he had been talking to Ron Perelman, the head of Revlon, on her behalf. Amazingly, in retrospect, Lewinsky's name never came up in our conversation, because neither of us knew the other guy was involved in trying to find a job in New York for Monica. Later, I discovered in the Starr transcripts that Clinton had coached her for our Watergate interview.

I WAS DONE with Monica Lewinsky, but she remained an uninvited party in my life through 1998. Clinton liked the phone late at night, and I wasn't averse to it either. Through the middle of the year, we talked regularly, conversations that rarely occurred before 11:30 in the evening and increasingly concerned his Lewinsky predicament. Maybe it was my imagination, but I got the distinct impression in these chats that he was fishing for a way to tell his wife that he'd had a sexual relationship with Lewinsky. "Billy, I'm telling the truth," he kept saying to me. But then, as I tried to cheer him up, he'd become morose and go silent for a time. We'd go on, perhaps for an hour, and I got the feeling, although the president never said it explicitly, that he would have liked nothing better than for someone to break the news to Hillary. If he had asked me directly, I would have said no directly: getting someone else to clean the stable was a lousy idea.

President Clinton told his wife the truth about Monica Lewinsky on August 15, two days before his closed-circuit testimony to the Lewinsky grand jury from the White House Map Room. Then they went on vacation on Cape Cod.

In September, at an informal meeting in the White House, Clinton finally apologized to his cabinet. It was pretty painful to watch a president talk about anger pent up from childhood and how he'd been praying in an effort to reconcile with God. He told us he was sorry. When he was done, Madeleine Albright spoke first, saying that he'd made some big mistakes, but that we were behind him and had to move forward. Others weighed in, invoking the Lord's forgiveness and human fallibility. Clinton had made some serious mistakes, I said, but I was going to remain in his corner, adding that this assault by Starr had as much to do with raw politics as it did with the law.

The most poignant moment, in my view, was when Carol Browner, the head of the Environmental Protection Agency, rose and spoke. Her nine-year-old son had asked her what she thought of the president's behavior, she said, and she found herself at a loss for words. Clinton was visibly moved by that. The president was also moved, but in the opposite direction, when Donna Shalala dressed him down, calling his behavior reprehensible and wondering aloud whether she still could believe in him.

Clinton was seething by the time Shalala sat down—I could see his jaw tightening. He expected to take some grief but not that much. It took cooler heads—Treasury Secretary Robert Rubin and Vice President Gore—to change the atmosphere in the room. Gore, seated next to Clinton, brought the meeting to an end and captured its mood very well. You made some terrible mistakes, Gore said, but we've got to put it behind us. We've got an agenda, we've got to go back to work for the American people. Clinton, with tears in his eyes, grabbed Gore by the arm in an expression of thanks, and we did what Gore urged: we went back to work.

Seventeen

As I was headed to the United Nations in late 1996, Federico Peña was getting ready to say goodbye to Washington after nearly four years as transportation secretary and head home to Denver, where he'd previously been mayor for eight years. Both Clinton and Gore were upset and wanted to keep Peña, the other Hispanic in the cabinet, in the administration. Each of them called me to see if I could persuade him to take over the Department of Energy, which had become vacant when Hazel O'Leary resigned to return to the private sector. Vice President Gore in particular pointedly said that an important reason to turn Peña around was that he was the *only* Hispanic in the cabinet. That's news to me, I said. Well, yes, Gore said, but the UN job isn't quite full cabinet status, just cabinet rank.

Technically, that was true, because no cabinet "department" had been created by an act of Congress. Carol Browner, the head of the Environmental Protection Agency, fell into the same category. I used to joke that whenever Browner and I marched through the House chamber for a State of the Union Address, we always brought up the rear of the procession and got the lousiest seats. Actually, she was last, which made her bristle.

It wasn't a big deal. There's a hierarchy in the cabinet ranks. The big four are State, Defense, Treasury, and Justice; now the Department of Homeland Security is way up there. The others vary in importance, depending on the issues that dominate the political agenda in an administration and the Congress.

Anyway, I got hold of Peña on an airplane heading for somewhere in Texas. "You know, the president wants you to take this," I said. "You've got to do it." "No, I don't," he said. "DOE's a snake pit. You know those people, Bill. You've worked with those DOE folks. They are an untouched bureaucracy—a lot of scandals waiting to happen." Los Alamos National Laboratory was in my congressional district, and Peña had a point—it was very difficult to deal with. "But if he wants you to do it, you can't say no," I repeated. Peña knew I was right. The next day, Clinton formally offered him Energy and he accepted. He was sworn in on March 12, 1997.

Peña made it a bit more than a year before he said he was calling it quits in the spring of 1998. I knew what to expect next. Sure enough, I got a call one night from John Podesta, the president's deputy chief of staff. With Peña leaving, there would be no Hispanic in the cabinet, he said. I'm giving you a heads-up that I told the president to talk to you. Podesta was a good friend. He'd visited us in New York, and knew that Barbara and I were enjoying the UN posting. More than that: Barbara loved the city and I loved the work at the United Nations and the avenues it opened up to settle real-world disputes. It was everything I had hoped for and more. Podesta said that there was a solid internal candidate for Energy, Deputy Secretary Betsy Moler, and that she might get it, but he wanted me to be ready if the president leaned my way.

Lean he did. Over the phone, Clinton acknowledged that things had been pretty rough for him, and he said he wanted to keep his friends close. Would I think about DOE? "You don't have to do it, but would you think about it?"

"Well, do you want me to do this?" I asked. "If you do, I won't say no."

"Well, yeah, I kind of do. But I worry they'll massacre you with the Lewinsky issue." Erskine Bowles, his chief of staff, who was favoring Moler, had told the president that a confirmation hearing for me would turn into another Lewinsky investigation. President Clinton asked me to think about it some more and said we'd talk again.

It was no secret I was being considered, so no one was surprised when I began to run some quiet reality checks with key figures on the Hill. If there were minefields, I wanted to know about them. My first stop was Pete Domenici, who was then the second-ranking Republican on the Energy and Natural Resources Committee and the chairman of the Appropriations Committee that funded Los Alamos and the other national nuclear laboratories.

I asked Domenici if he'd support my nomination if the president appointed me secretary of energy. "Look, I'll work with you," I said. "Plus, I won't run against you for the Senate." He was taken aback, so I plunged ahead: "Look, I'll write a little note here and you can put it in your desk." I whipped out one of my United Nations business cards and wrote on the back: "I, Bill Richardson, will not run against you, Pete Domenici, for the U.S. Senate." "There," I said, handing him the card. "Put that in your drawer." He did, and said of course he'd support my nomination if Clinton made it official. But remember one thing, he added: I control the purse strings of DOE. What he meant was that he'd be looking over my shoulder, not on occasion but all the time. Given DOE's considerable operations in New Mexico, Domenici took a proprietary interest in the department's budget and activities, to put it mildly.

The other major player in the Senate was the Energy and Natural Resources Committee chairman, Frank Murkowski of Alaska. Murkowski and Alaska's senior senator, Ted Stevens, had powerful voices on energy issues because of the federal government's huge land holdings in their state and Alaska's enormous oil and gas reserves. Murkowski wasn't wildly enthusiastic, but he conceded that I was okay on oil and gas, by which he meant that my record in the House reflected a balance between drillers and environmentalists; my knee didn't jerk either way. All in all, he said, I probably was better than the other potential secretaries. Some compliment, I thought.

Murkowski said he'd require two things. First, a commitment that I would visit Alaska with him for three days sometime during my first three months as energy secretary. "And do what?" I asked. Among other things, he wanted to show me the Arctic National Wildlife Refuge, an area about the size of South Carolina along the Beaufort Sea, less than a hundred miles from the oil wells at Prudhoe Bay. Murkowski and many other Alaskans, including leaders of its native people, wanted to open up ANWR to oil and gas exploration; environmentalists strongly opposed even limited drilling, and I had sided with them in the past.

"Aw, Frank, I can't do that," I told him.

"Sure you can," he said. "Your views will evolve."

The second thing he cited caught me by surprise, although it shouldn't have after what Clinton had said. I was going to get confirmed, Murkowski assured me, but he was going to have to screw with me on the Lewinsky stuff. "Bill, I know there's not much there," he said, "but we have to have a little fun."

Clinton wanted a face-to-face meeting to discuss the Energy

job before he made the final decision. In the Oval Office, he said again he wasn't going to force me to take the job. This was often the Clinton way: Instead of asking or demanding something straightaway, he would dance around to the outcome he wanted. "Do you think we ought to do it?" he asked me. Barbara was dead set against my taking this one, partly because we had been in New York only eighteen months, partly because she knew that Peña wasn't alone in thinking DOE a snake pit. But we made our peace. For me, the domestic part of Energy rounded out all the international experience I had. It was also a true cabinet-level job, unlike the UN post. What's more, my president was asking me to serve.

"Yeah, I think we ought to do it," I told the president.

"Okay," he said, "but coordinate with my people on the Lewinsky issue. They [the Republicans on the committee] are going to come after you."

Clinton nominated me on June 18, 1998. At the confirmation hearing on July 22, Murkowski was true to his word. He led off with two or three DOE-related softballs, then quickly segued to Lewinsky. After the first question, a member of my staff handed me a note saying that CNN was going live. Murkowski hadn't missed a beat. He made me go through the story again and took some shots at Clinton for the cameras, but there was nothing new to say. The panel voted unanimously to approve my nomination and sent it to the full Senate for a vote. The Senate confirmed my nomination 98–0.

But even that didn't end it. Barbara and I headed to Cape Cod for a short vacation in early August. While we were away, and before I could be sworn in, the *Washington Times,* a conservative newspaper in the capital owned by the Reverend Sun Myung Moon, ran a story saying that I did not have a staff opening when we offered Lewinsky the public-affairs position. The paper essen-

Here I am, the little soldier, on my father's shoulder at a Fourth of July parade in Mexico City. (AUTHOR'S COLLECTION)

Receiving my first communion, at age seven, in 1954. As ever, my *abuelita* (grandmother) keeps a watchful eye on me. (AUTHOR'S COLLECTION)

The Richardson family—
my father, me, my mother,
and Vesta—Christmas 1965,
Mexico City.
(AUTHOR'S COLLECTION)

Vesta, the *bebé*, with her big
brother Bill, nine years old,
at our home in Mexico City.
(AUTHOR'S COLLECTION)

With the Mexico City
Little League team, the
Tarascos. I am in the
front row, third from
the right.
(AUTHOR'S COLLECTION)

I played the best baseball of my life at
Middlesex, and dreamed of a professional
career. (AUTHOR'S COLLECTION)

At the plate in my Albuquerque Dukes
uniform at the annual congressional charity
baseball game. I was voted MVP of the game
more than once. (AUTHOR'S COLLECTION)

With Barbara at home in Mexico City. This was her first visit to my family, in 1966, when she was sixteen and I had just graduated from Middlesex. (AUTHOR'S COLLECTION)

With Barbara at the Democratic State Convention in Las Cruces during my first run for Congress, 1980. (AUTHOR'S COLLECTION)

Networking before my first run for Congress, with local attorney Robert McNeill, Bernalillo County chair Burt Lindsay, and Senator George McGovern, 1979. (AUTHOR'S COLLECTION)

The proud son stands before a portrait of his father, at the University of the Americas in Puebla, Mexico. (AUTHOR'S COLLECTION)

Yasser Arafat demonstrates the elbow-grab handshake to Congressman Richardson, Jerusalem, 1987.
(AUTHOR'S COLLECTION)

Walking with Yugoslav president Slobodan Milosevic on his country estate during a congressional visit.
(AUTHOR'S COLLECTION)

I was the first non–family member permitted to visit the remarkable Aung San Suu Kyi after she was placed under military house arrest. Yangon, Myanmar, 1994.
(© KRAIPIT PHANVUT)

Visiting with children at a refugee camp in Mogadishu, Somalia, 1993.
(AUTHOR'S COLLECTION)

Establishing the connection: meeting Fidel Castro to discuss the release of political prisoners, Havana, 1996.
(AUTHOR'S COLLECTION)

With Sudanese rebel leader Kerubino Kwanyin Bol, signing over medical supplies and jeeps in return for the release of Red Cross hostages, December 1996. Kerubino sits to my right; between us stands my invaluable aide Calvin Humphrey. (AUTHOR'S COLLECTION)

An extremely rare moment of levity with the Taliban, in Kabul in 1998. I visited the Taliban and their Northern Alliance enemies as U.S. ambassador to the United Nations. (AP PHOTO)

Meeting with Bobby Hall and his wife, Donna, back in the United States in January 1995, after he had been released by the North Koreans on New Year's Eve. (AUTHOR'S COLLECTION)

Crossing the DMZ between North and South Korea after the body of pilot David Hilemon had been brought across. (AUTHOR'S COLLECTION)

Lining up the votes with President Clinton and the majority whip, Congressman David Bonior, for a new budget in August 1994. (OFFICIAL WHITE HOUSE PHOTO)

The new guy says no. Casting one of the United States' two vetoes in my first weeks at the UN, March 1997, this one on a draft resolution regarding Israeli settlements in East Jerusalem. (UN/DPI PHOTO BY MILTON GRANT)

President Clinton announces my appointment as secretary of energy at the White House Rose Garden, June 1998. (OFFICIAL WHITE HOUSE PHOTO)

A formal picture taken in the Oval Office after the DOE announcement. From the left: my old friend Andrew Athy; Jane Walsh, Barbara's sister; Jane's husband, Bill Walsh; Barbara; President Clinton; me; Lisa and John Flavin, Barbara's sister-in-law and brother. (OFFICIAL WHITE HOUSE PHOTO)

My last act as congressman for New Mexico's Third Congressional District was to turn Blue Lake over to Taos Pueblo. Here pueblo officials and elders attend the ceremony. (© LAURENT GUERIN)

Meeting with Native American leaders, including actor Wes Studi, at the State Capitol in Santa Fe. (© MICHAEL JACOBS)

Part of my job is to help promote the great state of New Mexico. I'm staring down on Times Square in Manhattan from this billboard, spring 2003. (© MARY RYLAND)

My wonderful mother and my sister, Vesta, at a reception held in my honor in Mexico City, December 1998.
(AUTHOR'S COLLECTION)

Celebrating our first day on the job as Governor and First Lady of New Mexico with my beautiful wife and life partner. Barbara and I have been together most of our adult lives and have been married for thirty-three years. Here we are at the Governor's Inaugural Ball, Santa Fe, January 1, 2003. (© PILAR LAW)

tially called my sworn testimony into question, and Murkowski responded by asking the president to delay my swearing-in ceremony until a bipartisan staff investigation could be conducted. The investigation took a week and came up empty: it found "no basis to believe that Ambassador Richardson had misled the committee in any way," as Murkowski said in a letter to Clinton. I was sworn in the next day as the nation's ninth energy secretary. I did eventually tour the North Slope with Murkowski, in mid-May 1999. Murkowski later became governor of Alaska; since then, we've become friendly adversaries, always kidding each other about our past battles.

ON MONDAY, August 24, 1998, I walked into the Forrestal Building on Independence Avenue, near the Washington Mall, and into what would become by turns one of the most painful and also one of the most gratifying periods of my professional life. The Energy Department was a bigger beast than anything I had tackled before, with 11,000 government employees and nearly ten times that many privately contracted workers scattered at laboratories and other installations across the country. Its annual budget was nearly $17 billion, with roughly 15 percent of those dollars spent in my home state of New Mexico. Its responsibilities reached almost every nook and cranny of America's energy-resource base, but at its center was the research, development, and management of the nation's nuclear-weapons arsenal.

Morale was a problem at DOE. The place had suffered rapid turnover at the top, gone through some downsizing and budget cuts, and in the mid-nineties had weathered Republican efforts to kill it off. That first day, I needed to be as upbeat as I possibly could. I got there early and greeted employees in the lobby as they came to work. And I had lunch in the cafeteria, shaking

hands, squeezing shoulders, and letting them know that I believed in their public service and that we all wanted to do the best
job we could for the people who paid our salaries—the American taxpayers. That afternoon, I gave a speech in the Forrestal's
auditorium, simulcast to all DOE field sites, that was designed to
underscore what I had said to the headquarters' employees I'd met
that day. "There's nothing wrong with the department that can't
be fixed with what is right with the department," I said. I wanted
people to know that I would be accessible to them. "Come to
talk to me in my office, because we're a team here," I said. Then
I added with a chuckle, "Just don't overdo it."

We did many good things at DOE and, in my judgment, at
least one truly great thing. But my time at the department always
will be stigmatized by its association with nuclear-security problems at the national laboratories, particularly the one I knew best,
Los Alamos. At various times during that thirty-month period as
energy secretary, I got ripped by my former congressional colleagues and even accused of being a racist, as ridiculous a charge
as ever there was. I did make mistakes, but in the main, the raps
were unfair, because security concerns at the nuclear-weapons
labs were growing long before I got there. A big one exploded on
my watch, however, and it wasn't wrong that I took the heat for it.

It also was true that I wasn't fully up to speed on the recent
history of nuclear espionage, particularly efforts by the People's
Republic of China to spy its way to scientific parity with the
United States. China was especially interested in the W-88, a
miniature nuclear warhead that ranked as our most advanced yet.
If the Chinese could gain access to the scientific design work, it
was thought, they had a shot at replicating the W-88 and ratchet-
ing up their nuclear arsenal very quickly. Still, in the 1980s, we
had no concrete evidence that China had penetrated our defenses
against nuclear espionage at the national labs.

Those defenses proved less formidable than we thought. The labs, which are owned by the government but run by an outside contractor, the University of California, worked on the deadliest "product line" on the face of the Earth. They also were peopled by some of the best scientists in the world, men and women who believed in scientific freedom and the exchange of scientific ideas. And it didn't hurt that they had strong political support in Congress. But there was a fundamental tension—a tug of war, really—between science and security at the labs, and the allure of science often prevailed, especially after the end of the Cold War. We sent our scientists to conferences abroad, in China and Russia and elsewhere, and we invited foreign scientists to visit us at our nuclear-weapons laboratories. After all, part of what we did after the Cold War was to work with other nuclear nations to secure their nuclear weapons. But we did a lot of dumb things. In 1994, for example, the Energy Department granted waivers to the two national labs in New Mexico—Los Alamos and Sandia— from a DOE policy that required background checks for foreign scientists visiting the labs as part of a scientific exchange.

The following year, Notra Trulock, DOE's director of intelligence in Washington, sparked an interagency investigation of possible espionage at the nation's three nuclear-weapons laboratories— the third is Lawrence Livermore in California—based on an analysis of the results of Chinese nuclear tests and the mention of the W-88 in a Chinese government document. In 1996, federal investigators identified five possible suspects, including a Chinese-American computer scientist at Los Alamos—the lab that produced the first nuclear weapons and where spies for Russia first stole atomic-bomb secrets in the 1940s. Trulock and Charles Curtis, then the deputy secretary of DOE, briefed White House officials. Curtis ordered tighter security measures in November, just before he left the department, but most of them were largely ignored.

It didn't get much better when Peña became energy secretary in 1997. Trulock was screaming bloody murder, convinced that both the CIA and the FBI were underplaying the severity of what everyone seemed to concede were acts of espionage. FBI director Louis Freeh apparently didn't feel his guys had enough evidence to warrant a wiretap on the Los Alamos scientist, let alone make an arrest. But Freeh did argue that the suspected scientist, Wen Ho Lee, at least should be removed from his sensitive position in the so-called X Division, which among other things was where work was done on the government's "legacy codes"—the mathematical formulas for nuclear-weapons designs. Nothing was done.

That, basically, was the mess I inherited when I started work at DOE in late summer, 1998. Clinton had ordered the labs to improve security in a February presidential directive, and Edward Curran, a top FBI agent, had been brought in to run a new counterintelligence program, but not much else had changed. Right after I arrived, Trulock briefed me and Larry Sanchez on what had been happening over the past four years. Sanchez, who had headed my intelligence detail at the United Nations, had agreed to come aboard as DOE director of intelligence. It wasn't a vote of no confidence in Trulock, but I wanted someone I knew well and trusted in the top intelligence position. I asked Trulock to take the job as deputy director and he accepted.

Trulock also filled us in on the secret testimony he was giving to the Cox Committee—formally, the House Select Committee on U.S. National Security and Military/Commercial Concerns with the People's Republic of China. Chaired by Representative Christopher Cox, a partisan California Republican, the committee had begun life to examine the possible relationship between Chinese political contributions to the Democrats in the 1996 campaign and the Clinton administration's policies on the export of military technology, but its scope had grown to include Chinese espionage—related issues.

Trulock was telling the committee what he told us: that Chinese penetration of the labs was deep, serious, and very damaging. He wrote in his own book that it was his impression that Sanchez and I were stunned by what had transpired over the previous few years. That was a fair assessment, but we weren't paralyzed. In October 1998, after less than two months on the job, I ordered that background checks be reinstated on all foreign visitors; the FBI had recommended this perfectly sensible precaution seventeen months earlier, only to be ignored. I also moved enough money around to dramatically boost the counterintelligence budget within DOE and assigned more CI experts to the labs. The counterintelligence budget, only $3 million in 1996, went to $39 million within four years; there were 7 people in CI in 1998, 150 two years later. It had to be clear to everyone that DOE ran the labs, the labs didn't run DOE.

Were we getting a handle on things? I thought we were, but in retrospect, I suppose we were being reactive for the most part, not proactive. The Cox Committee was in overdrive, hauling Trulock, Curran, FBI and CIA people, and others before full hearings twice in December 1998. After one of the hearings, I received a private visit from Representative Norm Dicks of Washington, the top Democrat on the committee, who excitedly told his old House colleague, now the energy secretary, that I had to take action on the Los Alamos spy case. Immediately, if not sooner.

All of this was happening outside public view. There had been a few stories in the national media, but no one had published or broadcast anything that made much noise. That changed on Saturday, March 6, 1999, when two prize-winning reporters for the *New York Times*, James Risen and Jeff Gerth, wrote a long front-page special report entitled "Breach at Los Alamos." The piece described the theft of nuclear secrets as "one of the most damaging spy cases in recent history" and said the government response was "plagued by delays, inaction and skepticism." Almost everything in the *Times* report had occurred before I got to the Energy Department, but there was no question where this radioactive bear had come to rest. The *Times* story did not mention Lee by name, but I knew his anonymity wouldn't last into the following week. We had been preparing to act, and the *Times* story was the last straw. On Monday, March 8, I announced that Wen Ho Lee had been fired by Los Alamos director John Browne at my order.

Lee had been questioned by the FBI for three days before we fired him and had stonewalled his interrogators, I was told. He was fired, I said, because he failed to properly safeguard classified materials, attempted to deceive Los Alamos officials about security issues, and didn't notify his superiors about contacts with people from a "sensitive" country, China. During this period, I gave Notra Trulock a whistleblower-type award that amounted to a $10,000 bonus—a signal that we took his charges of spying at the labs seriously. Later, I came to doubt Trulock's data and his motives.

I also ordered that DOE begin a series of polygraph examinations of department and lab employees who worked in areas where nuclear secrets could be compromised. Previously, no government employees outside the CIA had to take lie-detector tests on a regular basis, and the scientists at the labs went nuts. But we did it right: We held several public hearings, listened to their concerns, and went through an elaborate rule-making process to make sure we weren't casting too big a net. In the end, we set in place a procedure to administer lie-detector tests only to lab employees with the highest clearances. Nonetheless, scientists throughout the DOE labs deeply resented these polygraph tests, tests that continue to this day.

The FBI said it didn't have enough to charge Lee with a crime, but he was still the bureau's chief suspect in the W-88 case from the late 1980s. Then we got more alarming news: According to DOE and FBI investigators, Lee had transferred enormous amounts of secret data on the legacy codes from a highly classified computer system to a widely accessible network, where the files were stored under different names. In February 1999, Lee tried to cover his tracks by deleting hundreds of files from the less secure network, the investigators said.

The legacy codes not only contained design information, they also included test and safety data. That went directly to our so-called stockpile stewardship program. As signatories to the comprehensive test-ban treaty, the United States and other nuclear powers no longer tested nuclear weapons in the atmosphere or in explosions below ground. Instead, we relied on complex computer simulations to determine the efficacy of our nuclear arsenal. We were well ahead of everyone else, but if the Chinese had access to our data and could replicate it, they could catch up fast.

I immediately shut down the classified computer systems at the three labs and ordered changes in security procedures.

The rest of 1999 was a nightmare of reports and revelations that detailed how sloppy security had become at the laboratories over the previous quarter-century. We were moving fast to address these shortcomings even as the Cox Committee and the president's Foreign Intelligence Advisory Board, headed by former New Hampshire senator Warren Rudman, added to the long list of recommended changes. Rudman's report actually gave us credit for trying to upgrade security and counterintelligence at the labs, and I said publicly that the Cox Committee had made a valuable contribution to our continuing efforts. Then, I made the mistake of adding my pledge to the American people "that their nuclear secrets are now safe at the labs." We weren't there yet, and that quote would come back to haunt me.

But we were getting closer, which is why I resented one particular effort by Congress to "reform" DOE. One of the leaders of this misguided plan was my old political competitor, Senator Pete Domenici of New Mexico. Domenici and others in the Senate were promoting the idea of a semi-autonomous agency that would be part of DOE but not subject to the full authority of the energy secretary. The National Nuclear Security Administration, as it was to be called, amounted to a fiefdom within a fiefdom—a replication of the duties of existing counterintelligence in DOE and a prescription for confusion and inefficiency. We had imposed dozens of changes, many of them recommended by the talented Ed Curran, and now Domenici and the others, however well-meaning, were doing something to screw it up. The legislation, wrapped into the defense authorization bill for the new fiscal year, mandated that the new NNSA go live on March 1, 2000. I wanted Clinton either to veto this half-baked plan or demand changes as the price for his signature; otherwise, I couldn't stay on as DOE secretary. We wound up with a compromise, and the president, in his signature message, gave me substantial latitude in administering the new law. Domenici and other conservative Republicans howled in protest.

In December, Wen Ho Lee was indicted by a federal grand jury on fifty-nine counts of illegally downloading restricted information to an easily accessible computer system, then copying much of the information onto portable, high-volume computer tapes. Lee, who proclaimed his innocence, was not accused of espionage. Even so, government prosecutors managed to persuade a federal judge that he posed a grave security threat and that he should be held in solitary confinement without bail.

Along with almost everyone else, we weathered the moment that life as we knew it was supposed to come to a halt, the stroke of midnight, Y2K, and moved into a new year optimistic that we were on top of DOE'S security problems at last. Meanwhile, Al Gore had cut former New Jersey senator Bill Bradley down to size in the presidential primaries and there had been some talk of a Gore-Richardson ticket. With the troubles at DOE, that chatter had come to an abrupt end.

On May 7, two computer hard drives at Los Alamos were discovered missing by two members of its Nuclear Emergency Safety Team, which was surveying the lab for damage and potential threats posed by forest fires that had begun on May 4. That was bad enough. But the Los Alamos scientists compounded the felony by waiting three weeks before they reported the loss to DOE headquarters. This was in unambiguous violation of a rule I had imposed that required potential security breaches to be reported to DOE within eight hours. Later, the FBI told me that its people believed the hard drives vanished in late March from an X Division vault. The hard drives were found on June 16 behind a copying machine in an X Division area that was supposed to be secure, and after a long investigation, we discovered that the information on the drives had not been compromised. Even so, there was no reason to feel vindicated. The episode meant that some people weren't hearing or were flatly ignoring the messages we had been sending about enhanced security at the labs. The damage was done, and I became the butt of jokes from Don Imus and other talk radio types.

Predictably, my appearance before the Senate Armed Services Committee in June turned into a bizarre spectacle. Despite avuncular assurances beforehand from Chairman John Warner of Virginia that this would be a dignified affair, CNN was broadcasting live and the senators—Republicans and Democrats alike—were taking turns bashing me like a piñata. Richard Shelby, an Alabama Republican who headed the Senate Intelligence Committee, and Robert Byrd, the long-serving Democrat from West Virginia, were in especially high dudgeon, in part because of my decision not to testify before Shelby's committee a week earlier. It wasn't that I was ducking Shelby's committee—I had committed to Armed Services, the DOE's principal authorizing committee.

Shelby said I'd lost "what little credibility" I still had on Capitol Hill; Byrd accused me of "a contempt for Congress" and said he'd never again support me for appointive office if it required Senate confirmation.

It was worth taking note, although few journalists did, that both senators also were angry with me because I'd carved some pork intended for their states from the DOE budget. But they were entitled to take their licks on the proximate breach in security at Los Alamos. I shared their outrage and said so. I also said that we had done more to enhance security and counterintelligence at the labs in two years than my predecessors had done over two decades. Curran, who wasn't my appointee, and Eugene Habiger, a four-star general who had run the Strategic Command and was my new security czar, backed me up. But the truth was that although we could set new rules and do our best to enforce them, we could not alter overnight a culture of resistance to authority, even one with admirable and necessary objectives, that had been embedded over the course of half a century.

The summer of 2000 was a low point in my public life. My accomplishments at the department had been overshadowed by people who thought they were above the law when it came to the security procedures I had instituted at the labs. Still, I received many calls and letters of encouragement from colleagues and friends outraged at my treatment by Congress. In the middle of the war of words, the phone at home rang one night at eleven. I answered it, hearing the voice of the one person whose encouragement and support I most needed at that moment—President Clinton.

"You're catching a lot of shit," Clinton said. "I want you to know I'm an expert on that." He said it with a chuckle, and I laughed aloud. He'd taken more of it than I could ever imagine. "I called to say I'm behind you and that this will blow over."

I was getting battered every day by congressmen and the press, with some reporters even suggesting that I was somehow responsible for the fires that broke out near Los Alamos. And I was removed from consideration for vice president. When I was down in the dumps, Clinton's call helped a lot. It was a remarkable quality about him: he knew when and how to connect. And that night he made a difference.

IN SEPTEMBER, Justice officials accepted a guilty plea from Wen Ho Lee on one count of mishandling secret information. The federal judge in the case, James A. Parker of Albuquerque, took the unusual steps of castigating government prosecutors for misleading him on the threat posed by Lee and apologizing to the defendant "for the unfair manner" in which he was held in custody by the executive branch. Lee went free, on condition that he explain over ten debriefing sessions why he downloaded the data and what he did with it.

I made my share of mistakes over those couple of years but I always acted to try to protect nuclear secrets. If I could do things over, I would have questioned Trulock more closely about the security breaches in general and Lee in particular; instead, at the beginning, I tended to believe Trulock completely about almost everything. I think he was ideologically motivated and that he wanted to embarrass the Clinton administration. As for Lee, he committed a crime, but he also was badly treated. Here was the government putting this skinny sixty-year-old guy into solitary confinement for nearly a year. I have to realize that it was wrong, and I should have spoken out more, although I did try to influence the Justice Department on their incarceration of Lee. Finally, I suppose I should have listened to Peña, Barbara, and others. In some respects, DOE *was* a snake pit.

But not in all respects. If I hadn't taken the job when Clinton offered it, I wouldn't have had the opportunity to address one of the great wrongs visited upon American workers by their government.

Eighteen

By THE TIME I got to DOE, it was no big secret that a disturbing number of those who worked for the department or one of its hundreds of contractors were sick, dying, or dead. These were the silent Cold Warriors, the tens of thousands of people who went into plants around the country and came into daily contact with the extraordinarily dangerous elements used to make nuclear weapons. When they were taken ill, most of them didn't complain about their working conditions; when they did, the government spent tens of millions of dollars fighting their lawsuits, effectively telling these patriots either to salute and get back to work making nuclear weapons to counterbalance the Soviet menace or find another job.

There were legitimate grievances brought into public view by the health coalitions and labor groups that sprouted around the country to represent nuclear workers. This was a human tragedy of immense proportions, and I saw it as a gigantic piece of casework. Shortly after my swearing in, I started to visit the installations in DOE's considerable orbit—some of the storied names in our nation's nuclear history. One of the first was the Oak Ridge facility in eastern Tennessee. Oak Ridge was one of three gaseous diffusion plants, where uranium was enriched to make plutonium for nuclear weapons. Part of the trip was to include a thirty-minute meeting with a local group representing sick workers, but the session was cut short because I had to return to Washington sooner than originally planned. Still, I heard enough and knew enough to realize that we had to get on this quickly.

One problem was that my assistant secretary for environment, safety, and health hadn't started work yet. David Michaels, an epidemiologist, actually was appointed to the post by Federico Peña, but his confirmation got held up—not because of his qualifications, which were superb, but because the White House and Congress were completely transfixed by the Lewinsky business. He finally was confirmed in October 1998. My guys kept asking when he'd show up, but he said he couldn't until he finished up that semester's teaching duties at City College in New York. At an Oak Ridge press conference during my visit there, someone asked when DOE would start paying attention to the concerns of sick workers. We already are paying attention, I said, but it would help if my new assistant secretary showed up for work.

He did show up and was sworn in on Friday, December 11, which happened to coincide with DOE's Christmas party. Michaels came to my office after his swearing in and said he was reporting for duty. "Great, Doc, I'm glad your vacation's over," I needled. "Now, I want you to go to Oak Ridge Monday and talk to those workers and tell them I want to help them." I gave him until the end of January to come up with a plan for dealing with what was a moral issue: How should we compensate nuclear workers made ill and deceived by their government?

Michaels had been doing his homework already. Our nuclear infrastructure had become so huge in part because policymakers, worried about Soviet espionage or even nuclear attacks, insisted on redundancy. Thus, the Hanford facility was built in the 1940s to produce plutonium, and Savannah River was built in the 1950s to do the same thing. Oak Ridge was built in the forties, and the two other gaseous diffusion plants, at Paducah, Kentucky, and Portsmouth, Ohio, were built in the fifties. In the 1980s, under President Reagan, nuclear production really revved up, with serious environmental consequences. But everyone focused on what went into the air and water, not what was going into the bodies of workers in the plants.

Michaels met with workers at Oak Ridge on Monday, December 14, and got two earfuls. The meeting began at six in the evening and didn't finish until one in the morning. He didn't offer them anything—he couldn't at that point—but he told them on my behalf, Let us know about your problems, because we want to help. Apparently, no one from DOE had said these words before. The stories they told him were repeated elsewhere over the next eighteen months. How people would ask for their medical records and get them with huge parts blacked out, including the names of chemicals they had been exposed to. How complaints were met with removal of security clearances and no security card meant no work, which was no small thing given good pay that could run to $25 an hour. How distrust of DOE and its corporate contractors ran a mile wide and two miles deep.

The vast majority of people in these facilities were contract employees, covered by state compensation programs that provided lousy protection compared with the federal system. But they were federal employees in everything but name. Politically, we wanted to be the ones to frame the issue, because what we were proposing was a new entitlement program—not exactly a popular concept in Congress or, for that matter, in the White House. In one sense, the timing was perfect: the Cold War was over and, with it, the arms race against the old Soviet Union. Those in the entitled group, we said, were civilian Cold War veterans; what we were proposing for them was not something special but something that put them on a plane roughly equal to that of the federal employees who supervised them.

The plan Michaels brought to me in January was a no-fault system of compensation for occupational illness that put contract employees on a par with federal employees. DOE, given the decades of distrust, wouldn't run it; instead, Michaels proposed that it be run by the Department of Labor, which had the experience and expertise to set rules and manage such programs. But there were implications for agencies all across the government. We took our program to the White House in March 1999. That began a remarkable eighteen-month period of interagency cooperation and bickering, public hearings, and listening sessions around the country that brought what the government had done into sharp focus and yielded a measure of long-overdue justice.

We were helped by some enterprising journalism. Local papers with nuclear facilities in their regions had done stories in the mid-nineties about sick workers and the government's inattention to their plight. But it wasn't until August 8, 1999, that the issue went truly national. That's the day *Washington Post* reporter Joby Warrick did the first of a series of articles on the plant in Paducah, Kentucky. The lead sentence of that first article: "Thousands of uranium workers were unwittingly exposed to plutonium and other highly radioactive metals here at a federally owned plant where contamination spread through work areas, locker rooms and even cafeterias, a *Washington Post* investigation has found."

Warrick also said that DOE, under fire in a lawsuit, still contended that "worker exposure was minimal."

I was on the phone to Michaels by nine that Sunday morning, ordering him to Paducah immediately. Michaels held a town meeting in Paducah the next day, and we launched a new investigation of the Paducah plant. I went to Paducah myself a month later to preside over another town hall meeting and to do what should have been done years earlier: I apologized. "On behalf of the United States government, I am here to say I am sorry." The government recognized what the men and women who labored in the Paducah plant had contributed to their country, I added, and will meet its obligation to them. Joe Harding, a Paducah worker who died in 1980, had been featured in one of Warrick's *Post* pieces. Harding had written eloquently just before his death of a futile struggle to get the plant to acknowledge that it was responsible for his fatal illness. It was, he said, "like fighting a tiger with a toothpick." I cited Joe's widow, Clara Harding, who had taken up her late husband's struggle, and presented her with a gold medal "as a symbol of our sincere appreciation."

These town hall meetings and listening sessions around the country were often heartbreaking. We always tried to include Senate and House members, and they usually showed up. In Portsmouth, Ohio, with Senators Mike DeWine and George Voinovich, both Republicans, and Representative Ted Strickland, a Democrat, in attendance, a man rose to recall how he used to come off his shift coughing and wheezing because he'd inhaled uranium hexafluoride gas, which causes major lung damage. Voinovich asked him whether he'd do it again, knowing what he now knew. Of course, he said. I did it for my country.

In Burlington, Iowa, where there had been a final-assembly plant for nuclear weapons, Senator Tom Harkin, a Democrat, joined me in a meeting with former workers. One guy said that the workers were sworn to secrecy by the Atomic Energy Commission. "I never told my wife or my doctor what I did for a living," he said. Even after the AEC left in the mid-seventies, this worker remained silent and was reluctant to that day to talk about the plant. Harkin and I told him, It's okay, you can talk about this now.

The burst of journalism and a growing bipartisan coalition in Congress helped to push us forward, but the clincher probably was the release in early 2000 of a study by the White House's National Economic Council (NEC). When we first made our pitch to the White House in early 1999, we pressed strongly for immediate action on beryllium, a strong, lightweight metal used to "clad," or encase, nuclear weapons; in dust form, inhaled beryllium can cause deadly lung diseases. We had hundreds of people who had beryllium disease from exposure in plants that sold the fabricated metal to the Atomic Energy Commission. The problem was that most of these plants were long since closed, leaving the ill workers to the mercy of state workers' compensation programs. We argued that they had been making beryllium for nuclear weapons, even though they weren't contract employees, and ought to be covered by the federal government. The White House said we could move ahead on beryllium, even setting a tougher new standard to gauge exposure, but on the larger issue of exposure at the government's major nuclear plants, an interagency study would be needed. The NEC was designated to lead it.

Nearly every department of the executive branch was involved. The NEC report said that workers at the government's major nuclear-weapons plants were placed at heightened risk of getting cancer because of their exposures on the job. On April 12, 2000, three months after the draft report of the NEC study was released, I announced our compensation plan for America's ill-treated nuclear workers. The program would go through some congressional hoops before a final version landed on President Clinton's desk, but the basic program held up—thanks to the hard work of many lawmakers, including Senators Fred Thompson of Tennessee, Jeff Bingaman of New Mexico, and George Voinovich of Ohio.

The Energy Employees Occupational Illness Compensation Act, which Clinton signed into law on October 30, 2000, covered beryllium workers and employees at DOE, contractors or subcontractors who had developed cancer after beginning work in nuclear-weapons facilities. A so-called Special Exposure Cohort included workers at the three gaseous diffusion plants at Oak Ridge, Paducah, and Portsmouth, plus employees exposed to radiation in Amchitka, Alaska, where underground nuclear tests were conducted. Assuming certain criteria were met, all these workers or their survivors would receive benefits.

The Labor Department's idea in drafting the compensation scheme was based on a cash-payment model that would liquidate any damage claims and end any and all litigation. The amount was set at $150,000 and payment of medical expenses from the date a claim was filed. It wasn't perfect, but I thought it was a just outcome. The government finally had done the right thing, apologizing for what it had done in the past and trying to make amends with a concrete program of compensation. By now, thousands of workers or their survivors have filed their claims and the government has dispensed more than $2 billion. As I said earlier, the Wen Ho Lee business and the missing hard drives tarred my tenure at DOE, but there was another legacy, too, and it was the one that I cherished.

One final note. Elaine Chao, President Bush's labor secretary, didn't seem too thrilled about administering the compensation program and proposed in early 2001 that it be shifted to the Justice Department. She backed off quickly under a withering attack by members of Congress—Republicans and Democrats alike—who had participated in listening sessions and in the drafting of the final legislation. The program took effect on July 31, 2001. On August 6, 2001, the fifty-sixth anniversary of the dropping of the first atomic bomb on Hiroshima, Chao flew to Kentucky and presented the first check to Clara Harding, the widow of Paducah Cold War hero Joe Harding. Today, unfortunately, the program is still hampered by bureaucratic inertia and resistance. Nonetheless, it is the law.

IN LATE 1998 and early 1999, with the global market awash in oil because of overproduction by Saudi Arabia, the price of a barrel of crude slipped to around $10. American motorists loved it. On August 24, 1998, my first day as DOE secretary, the average price for a gallon of regular gasoline was a buck, and for seven months or so, it headed even lower, dipping just below 90 cents a gallon in March 1999. For U.S. oil producers and for oil-producing states like New Mexico, however, $10 crude was a complete disaster. It meant capping wells and pulling offshore rigs out of service because there was no profit to be made at that price.

The American economy was already well into one of the longest booms in history, and it now went into overdrive. Saudi Arabia, the biggest player in the Organization of Petroleum Exporting Countries, finally seemed to hear the market's signal and led a global production cut. In fact, my friend Luis Telles, by then Mexico's energy minister, talked OPEC into cutting production substantially; Mexico wasn't an OPEC member, but it had a lot of oil reserves and often played the broker in petropolitics.

The combination of accelerating demand and reduced supply had the predictable effect. By late 1999, crude oil was $26 a barrel, gasoline prices were rising, and supplies of home-heating oil—

essential to the frigid Northeast, where 70 percent of households used oil heat—were tightening.

A cold snap in mid-January 2000 made matters worse. At one point, Jay Hakes, who headed DOE's Energy Information Administration, said there might be an actual shortage of home-heating oil if the weather didn't break soon. Fortunately, it did break, but prices were more than twice what they had been the previous winter, and we were getting hammered by lawmakers from the Northeast to do something. What many of them wanted us to do was either to use the Strategic Petroleum Reserve or to establish a separate reserve for home-heating oil. I thought a home-heating oil reserve was the right thing to do, but the economic types at the White House and at the Treasury wanted nothing to do with it. It was against that backdrop that I hosted the first New England Heating Oil Summit.

Senator John F. Kerry of Massachusetts and a few others had called for the conference, and I was happy to accommodate them and anyone else with an interest in the issue. As it turned out, we had a pretty diverse crowd at Boston's Faneuil Hall on February 16—not only other elected and appointed officials from the region, but also a couple of dozen truckers concerned about a spike in diesel fuel, oil wholesalers and retailers, environmentalists and consumer groups, an investment banker or two, and a smattering of senior citizens. On one point, at least, everyone was in agreement: "It's obvious the federal government was not prepared," I told them. "We were caught napping." Once again, I was candid to a fault and got us into trouble. I should have kept my mouth shut.

Three hours of browbeating the Clinton administration for screwing up by not anticipating the price increase didn't get us very far. There were some suggestions about what we could do. One idea came from Joseph P. Kennedy II, son of the late Rob-

ert F. Kennedy and a former House colleague. Joe Kennedy had
returned two years earlier to Citizens Energy Corporation, the
nonprofit Boston firm he founded in 1979 that, among other
things, worked to get heating oil to the poor and the elderly. He
thought tougher regulation was the answer—specifically, a requirement that oil wholesalers keep a fixed minimum supply of
heating oil in storage as a cushion against fuel shortages and price
spikes.

I said publicly that we would consider Kennedy's proposal.
Clinton liked Joe a lot and later pressed me to make his proposal
happen. Privately, I had my doubts. More regulation was not the
answer to a market-driven problem, and I told Clinton to give
me a little more time to deal with the issue. What we faced was a
combination of OPEC power in the marketplace, our dependence on imported oil, and demand pressures, not only from a
strong United States economy but from a booming China as well.
It was clear that we needed an energy policy that would begin to
wean us from our dependence on OPEC, but so far, the executive
and legislative branches of government over nearly three decades
had failed to reach any consensus on what the components of
that policy should be.

In the shorter term, however, I thought there was much we
could do. One step was the reserve for home-heating oil. We won
the internal battle, finally, because there was no persuasive reason
to oppose the idea. And we were aided in the spring and early
summer by fresh data that implied shortages in heating oil during
the winter of 2001. Inventories were 41 percent lower than those
of the previous year; in New England, they were 70 percent
lower. When I met with energy people from the Northeast during this period, I used the smaller number because I just didn't
have the heart to hit them with the bigger sledgehammer. President Clinton backed me when I pressed the case, and on July 10,

2000, he issued the order to set up a 2-million-barrel reserve of home-heating oil, to be stored at four sites in New Jersey and New England. Within three months, the oil had been delivered and placed in storage. Two million barrels didn't sound like much, but it amounted to a ten-day supply for the Northeast—enough time, we thought, to get shipments from the Gulf of Mexico to New York Harbor in the case of a genuine emergency.

Other elements of our strategy for 2000 were more controversial. In September 1999, OPEC decided to maintain the production cuts it had imposed six months earlier, even though prices had doubled during that period; the oil ministers would review their decision, they said, in March 2000. It was important that these guys hear directly from us that the time had come to rethink their production cuts. Over the course of the year, I made four trips to various OPEC countries, principally the ones in the Middle East, to jawbone for hikes in output that would moderate the increase in prices. In the process, I became an easy target for politicians and pundits eager to take potshots and turn a phrase. Alaska senator Frank Murkowski called my trips exercises in "tin-cup diplomacy." *Washington Post* columnist David Ignatius called a visit to Kuwait and Saudi Arabia my "Hat-in-Hand Express."

I wanted OPEC ministers to act, but I wasn't pleading. I stressed that oil at around $25 a barrel was an equitable price for consumer and producing countries. A high price for crude oil could be inflationary, hurt economic growth, and unnerve the financial markets. Meanwhile, I tried to rally other big consuming countries—Japan and the members of the European Union—to get behind our position of price stability for oil.

OPEC oil ministers hated to see us pressing them so openly for production increases to lower oil prices, because they didn't want to be portrayed as the bad guys. Once, I placed a phone call to an oil minister during an OPEC meeting in Vienna. News of the call got out, and some ministers went public, screaming about the pressure from the gas-guzzling Americans. In the end, however, they felt compelled to take measures that gradually would reduce prices. On four occasions—in March, June, September, and October—OPEC agreed to increase oil production. Several large non-OPEC producers, such as Mexico and Norway, which I also visited, agreed to do the same. Sadly, crude-oil prices continued to rise through the first eight months of 2000, as the global economic boom continued to drive demand ever higher. By August, the price of crude topped $32 a barrel and the average price for regular gasoline was around $1.60 a gallon, close to double what it had been less than eighteen months earlier.

But within a few short months, both crude and gas prices were headed south. Perhaps the principal reason was our use of the Strategic Petroleum Reserve (SPR). After the Arab oil embargo in 1973 and the subsequent quadrupling of oil prices, policymakers in Washington realized just how vulnerable the United States was to a major supply disruption. In late December 1975, President Gerald Ford signed the Energy Policy and Conservation Act into law, creating the SPR. By the year 2000, it contained more than 570 million barrels of crude oil, stored in huge salt domes in Texas and Louisiana. The conventional understanding was that the SPR could be tapped only in the event of an emergency or a severe supply disruption. But the conventional wisdom was wrong. In fact, the president can order its use under other circumstances. One is so-called anticipatory authority—an order to release oil based on the expectation of a significant problem. We were considering doing it for Y2K, for example.

An energy secretary also can order test sales of up to 5 million barrels anytime he or she wants. A test sale of slightly more than one million barrels was done in 1985. And at the president's order, the government can exchange SPR oil to acquire oil later on. That's what I advocated within the administration. We could move oil to refiners at the most advantageous price we could manage, I said, in an arrangement that would require the buyer to replace the oil by a specified date. We might even be able to strike deals that required a replacement premium, assuming the refiners would use the futures market to hedge their risk and make a few bucks in the process.

The notion of using the SPR was out there in late 1999, when prices were rising and the presidential primary season was beginning to heat up; candidate George W. Bush, for one, said using the reserve was an option worth considering. My folks at DOE were thinking about it, too, and my interest even in the *possibility* of using the SPR gave fits to the economics people in the administration when they read about it in speculative press pieces. This would be an attempt to manipulate the market, they said, which wasn't the purpose of the SPR and wouldn't work in any event.

Prices continued to rise over the summer. In early September, the president asked for memos from Treasury Secretary Lawrence Summers, the chief opponent of using the reserve, and from me as the chief advocate of its use. Make your best case, he said, and then he'd make the call. Melanie Kenderdine, my chief policy adviser on oil and gas issues, and Gary Falle, my chief of staff, drafted our memo. We argued that psychological elements had come to dominate a frothy market that apparently assumed there wasn't any crude oil available, even at the margins. On September 10, the market made our point: OPEC announced that it would increase production by 800,000 barrels a day and the crude-oil price *increased* $4 a barrel. Using the reserve in a timely way could alter market psychology, we insisted, and drive oil prices down.

The International Energy Agency, based in Paris, was urging us privately to act, but we needed to hear from someone else before we moved. President Clinton, at a United Nations General

Assembly meeting in New York, told Prince Saud al-Faisal, the Saudi foreign minister, that we might use the reserve and wanted me to brief Saud immediately. A few days later, on September 15, Kenderdine, Rachel King (a senior policy adviser on international affairs), Natalie Wymer (a press officer), and I piled into a small government jet at first light and flew to California. This was figuratively under the radar screen; even Kenderdine's counterpart in the White House, Ron Minsk, didn't know about it.

Prince Saud was by then in Beverly Hills, and we needed to know what the Saudis might do if we surprised the oil-producing world with a sale from the petroleum reserve. I told him that we appreciated the latest OPEC announcement and his country's efforts earlier in the year to moderate oil prices. Then Kenderdine made our presentation, which essentially was a variation on the memo we had submitted to the president. Prince Saud, a nephew of King Fahd, took it all in and then told us what we wanted to hear: The Saudi government, he said, would regard the use of the U.S. Strategic Petroleum Reserve as an internal American matter. In other words, it wouldn't affect Saudi oil policy one way or the other. We certainly didn't need Saudi Arabia's approval, but it was good to know in advance where the kingdom stood.

We returned to Washington late that same day and I delivered the memo to the president. A few days later we got word that the president was backing my play and was ordering us to move ahead with the sale on September 22. That gave us a full working day, September 21, to put everything in place and push the button. Kenderdine, who would meet with the department's SPR people the next morning, counseled what I already knew—that this was going to be a political hot potato, that the opposition would go after Gore and me, and that I had to leave the execution of the policy in the hands of the professionals.

The next day, the *Wall Street Journal* carried a story, leaked to one of its reporters, on the contents of Larry Summers's memo to Clinton. Summers maintained that the release from the reserve would have only a "modest effect" on prices, if it had any effect at all. Further, he said, he and Federal Reserve Chairman Alan Greenspan concurred that use of the SPR would be "a major and substantial policy mistake," because it would set a dangerous precedent. Summers thought I was the source of the leak, but he was wrong. The last thing I wanted was to give exposure to Summers's position. It seemed to give credence to our critics' claim that this was all about presidential politics, especially when Gore later in the day proposed a series of 5-million-barrel test sales, with no advance notice to me and my staff.

I originally had argued for the release of up to 60 million barrels, but Clinton didn't want to go quite that far. Prince Saud also had asked that the president himself not announce the move, in the hope that it would get somewhat less attention. So on September 22, we formally announced that 30 million barrels of oil would be released from the reserve over the next month. The release meant that as much as 5 million extra barrels of home-heating oil would wind up on the market, helping to beef up inventories that were then much lower than they had been a year earlier. We suffered a few glitches, but we managed to get all the oil into the marketplace on our timetable. Our daily crude-oil consumption was running about 20 million barrels a day, so the release over this period of time represented about 5 percent of what we used. It was enough, and the market softened. That day, the price of crude oil for delivery in November dropped 4 percent on the New York Mercantile Exchange, to $32.68 a barrel. By Christmas Day, OPEC crude had slipped to $21.50 a barrel. And the SPR eventually got 33 million barrels from refiners in return for the 30 million we released.

There had been a bubble in the oil market, I felt, and our

policy had pierced it. But I also knew we would be deluding ourselves if we thought we had somehow gained control of our energy future. We still get most of our crude oil from abroad, which means that while we can complain about oil and gasoline prices at unprecedented levels, we lack the leverage to do much about them.

THE POST–COLD WAR world was supposed to be a safer place, and in one important sense, it was. We were no longer concerned about a direct nuclear confrontation between the United States and the Soviet Union. But Russia still possessed a formidable arsenal of nuclear weapons, and our concern was whether anyone was minding the store. Would hard-pressed Russian scientists succumb to rogue nations and terrorist groups that might pay top dollar to get their hands on even a small piece of the stockpile?

DOE is the steward of America's nuclear-weapons program, and it made sense for the department to play a big role in helping to address what everyone called the "loose nukes" problem. In fact, we were able to take some effective steps over the thirty months I headed the department. In late 1998, I started the Nuclear Cities Initiative, a program designed to open up Russia's ten closed nuclear cities and generate private-sector jobs for the thousands of nuclear scientists who worked at them. One of these cities was Sarov, a gigantic complex a couple of hundred miles southeast of Moscow where nuclear weapons had been designed and assembled. I visited on two separate occasions, and we managed to kick-start a couple of civilian enterprises there, including a joint open computer center in partnership with the Russian Atomic Energy Ministry and a German-American company to manufacture kidney dialysis equipment and supplies. These would employ a few hundred people, a relatively small percentage of Sarov's nuclear workforce, but at least we were moving things in the right direction.

Similarly, I made a couple trips to nuclear submarine bases in the Russian Far East. On one occasion we went to the formerly closed port city of Vladivostok during a full-blown typhoon. We didn't make as much progress as I would have liked in helping the Russians decommission and "denuke" these aging subs, many of them so decrepit they were no longer seaworthy. Access at these bases and at other sensitive Russian nuclear sites remained a problem for us, but by our internal estimates, we figured that DOE had improved security for nearly 70 percent of the estimated 750 metric tons of weaponizable nuclear material in Russia. That didn't mean these stocks were completely secure; it meant that we were closer to that ideal than we had been a few years earlier.

For all the progress, I felt it was important to get an independent assessment of our nuclear nonproliferation activities. In March 2000, I appointed a special task force, cochaired by former senator Howard Baker of Tennessee, a Republican, and the late Lloyd Cutler, a prominent Democrat who had served in several administrations. They headed a mighty distinguished group that included several former senators (Republicans Alan Simpson of Wyoming and Jim McClure of Idaho, and Democrats Gary Hart of Colorado, David Boren of Oklahoma, and Sam Nunn of Georgia) who were tough-minded and who knew their way around foreign-policy and nuclear issues. Andrew Athy, an old friend, also served on the panel. Andy is a trusted adviser with a rich background in energy issues who has helped me in a variety of ways during my time as energy secretary and as governor.

The task force delivered its report to me in January 2001, ten days before we left office. Its findings confirmed my instincts: We had registered some successes in the battle to contain nuclear proliferation, but there still was a long way to go. Our efforts and, crucially, the Nunn-Lugar cooperative threat-reduction program, based on 1991 legislation sponsored by Nunn and Senator Richard Lugar of Indiana, had reduced the Russian arsenal and improved the security at sites where nuclear materials were stored. Even so, the panel urged a quadrupling of funding for this work, to an average of $3 billion a year over a decade. And it underscored a glaring problem—the sale of so-called dual-use technology, including nuclear technology, by Russia to Iran. It is a problem that remains with us to this day.

When I was at DOE, we made a trip to Turkmenistan, one of the new nations of the former Soviet Union, and met President Saparmurat Niyazov, whose hospitality was almost overwhelming. He was important to us because of his part in the proposed trans-Caspian pipeline to transport Turkmenistan's natural gas via Azerbaijan to Turkey.

Rebecca Gaghen, who worked for me at the UN and at DOE, reminded me of a lot of the details of the visit. We flew into the capital, Ashgabat, from Baku in Azerbaijan. Ashgabat is pretty much the end of the line. The planes stop there and go back to Baku, because there's nowhere else to go. The city feels stuck in time. Even in 1999, statues of Lenin stood in the squares, as well as portraits of the "beloved" leader Niyazov.

Niyazov is quite short, with obviously dyed hair. The night we arrived he took our delegation to have dinner with his cabinet in one of his palaces. When you're on official business, you have to be careful not to offend anyone by turning down food you're offered.

This is especially true in Hispanic and Native American areas in my state. But Niyazov's dinner was well beyond my capabilities.

When we sat down, the table was already groaning with piles of caviar, fish, and other dishes. These were the appetizers. We were given a menu with twenty-three items, and were served, over the course of a long night, a twenty-three-course dinner. Our host gave a vigorous vodka toast before each and every course. He got more and more animated and danced with the attractive young women who were providing the entertainment. Rebecca says Niyazov did a dance that looked like the pony in slow motion. I had a lot of women on my staff, and they were horrified at the whole spectacle. They wanted to get me out of there. I tried to bring the curtain down on the proceedings more than once. We'd flown in overnight and were ready to pass out. No one paid any attention.

The next morning I was supposed to officiate at a wreath-laying ceremony but I just couldn't get up I was so exhausted. They moved the event back an hour. During the trip I was given various gifts, none of which I could accept. (This happened quite often. In Kinshasa, we were given a box of carved elephant tusks we had to leave behind.) In Turkmenistan the least practical was a beautiful horse Niyazov gave me. I said it was far more valuable than I was allowed to take, not to mention impossible to transport home, but he insisted.

We repaired for lunch to the horse stable. Niyazov wanted to drive me himself in one of the new black Mercedeses we were using, but he managed to drive the car right off the road on the very short trip and tear up the side of the vehicle. He just kept going as if nothing had happened. When we sat down for lunch, we picked up our menu and realized it was the same deal as the night before—all twenty-three courses. Niyazov proposed a toast and asked me to do the same. I said it was too early for me to start drinking and that I'd just have water. Niyazov clearly wasn't pleased, but I wasn't going to go through the whole banquet again. I said we'd just eat the food that was on the table and call it a day.

In the Clinton administration's waning days, we worked nonstop on the California energy crisis. I issued several emergency orders mandating that Enron and other energy suppliers could not turn off California's lights for nonpayment of bills. Larry Summers and I teamed up to try to advise then-governor Gray Davis how to manage and respond to the crisis. Davis had been claiming that the energy companies were manipulating prices and screwing California in the process. Two years later, he was proved right when Enron traders in electricity contracts were caught jacking up prices and manipulating the markets. At one point, an Enron guy, on a tape transcript, said that maybe we can get rid of that "fucking Bill Richardson" as energy secretary.

We worked flat out to the very end of the Clinton administration, and my chief of staff, Gary Falle, turned off the lights in our offices just past midnight on the day of George W. Bush's inauguration. We had won a significant environmental victory our last day at DOE when we convinced the White House to increase energy-efficiency standards for air conditioners by 30 percent. The Bush White House wasted little time in administratively overturning our last-minute order. Four years later, a federal court upheld our decision. I quietly lifted a Champagne glass with Barbara at the governor's residence in Santa Fe when we heard the news. Once again, I had made a small difference in our efforts to become a more energy-efficient nation.

. . .

WHEN I WALKED through the door at DOE in 1998, I told employees that I would be accessible to them, and I believe I was. DOE's career employees had been buffeted by political turmoil for years. We needed to demonstrate in concrete terms that we valued their public service and that we intended to make DOE a better and more rewarding place to work. In many ways, we succeeded. I utilized career employees and vested greater responsibilities in many of them than my predecessors and, for that matter, my successor. We made significant workplace improvements, making in-house child care more affordable for our people, doubling the subsidy for employees using public transportation, and opening a fitness center at our Germantown, Maryland, headquarters. We must have done something right, because I received an award from the government's Office of Personnel Management for the most dramatic improvements in the quality of work among all federal agencies.

Toward the end of my time at the department, I was able to do something to honor a man who'd been very important to me when I was in Congress. Mickey Leland, who represented Houston, was a very flamboyant guy and a genuine maverick. He and I had a lot of fun together, and Barbara was very fond of him, too. Mickey had a tremendous compassion for Africa. He died in a plane crash in August 1989 on a trip taking food to Ethiopia. Mickey's wife, Allison, was pregnant when he died.

Mickey had been very interested in renewable energy, and I wanted to leave a legacy in his name at Energy. The department had something they called the Office of Fossil Energy's Minority Education Initiative. I had it renamed the Mickey Leland Energy Fellowship, and the young people benefiting became Mickey Leland Energy Fellows. I think it is very important to celebrate the lives of our best people. I was delighted to be able to do this for Mickey.

It is traditional for all cabinet secretaries to have a portrait done. When my portrait was unveiled by my successor, Spencer Abraham, career employees turned out in force and cheered. That made me feel good. I made mistakes at DOE, no question about it. But I also made a positive difference, turning DOE into a better department by the time I walked out the door in January 2001.

Nineteen

IN LATE DECEMBER 2000, Thomas F. "Mack" McLarty III, Clinton's first chief of staff and special envoy to Latin America, approached me to discuss my options in the private sector after the Clinton term wound up. Mack went farther back with Clinton than anyone, back to kindergarten, and he made a big name for himself in Arkansas politics and business before he got to Washington in 1993. After he left the administration in 1999, Mack helped to found and build Kissinger McLarty Associates (KMA), a successful consulting firm in Washington. Now he was very interested in having me join his expanding team, and I was, frankly, intrigued.

The benefits of public service are intellectual and emotional, not financial. Barbara and I were comfortable, but we were in our early fifties and we hadn't built up any real savings. Mack was offering an opportunity to sign on at a high level, with the flexibility to supplement my income through lectures, teaching, and other part-time assignments. I would make good money as a consultant, concentrating in areas such as energy and Latin America that

I knew well. He also understood I still had a lingering itch I might want to scratch—a run for governor of New Mexico. I accepted Mack's offer and agreed to make a decision on the New Mexico governor's race by December 2001.

My energy level was as high as ever, and before long I was working three days a week on KMA business and giving paid speeches, sitting on a dozen corporate and nonprofit boards, making plenty of media appearances, advising Citigroup on energy issues, teaching a course on practical politics at Harvard's Kennedy School of Government, and traveling around the nation and the world. I love motion. I think well on my feet and I'm reasonably adept at keeping several balls in the air at once. This was a portfolio that played to my strengths.

Still, as the summer of 2001 wore on, I was hearing the call of politics more strongly. In New Mexico, the governor, Republican Gary Johnson, was approaching the end of a second term and was term-limited from running again. I'd been doing some groundwork already, and it was time to take some readings. I flew back to New Mexico over the Labor Day weekend and took political temperatures in seven or eight counties outside my Santa Fe base. The results looked good. After nearly eight years of Governor No, as Johnson's frustrated opponents called him, many New Mexicans in both parties said they were ready for more aggressive leadership, and plenty of Democrats, at least, were urging me to provide it. Barbara reminded me that we'd left a comfortable life in Washington and moved to New Mexico nearly a quarter-century earlier. Was I certain I wanted to do it again? The answer was a definite maybe.

My CALENDAR for September 11, 2001, listed an 8:30 A.M. meeting at KMA to discuss our objectives for our clients. It was an important session, with Mack himself presiding, and I arrived a few minutes early, grabbed my morning coffee, and wandered into the conference room where the meeting was to be held. We started promptly, but barely fifteen minutes into our discussion, one of our partners, Richard Huber, on speakerphone from New York, broke in and said matter-of-factly: "CNN is reporting that an airplane has just hit one of the World Trade Center towers." His television had been on, with the sound muted. It must be a small plane, everyone figured, and we moved back to our discussion.

A few minutes later, Huber interrupted again. "This is serious; a second plane just hit the other tower." It was 9:03 A.M., and events that disrupted forever the world we knew were unfolding fast. This second plane was United Airlines Flight 175, we would learn later; the first American Airlines Flight 11. Huber found the right words first: "Holy shit, this is an attack on our country." Then the phone line to New York went dead.

We scattered to our own offices, but I darted back to the conference room to pick up some papers I'd left. Through the window, I had a clear view of Pennsylvania Avenue in chaos— hundreds of people streaming out of the World Bank, the International Monetary Fund building, and around the corner from our offices, the White House and the Old Executive Office Building. They were all evacuating, and moments later Mack said we were being advised by security personnel to evacuate as well. Any nearby explosions, we were told, could turn the windows of our offices into deadly shrapnel.

Soon, only a handful of us—Mack, Nelson Cunningham, a Latin American expert, communications director Richard Klein, a couple of interns—remained in the building. I was too intent on following the news to leave. Klein and I moved to another conference room, the only one with a television, and it took a few seconds before I realized the projectiles falling from the windows of the towers weren't pieces of debris but human beings. The shocked mind denies what it cannot accept, which may be why a childhood memory suddenly popped into my head—an image of toy soldiers, two or three inches high, that little boys use to stage their mock battles. But this was the real thing, and those tragic souls in the towers, at the Pentagon, and on United Airlines Flight 93, which crashed in a Pennsylvania field, weren't soldiers but a new war's first innocent victims.

Just past noon, Mack and I compared notes. We'd each talked to some foreign leaders and to former colleagues in the Clinton administration—in my case, Sandy Berger, the former national security adviser. The media calls, beginning with Dan Rather of CBS, started to come in a flood. Osama bin Laden's name was coming up in connection with the attacks, and I was the last cabinet-level official of the United States to visit Afghanistan, where the Taliban government had harbored bin Laden and his terrorist training camps.

What I said was that bin Laden's al Qaeda network was large and growing. But we had time to fix blame for these unspeakable acts. Right now, Democrats and Republicans needed to put politics aside, pull together, and support the president. This massive attack, I added, deserved a massive response, including the use of substantial military force.

Barbara called with alarming news. She had just spoken with one of her closest friends from our UN days in New York, Christy Ferer: "Bill, Christy says Neil's missing." Neil Levin, her husband, was executive director of the Port Authority of New York and New Jersey, the World Trade Center's landlord. He had become one of my best buddies in New York. Neil had been in his new job only five months and had been attending a breakfast meeting at Windows on the World, the 107th-floor restaurant in the North Tower, when the first plane hit. Two weeks later, we attended a memorial service for Neil in New York, but it would be another seven months before his remains finally were identified.

I called Larry Sanchez, the man who had been my intelligence adviser when I was at the United Nations. He was now back at CIA headquarters in Langley, and he confirmed what I suspected from the start: "It's bin Laden, boss, fucking bin Laden."

Then Sanchez hit me with the crowbar: "Boss, they can't find John O'Neill." O'Neill was ex-CIA, one of the top terrorist experts at the New York Police Department. I knew him because he was our NYPD terrorism contact during my UN days. He was a good guy who often managed to bring me delicious cigars from undisclosed countries. John was gone, too.

Only later that day, after absorbing the full magnitude of these horrific acts, after learning of the probable deaths of two close friends, after going home past midnight to my wife, life partner, and best friend, did my armor against emotion begin to weaken and slip away.

OUR WORLD was turned upside down. Every premise I had cultivated about the international system was now at issue. That we could resolve disputes at the United Nations and in other international institutions. That diplomacy could serve as a counterforce to terror. That our intelligence was so strong we could prevent such acts from happening here. I previously thought the biggest challenge in the post–Cold War world was nuclear proliferation, but we had a new enemy, international terrorism, and its practitioners were using what the military types called asymmetrical warfare. That meant all sorts of unconventional arms, from suicide bombs and airplanes as guided missiles to potentially much worse—chemical, biological, and even nuclear weapons.

The tragedy convinced me that it was time for me to return to public service. I could get back in the arena, run for governor, do my level best for New Mexico, and try to offer leadership on national and international issues. In the post-9/11 world, governors were bound to assume a greater role in homeland security, and New Mexico had more than its share of prime targets for terrorists—stockpiled uranium, nuclear-weapons laboratories, military bases, and more. If I don't take this on, I told Barbara, I'm not sure I'll ever make a difference again. I felt bad for asking her to uproot herself yet again.

I had always been intrigued by the job of governor. When I was in Congress, several senators told me it was the best job they ever had. You get to set the agenda and then follow it through. Besides, neither Senator Pete Domenici nor Jeff Bingaman, New Mexico's junior senator, was going anywhere, and I didn't want to go back to Congress anyway. If I wanted to reenter the public sphere, running for governor was my only option. The political juices were flowing again; I desperately missed politics—the campaigning, the issues, the people, and especially, the ability to make a difference through public service.

Almost from the moment I got involved in New Mexico elective politics, there were rumors that I was going to run for governor. I did think about a primary run in 1994, against Democratic incumbent Bruce King, who had been elected three times over three decades, but I decided against it, partly because I had become a bigger player in Congress and partly because Barbara thought the timing was wrong. King wound up losing to Republican Gary Johnson, a conservative with a strong libertarian streak, who was reelected in 1998.

King's money guy had been James H. "Jamie" Koch, a native New Mexican who served four terms in the state legislature in the late sixties and early seventies. Koch and I had clashed over the use of federal funds I had raised while in Congress that I wanted to use in my prospective run against King. With help from his pals in the legislature, Jamie had inserted language in a bill prohibiting me from transferring the federal funds to a state campaign. It took a long lawsuit to settle the issue in my favor. But that was then; there were no lingering hard feelings.

In the spring of 2001, at his instigation, Koch and I got together at the 40,000-acre ranch of David Salman, another former politico who had served as the New Mexico House majority leader. Jamie said that if I wanted to run for governor, I could count on him in my corner; he would do whatever he could to get me elected. I thanked him, because I knew anybody smart enough to block me as he had on that funds transfer was a good guy to have on the team. I told him that I was thinking about it but hadn't committed. Still, we had to proceed as if my candidacy was a real possibility.

I asked Koch to produce a list of the financial heavy hitters who had contributed to King's gubernatorial campaigns over the years, and I called them all. I had Paul Bardacke, a prominent lawyer and former New Mexico attorney general, put together an exploratory committee. Most important, I assigned Koch the job of identifying the best person in the state to run the campaign if I decided to run.

Jamie told me the guy for me was Dave Contarino, a fortyish guy from Boston who had been in the state less than a decade. He had cut his teeth in politics as chief of staff to the late representative George Brown Jr., a California Democrat, in the early nineties. During that time, he got to know some top staffers for Jeff Bingaman. Contarino as campaign manager had helped Bingaman survive a tough challenge from Colin R. McMillan in 1994, the year a lot of Democrats lost their seats.

Contarino and his wife became enchanted with New Mexico and decided to stay. They started a title-and-escrow company in Santa Fe, but Dave kept getting pulled back into politics. I had met him in 1996, when I was chairman of Clinton-Gore for New Mexico and he was coordinating the campaign, but I didn't know him well. Bingaman said Contarino was a great campaign strategist and he also got high marks from other people I asked. Bingaman also said that Contarino liked to spend all your campaign money, so watch him. Jamie Koch sounded Contarino out and he said he'd talk to me.

Koch asked Contarino to work up a strategy memo. It was an impressive document, urging me to stress that my experience and accomplishments in Congress and as a negotiator were the ingredients needed to make a difference for New Mexico. We met for an hour to talk strategy and tactics, and I told Dave I'd get back to him. In late September we met, and I told him I wanted him to run my campaign. To my astonishment, the punk turned me down. Contarino said he'd construct a campaign organization and work on strategy, operations, and policy but he didn't want to do all the day-to-day stuff. He had a life apart from politics, he said—a business, a wife, two small children—and he didn't want it ruined. The guy had *cojones,* I thought. Fine, I said. I thought we could suck him in later. I did. Lock, stock, and barrel.

Contarino started to put together a campaign-in-waiting, and for the most part, I cut him plenty of slack. Even talented people should be held accountable, of course, but they deserve a lot of leeway, too. He signed up Billy Sparks as our communications guy. Sparks, a North Carolinian who is half Cherokee, started in politics as a U.S. Senate page, a sixteen-year-old protégé of Senator Sam Ervin's of Watergate Committee fame, and worked for a succession of Democrats and Democratic groups over the years. In the process, he became an expert in rapid-response politics—the art of instantly turning an opponent's attack around. Sparks helped Contarino on Clinton-Gore in 1996 and came to New Mexico to stay in 1997. He became the state legislature's first communications director and helped boost its approval rating from 19 percent to 50 percent in three years. We hired a husband-and-wife team of Ted Osthelder and Jill McNaughton as operations director and finance director, respectively. We also hired media expert Thomas "Doc" Sweitzer, one of the principals in the Campaign Group, an outfit based in Philadelphia. Sweitzer's firm went on to exceed our high expectations with some brilliant advertising. We didn't have Bob Shrum, the D.C.-based campaign legend and my old friend, because I felt his numerous commitments would not permit him to give my race priority. Today, the relationship is strained, to say the least.

In the fall of 2001, we were still in the so-called exploratory period, with no official declaration of my candidacy. I made a point of visiting every one of the thirty-three counties in the state. We were rounding up volunteers, raising money, and starting to get some preannouncement momentum. We planned the official announcement for the second week in January as a one-day road show, launching in Santa Fe in the morning, flying to the southern city of Las Cruces, the state's second-largest metro area, for a noon speech, then winding up in Albuquerque—the state's biggest market—in the early evening. Two of three events would include big fundraisers as well.

But Contarino sensed there was something missing in the unofficial campaign. It was moving forward like clockwork, but there wasn't enough tension and excitement, not enough buzz. So my reluctant campaign manager, who was formally a senior adviser at the time, decided unilaterally to goose the entire enterprise. "You can be 100 percent sure he's going to be announcing for governor," Contarino told an Associated Press reporter on January 3. The formal announcement will come January 12, he added. He hadn't cleared this with me in advance and couldn't reach me directly right after the fact. Instead, he left a message on my Washington voice mail: "I've just announced you're running for governor."

I got back to him the next day. "I just got your message, after I'd read it in the *Washington Post,*" I told him.

There was a pregnant pause. "Well," he said with a hint of apology in his voice, "I thought we needed something."

"No, no, I love it," I told him. "It's just what we need." And it was. The story went national and, boom, things took off. We were the talk of the state, the number of volunteers rose sharply, and we rocketed to my formal announcement on January 12.

EVERY STATE IN AMERICA has unusual, even unique, traits, and New Mexico has its fair share. We are the nation's first majority-minority state, where Hispanics and Native Americans make up 52 percent of the total population. New Mexico's regions often seem like separate mini-states, with sharply differing characteristics. North-central New Mexico, for example, is heavily Hispanic, with its people embracing a deep connection to the land, their culture and heritage, and religion. Northwestern New Mexico is oil-and-gas country, with large Mormon and Indian populations. Big swaths of the southeast part of the state—cities such as Clovis, Hobbs, Roswell, and Carlsbad—are heavily influenced by neighboring Texas; their politics tend to be conservative and Republican. Southern New Mexico, centered in Las Cruces, is the fastest-growing part of the state, with a significant military component because of Holloman Air Force Base and the White Sands Missile Range. Metropolitan Albuquerque, home to a third of the state's population, and Santa Fe are worlds unto themselves—the former an increasingly diverse area of high-tech and aviation, and home to half of the state's swing voters, the latter a liberal community that has become one of America's leading centers of the arts and Southwestern culture.

New Mexico ranks first in the country in the category of federal funds per capita, thanks to its two national laboratories, Los Alamos and Sandia, and its military installations. But when it comes to many lists, as I suggested when I declared my candidacy, New Mexico has little reason to be proud. We rank forty-eighth in teacher salaries, forty-ninth in per capita income, and dead last in the percentage of children without health insurance, I reminded New Mexicans. "By any standard," I told them, "our state government is failing us." I promised to end years of gridlock and political infighting in Santa Fe, the state capital, and pledged to work with the legislature. I meant it, too. I knew I would ruffle some feathers. So be it: If elected and reelected, I would have only eight years to move the needle for my state, and I intended to make the most of them.

First, of course, I had to secure my party's nomination for governor. Two other candidates had declared, state commissioner of public lands Ray Powell and former state representative Gary King, son of former governor Bruce King. A primary was set for June 4, but first the Democratic Party would have a nominating convention in March. There would be 1,500 delegates at the convention in Albuquerque, and any candidate who received at least 20 percent of the votes automatically qualified for the primary ballot. I was the odds-on favorite, no question about it, and I could have ignored the convention and probably won the largest number of votes anyway. But that's not how I wanted to do this. The convention was a test of power, and we needed to demonstrate our dominance. I wanted to score such an overwhelming victory that the possibility of an opponent in the June primary was eliminated. If that happened, it would be the first time in New Mexico since 1964.

We worked to corral our forces in the two months between my announcement and the convention. We identified every delegate and every alternate in every county and found out who they supported. I called the delegates, meeting with them in small groups or individually, if that's what it took; the uncommitted would hear from me more than once. The head of the state AFL-CIO, George "Jeep" Gilliland, was in Gary King's corner because of my role in the NAFTA vote. So we tried an end run by enlisting Brian Condit, head of the building-trades union, to plot our labor strategy. Brian was a blessing throughout the campaign, and when I took office, he joined my administration as deputy chief of staff. Condit got the state public employees union, the American Federation of State, County and Municipal Employees, to come on board.

We worked even harder at the convention itself. Osthelder had put together a strong on-the-ground operation, and maybe fifteen of our people were on the uncommitted delegates from the moment they signed in. I sat in a Winnebago outside the convention center, and my operatives would bring delegates in for a private visit. What seemed to impress the delegates was my love of campaigning and grassroots politics even after the fancy high-profile positions I had held. One on one, I would ask wavering delegates for their support. I tried not to push too hard. One King plant, who visited me in the Winnebago but had no intention of supporting me, told the press later that I was bullying him. It was baloney.

The vote on March 9 went according to plan. I got more than 75 percent of the delegates, Powell was in single digits, and King fell a few votes below the 20 percent threshold. Either one of them could still get on the ballot by submitting the requisite number of valid signatures from voters, but the message from the convention was clear: Democrats wanted what I wanted—an uncontested primary. By early April, both Powell and King had dropped out and I could concentrate exclusively on the general-election campaign.

While the Democrats were united, the Republicans were mud wrestling. Their primary was between Walter Bradley, the sitting lieutenant governor, and John Sanchez, a first-term representative and the state GOP's golden boy, who looked like the favorite. But Sanchez made a big tactical mistake when he attacked Bradley, trying to associate him with the policies of a prominent liberal Democrat in the legislature. That pissed off the Republican governor, Gary Johnson. We spotted a target of opportunity.

After the party convention I signed up David Harris to be my top fiscal adviser. David is a Democrat, but he had been Governor Johnson's first cabinet appointee and had headed his Finance and Administration Department for nearly six years. Harris and Johnson had tried unsuccessfully to cut personal income taxes over two terms in office. I'd gone on record with an op-ed piece in the *Albuquerque Journal* advocating a tax cut to make us more competitive with nearby states and to stimulate our state economy. I thought Harris could help us make a pitch to Johnson.

Contarino, Harris, and I met with the governor to convey two related ideas: Bill Richardson would be a fiscal conservative as governor, and in busting the gridlock in Santa Fe he could achieve what we both wanted—a cut in income taxes. We didn't think there was much chance Johnson would endorse me, but given his anger toward Sanchez over his attack on Bradley, we thought there was at least the possibility he'd stay out of the fray. Sanchez, however, hit one of Johnson's hot buttons when he came out big for a school-voucher program. After a nervous waiting period for the Sanchez camp, Sanchez triumphed over Bradley by 20 points in the GOP primary, and the governor and Bradley himself swallowed deeply and endorsed him.

At first, we aimed to keep my campaign on a positive footing. Of all the themes and issues tested on focus groups, by far the most popular was my success in negotiating the release of hostages, in particular getting Saddam Hussein to turn over David Daliberti and William Barloon to me. I had brought in Rick Homans, the guy who ran Tom Udall's campaign against me in the 1982 congressional race, as my principal policy adviser. Homans tracked down Daliberti and Barloon and got them and Daliberti's wife to Santa Fe, where Doc Sweitzer's partner at the Campaign Group, Mark Moskowitz, taped them in a sixty-second ad that became a central part of my campaign.

Meanwhile, Contarino and Homans and his group helped me develop what we believed was the most substantive, policy-rich campaign in the country. We rolled out thirty detailed policy initiatives on everything from taxes and education to domestic violence and health care. One of our highest priorities was taking aim at New Mexico's epidemic of DWI—driving while intoxicated. I proposed to toughen the penalties for those convicted of DWI offenses and to institute an education campaign and enhanced treatment programs.

Homans and his people also put together a 200-page plan to save $90 million in operating expenses. We contrasted it with Sanchez's proposals, which we said could well bankrupt the state. I was the fiscal conservative in this race, not my Republican opponent. The difference was between balanced budgets and insufficient funds, I said, and I praised outgoing governor Johnson for his fiscal probity. All along, we kept hammering on the gridlock in Santa Fe and my demonstrated ability in Congress, as an international negotiator, even at DOE to get things done.

Sanchez and his campaign went negative in a big way. Richardson was a tax-and-spend liberal, they insisted. He had ties to the evil Bill Clinton and the Lewinsky scandal, and he made a mess of things at the Energy Department. They dusted off the Bobby Byrd quotes from that Senate committee hearing in June of 2000 and used those, too. I had some potential vulnerability because of my association with a company called Peregrine Systems, a software firm based in San Diego that was run by Barbara's brother-in-law, Stephen Gardner. I was a Peregrine director from February 2001 to June 2002, when I resigned after the primary. Peregrine was an Internet high flyer during the bubble years, but there were accounting irregularities and it had filed for bankruptcy protection. I got hit for not participating in all the board meetings or reading every single corporate report. But I believed I had met my fiduciary responsibilities as a director and voted along with other outside directors to fire the Arthur Andersen accounting firm and replace it with KPMG, the outfit that conducted a new audit and discovered Peregrine's accounting problems.

Dave Contarino told me the only thing that could hurt me was the Peregrine association. My lead was eroding. I knew Sanchez was planning attack ads, so we had to strike first and take him out. Fortunately, John Sanchez wasn't all he claimed to be. I've made it a point throughout my entire career to work harder and longer than the people who work alongside me—especially people who work for me. I don't think even my political adversaries can challenge my work ethic. But Sanchez had a tendency to skip votes in the legislature. We ran an ad saying as much and citing his voting record. We even created a website—www.johnsanchezdoesntshowupforwork.com—and got a fair number of hits on it. We also chipped away at Sanchez's credibility and negated anything he had to say about Peregrine.

In a political race, I am almost reflexively paranoid. It doesn't matter what the polls show. You have to work every minute of every day as hard as you can and leave nothing to chance. We raised $7.5 million, and my finance chairman, Paul Blanchard, said he took in as much from Republicans as he did from Democrats. Over the course of the campaign, I probably shook a hand for every one of those dollars. In fact, I shattered Theodore Roosevelt's long-standing record for handshaking and made it into the *Guinness Book of World Records*. On New Year's Day, 1908, TR squeezed 8,513 hands; on September 16, 2002, BR touched 13,392 of them in an eight-hour period at the New Mexico State Fair.

My objective wasn't simply a win. I was running against the numbers, and what I needed was the general-election equivalent of that preprimary convention—a victory so commanding that no one could question its authority as a mandate for change.

On November 5, 2002, ten days before my fifty-fifth birthday, the people of New Mexico gave me the greatest gift I could ever imagine. My victory margin was over 16 percentage points—56 to 39, with 5 points going to the Green Party candidate. "As governor I will be on the side of ordinary New Mexicans and I will work every hour of every day to make a difference in the lives of our people," I said after it was clear I'd won and won big. What I didn't say was what my people already knew: I intended to start governing at a dead run and pick up speed from there.

Twenty

I WAS THE GOVERNOR-ELECT of New Mexico and was in my Jeep on the way to drop off laundry, when my cell phone rang. I answered, figuring it was Barbara or Dave Contarino or one of my other staff people. No: It was Han Song Ryol, the United Nations deputy ambassador from the Democratic People's Republic of Korea—known more familiarly as North Korea, now anointed a member of President Bush's axis of evil.

This was very weird. I had dealt with the North Koreans on several occasions. They apparently thought of me as an honest broker, someone they could trust as a negotiating partner or an intermediary or both. I knew Han, of course, but I didn't think he was calling to congratulate me on my recent election victory.

"Han, how did you get my cell phone number?" I asked him.

"I have friends."

"Well, what do you want?"

"I want you to help us with the Bush administration."

This guy just doesn't get it, I thought. "Han, there was an

election two years ago. I am a Democrat. My guys lost. I was just elected governor of New Mexico. What the hell can I do?"

"We want to pass along a message through you that we're prepared to talk."

"Okay, let me see what I can do. But I don't have a lot of time for this."

A few days later, I was in Washington at a how-to-be-governor conference. The agenda included a series of meetings at the White House, and one meeting involved Andy Card, Bush's chief of staff. I liked Card, although I didn't know him that well. On a little White House napkin, I scribbled that the North Koreans had contacted me to pass a message to the administration. I handed it to Card, who stuffed it into a pocket without a glance.

Two weeks passed without a word. Meanwhile, the North Koreans were calling nearly every day. "I did what you asked," I told Han. "That's all I can do right now."

Finally I got a call from Steve Hadley, who was then the deputy to National Security Adviser Condoleezza Rice.

"Governor," Hadley said in a serious voice, "I have your napkin." It cracked me up, and he laughed, too. "We'd like you to follow up on the message."

"You're sure?" We both knew a lot of people might not like it. I also had a new day job that would require my complete attention, especially over the first few months. My appetite for work was voracious, but there still were only twenty-hours in the day.

"Yes," he said. "Colin Powell will be calling you in a few minutes." I told him I had known the secretary of state for years and looked forward to hearing from him.

Powell reiterated that they wanted me to be involved. "Our channels to the North are not always working. See what's on his mind."

I told him I'd be happy to do what I could.

Then it was Han's turn. I said the administration was willing to let me play unofficial intermediary, if that's what his government wanted, but I was not an administration envoy. It was a familiar story.

He said his instructions were to deliver North Korea's message to me personally. "How about New York?" he suggested.

"No, Santa Fe," I said. I knew his travel in the United States was restricted essentially to the New York metropolitan area unless he got a special dispensation from the U.S. State Department. He said he'd get back to me.

I called Powell: "The good news is the North Koreans want to talk to me," I said. "The bad news is that they don't want to talk unless it's face-to-face."

"Oh, shit. Can you come to New York?" Powell asked.

There was no chance of that. I was about to be sworn in as governor of New Mexico, and I thought I should show up for that. Powell said he'd look into getting permission for Han and others to travel to Santa Fe. "That would be a gesture of goodwill," Powell said. "Can you keep it quiet?"

"Sure, but it'll get out."

"We'll do it very quietly," he said. "A visa to Santa Fe and nowhere else. We'll try to keep it under wraps."

"Great, but it'll get out."

The moment the North Koreans boarded their plane, it got out, on CNN no less. By then, it was my ninth day as governor, and the most covered story in the world featured my state, my capital, and me. We had fifty or sixty camera crews set up outside the governor's mansion in Santa Fe—from Europe and China and Japan and, of course, South Korea.

Han arrived, and I escorted him into the living room of the mansion. The only thing he had to say the first day was that the North Koreans were ready to talk.

"That's just great Han. That's what you said on the phone. But now that you're here, some details would be nice," I told him.

"We want to propose talks in New York or Pyongyang or some neutral place," he said.

The second day, the North Koreans announced in Pyongyang, their capital, that they were withdrawing from the Nuclear Non-Proliferation Treaty.

"Han, this is not good," I told him. "The atmosphere is not good. You're telling me you want to talk to the United States and you're withdrawing from the treaty? There are going to be huge headlines tomorrow: 'Governor of New Mexico Talks to North Koreans, North Koreans Withdraw from Treaty.' This is not the kind of spin that helps me."

"No, no, these are just tactics," Han said. "Tell Powell they are just tactics to improve our negotiating position." I was going back and forth on the phone with Powell, and in the end, we got a small breakthrough. Fortunately, it was never announced.

We had agreed on a broad framework for progress—an economic assistance package and a still-to-be-defined security guarantee against a U.S. attack in exchange for verifiable movement on the dismantling of North Korea's nuclear program. The North Koreans also backtracked on several other issues. A final deal would involve heavy negotiations. The administration, pushed by Powell, initially approved bilateral discussions. But apparently Vice President Dick Cheney and Defense Secretary Donald Rumsfeld went ballistic. No way, they said. The talks had to be multilateral, and that became Bush's position. Over a period of time, Powell faithfully and effectively executed the six-party talks among the United States, North Korea, China, South Korea, Japan, and Russia. Then the North Koreans balked again.

When the North Koreans came calling, I'd been governor less than two weeks and the state government's two-month legislative session had been due to begin in a few days. We thought the New Mexico press would roast us along with the right-wing radio types, saying Richardson was bringing the hated United Nations to New Mexico. But the press in Albuquerque and Santa Fe said the right thing—in effect, we're proud that this happened in our state. In my contacts with the North Koreans, I have been helped immeasurably by the sage advice of an old friend, K. A. "Tony" Namkung, an Asian scholar from New York.

It seemed fitting somehow that this would happen now. It drew a line between my past political life as a globe-trotting congressman, UN ambassador, and energy secretary and the political life that was about to unfold in the state I called home. I was proud, too. Still, it was a strange way to begin work on behalf of the people of New Mexico.

FORMER NEW YORK GOVERNOR Mario Cuomo once said that when you move from campaigning to governing, "you move from poetry to prose." It's true that the hard work of governance often can be mundane, even though you may be pushing for dramatic change. But in my view, politics without poetry—without the symbols, gestures, and retail elements—removes the visceral connections to your constituents, the things that give meaning to the proper prose of your official acts.

To honor my state's heritage and send a signal of the unity among its cultures—in effect, to extend the poetry of the campaign for one more day—I decided to begin my tenure as New Mexico's chief executive not in the Roundhouse, as the four-story circular state capitol is called, or in some grand hall or open-air ceremony, but in a room at the Palace of the Governors on the north side of Santa Fe's Plaza. The palace was built by the Spanish in 1610, the first official seat of government in what is now the

United States of America. At one minute past midnight on January 1, 2003, I raised my right hand, placed my left on a Bible, said the prescribed words, and became the first governor since statehood in 1912 to take the oath of office in that place.

I felt I'd completed a circle. I finally had a job where I was coming home. As a congressman, I didn't live here full-time, and neither did I as UN ambassador or energy secretary. Now New Mexico was my total focus. Perhaps I could even develop some hobbies and Barbara and I could spend more time together.

After a few hours of sleep, I appeared at the formal inauguration ceremony, a series of other events, and three inaugural parties. But the private ceremony at the palace—attended by 130 people, including my mother, my sister, and other family members from Mexico and from Barbara's side, as well as Governor Patricio Martinez of our sister border state, Chihuahua—had been the actual swearing-in.

The prose part of governance started the next day. The New Mexico legislature—seventy members in the House, forty-two in the Senate—convenes on the third Tuesday of January and conducts business for sixty days in odd-numbered years, thirty days in even-numbered years. Members are citizen-lawmakers; they receive no pay, except for a per diem when the legislature is in session, although many of them seem to dine especially well, thanks to the swarm of lobbyists who come to Santa Fe. During much of the eight years before I took office, relations between the Republican governor and Democratic legislature often turned nasty. As a result, not much got done. I intended to change the dynamic and get a lot done fast.

By the time I was sworn in, I already had named a cabinet. Now I wanted to do what I could to consolidate the instruments of power in state government so we could break the bureaucratic inertia of the past. New Mexico, like most states, differentiates between so-called exempt employees—in effect, political appointments—and classified employees, who fill positions with civil service protections against arbitrary dismissal. I replaced the previous administration's appointees with my own and converted vacant classified positions to exempt, which meant that the people filling them served at the pleasure of the governor.

Then I demanded resignation letters from each and every member of the state's three hundred or so boards and commissions. The majority of these people also served "at the pleasure of the governor." But over the years, the connection between the chief executive and the board and commission members had been diluted, in part because others—cabinet secretaries or even an industry or special interest groups—had made the appointments. Gary Johnson, my predecessor, had cared little about the boards, and legislators saw them as tools to pursue their parochial interests.

I rejected some of the letters because I thought the people were doing good work, but by the time we were done, every single board and commission member—more than two thousand in all—had been approved by me. I was determined these people all be competent. The positions were unpaid, for the most part, but I didn't think they should be filled by anyone who simply wanted a decoration for a résumé. We also got rid of boards that were ineffectual and we created new ones that I expected to perform: a Sports Authority to stage sports events, a physical education council to promote fitness, a film advisory board to stimulate moviemaking in New Mexico.

Many legislators, particularly Republicans, didn't like what I was doing, but they conceded that it was within the governor's authority. They got cranky, though, when I asked all the people I had appointed as regents to submit signed, undated letters of resignation that I could exercise if and when I saw fit. The regents were not obligated to do so, and only a few did. But I did require an undated letter of resignation from every new regent I appointed. That crossed the line for some lawmakers, who groused that what I was doing was unconstitutional, an opinion supported by the state attorney general. Fine, anyone who wanted to challenge me was welcome to do so. But I was the one who was elected with a clear mandate and I was the one who would be held accountable if my appointees screwed up. In December 2004, I decided to end the practice and ripped up the letters I already had received. I had achieved my goal: the regents were working hard and coming up with bold proposals and new ideas.

The people I was appointing to my administration and to the boards and commissions represented a broader cross section of the state's population than ever before. I wanted to expand the talent pool beyond Anglo men and Hispanics, who have played a prominent role in New Mexico's politics and government from the beginning, to include women, African-Americans, Asians, and especially Native Americans, who had been largely ignored in past state governments. My relations with New Mexico's Indians went back two decades to my first successful run for Congress. Within the first couple of months as governor, I had named a dozen Indians to top positions in the administration, including two cabinet secretaries, and a couple of dozen more to the boards and commissions. But we weren't playing any numbers games: These people were in their positions because of their qualifications and demonstrated leadership abilities, not because they were Native Americans.

I WAS DETERMINED to deliver quickly on my promise to cut taxes for New Mexicans. Most states in early 2003, hurt by a recession and unfunded mandates from Washington, were trimming

spending, raising taxes and fees, and employing creative accounting to close budget deficits. In New Mexico, eight years of political gridlock had yielded, paradoxically, a different outcome. The
Democratic legislature had refused to give the Republican governor any of his tax cuts, and the governor refused to spend on Democratic programs. The result was stagnation for the state but a
relatively sound financial picture. Now state revenue estimates,
driven higher by oil and gas royalties to the state, suggested we
could afford tax cuts and still meet our spending obligations.

I was convinced that tax cuts would improve the prospects for
keeping talented people and businesses, attracting new enterprises,
and kick-starting the entire state economy. It was vital that we be
competitive with nearby states. Our state personal income tax before I got elected was more than 8 percent, compared with 5 percent in Colorado and Arizona; Texas and Nevada, two booming
states, had no state income tax at all. My plan was to phase in over
four years a reduction to below 5 percent. Taking on the tax issue
first, I thought, would reinforce the idea that I was a different
kind of Democrat and create the momentum for everything else
we wanted to do.

Still, two key Democrats, Manny Aragon, majority leader of
the State Senate, and Ben Lujan, speaker of the House, weren't
quite on board. These guys were traditional liberals, and they
wanted to include an automatic trigger that would cancel the tax
cuts if revenues slipped below a certain threshold. You want as
much certainty in financial planning as possible, we countered,
and the trigger would undermine investment, because it amounted
to a permanent threat to rescind the cuts. I stressed that we had an
opportunity here to refashion the image of our party in the state—
and in the end, they got it.

The legislature took up my tax package, which included the

four-year cut in the personal income tax from 8.2 percent to 4.9 percent and a 50 percent cut in the state capital gains tax, as its first order of business after it convened on January 21. The package passed the House without a single dissenting vote and the Senate by a margin of 39 to 2. After a short House-Senate conference committee dealt with small differences, the final bill passed in both chambers on a unanimous voice vote. I signed it into law on Valentine's Day, 2003.

We followed this up with a pitch to corporate leaders in Chicago and a national advertising campaign in the *Wall Street Journal* and *Inc.* magazine. Then, in March, my mug, supersized on a billboard, showed up in New York's Times Square, extolling the virtues of New Mexico. I got needled, of course, but this was no ego trip—I already had a national profile. New Mexico would have been foolish not to capitalize on it and send a signal that my state was open for business.

We were especially eager to attract high-technology, high-valued-added business, with an open door to start-ups. The state had suffered one classic missed opportunity. In 1975, a couple of young guys named Gates and Allen had developed a language for the first personal computer, which happened to have been invented by Micro Instrumentation and Telemetry Systems, of Albuquerque. The following year, the trade name Microsoft was registered with the state of New Mexico. Bill Gates and Paul Allen retooled their software and signed up new customers such as General Electric and Citibank. By the end of 1978, Albuquerque-based Microsoft, with Gates as president and Allen as vice president, had thirteen employees and sales of slightly more than $1 million. Then it was gone. Why Gates and Allen left is a matter of some conjecture. Whatever the reason, Microsoft decamped and become the catalytic agent that helped to transform the entire Seattle metropolitan area. There are no guarantees, but I wanted to do everything I could to make sure that a future big fish didn't slip through our nets.

That's why I pushed for and got through the legislature in 2005 a research-and-development tax credit. It's basically a three-year tax holiday for new technology companies. These companies are laying scarce capital on the line, and we want to invest in their success, hence the period of tax relief. If they qualify, they can also take advantage of the tax credit we instituted for companies that provide high-wage jobs.

It was no accident that my first trip after the election was to Silicon Valley to let the companies and venture capitalists there know that we were a place friendly to business and eager for their investments. The most important visit was with the one that didn't get away. Intel, the world's largest manufacturer of computer chips, headquartered in Santa Clara, California, built a plant in Sandoval County, New Mexico, in the early 1980s and has expanded it steadily over the years. It employs more than five thousand people and has a payroll of $400 million, making it the largest private source of jobs in the state.

I sat down with Craig Barrett, the company's chief executive officer, and Paul Otellini, its president, and told them I was there to deliver two words from my incoming administration and the state of New Mexico: Thank you. That was it. Everybody who approaches these guys wants something, but I wanted them to know that we considered Intel to be a long-term partner and that we intended to do what we could to nurture the relationship.

Later, I invited Otellini to be a keynote speaker at the annual meeting of the Western Governors' Association in Santa Fe. He pitched the governors on tax policy, saying the United States was hurting itself and driving business to other countries by its corporate tax policies. Within a year, the governors had adopted my resolution, cosponsored by Utah governor John Huntsman, calling for U.S. corporate actions to reflect international competition.

I believe this had an impact on the state-supported collaboration between Intel and Sandoval County on a fifteen-year industrial revenue bond of $16 billion announced in 2004, the largest in the nation at the time. Intel wasn't promising to increase the number of jobs at the plant. But the company was saying that it would invest billions in its plant and effectively commit itself to New Mexico at least for another fifteen years and probably longer than that. Those high-paying jobs were going to remain in our state, not fly off to China or India or somewhere else where labor could be purchased for less than a dollar an hour. It was a huge vote of confidence.

We went after every piece of quality business we could. Even before the election, I had committed to attend the annual meeting of the World Economic Forum in Davos, Switzerland—a weeklong affair in January that brings together top political and business leaders from nations far and wide. The timing wasn't very convenient for me, given the start of my first legislative session in New Mexico. I'd been invited to participate in a discussion on North Korea. I also took the opportunity to promote my state to people who controlled significant investment dollars.

We put packages together on the fly when we had to. Early on, for example, we were fencing with Texas for a cheese manufacturing plant that Glanbia Foods, a big outfit based in Ireland, wanted to build in collaboration with the Dairy Farmers of America and Select Milk Producers. Rick Homans, the campaign policy guy I'd made my Economic Development Department secretary, was working with officials in the city of Clovis and Curry County, out on the plains of east-central New Mexico, to land this one. Glanbia planned to spend $200 million building the plant, which would generate 700 construction jobs over two years. After that, the plant would employ 225 people full-time, at good wages.

When Texas offered $6 million in state funding, we had to scramble to match it. Homans suggested that Clovis, Curry County, and the New Mexico Finance Authority, which we controlled, would be responsible for 75 percent of the $6 million; the rest, he said, would come from my capital budget, if I agreed. The numbers looked unassailable. The cheese plant figured to generate $10 million a year in gross receipt taxes statewide. Over ten years, according to his department's figures, $45 million in revenue would flow to Clovis and other communities in the area. Homans came to see me even as the Glanbia people were waiting in the reception area outside my office.

"So a million-five from my capital outlays gets this deal done?" I asked Homans.

"Yes."

"Do it, Dickie," I said. Homans prefers Rick, but sometimes has to suffer through the inevitable alternatives—Dickie, Rich, Richard, Ricky. So Dickie did the deal.

NEW MEXICO is the nation's fifth-largest state in land area, but it ranks down there in population—thirty-sixth. I felt we were simply invisible across too much of the country and the world, a place for arts-oriented tourists and downhill skiers but not much else. We needed to push harder than the other guys, to be out there where we weren't expected, demanding the consideration we deserved.

Early on, I made a trip to California to ask moviemakers to think about New Mexico as a location for films. To sweeten the pot, I pushed through some special incentives for filmmakers— tax rebates for movies and loans from the state of up to 60 percent of the cost of production. The industry responded: Movies like *The Missing* and *The Longest Yard* were made here along with television series, including Steven Spielberg's *Into the West*. Warner Bros. is filming *Astronaut Farmer* here in the fall of 2005. In my administration's first two and a half years, movies were being made at a rate of one a month, and the economic impact of filmmaking in New Mexico rose from $9 million to over $420 million during that time.

GOING BACK to my days in Congress, I always believed that economic growth and environmental protection were not mutually exclusive—that it was possible to strike a reasonable balance between them and even produce a win–win situation. New Mexico depended on oil and gas drilling to produce jobs and revenue for the state, and when possible, we needed to ensure that this important part of the state economy continued to flourish. As I had in Congress, I told oil and gas people that my door always would be open. But I also said that drilling wasn't an unfettered right, even in a business-friendly administration, and that there were lines I would not cross. One of them was on a tract of federal land called Otero Mesa.

Otero Mesa, in the Chihuahuan Desert of south-central New Mexico, features one of the most sweeping areas of native grasslands in North America. It is environmentally important for several reasons, not least because it carpets a vast groundwater system that should not be exposed to the risks of contamination. It is also a major hunting ground important to the state's sportsmen. For nearly a decade, the oil and gas interests have wanted to open up Otero Mesa, and in January 2005, they got a big leg up when the federal Bureau of Land Management approved a plan to drill a maximum of 141 exploratory wells on a couple of million acres that included the grasslands. The individual "footprints" of the wells wouldn't be huge, and there was a cap on the total acreage that could be disturbed. But the likely outcome was that wells would be dotted throughout the half-million-acre Otero Mesa, making a mess of this pristine part of New Mexico.

A year earlier, I had submitted my own plan for Otero Mesa, which would create a National Conservation Area, zoning off 300,000 acres from development, and impose restrictions on the rest of the land. The BLM director for New Mexico said no, and the national BLM's decision made it official. But that won't be the end of it. We're taking on BLM in court, and I'm going to do what I can to turn Otero Mesa into a national issue. The Bush administration has continued to observe a moratorium on oil and gas leasing off the coasts of Florida and California. Now the administration and Congress ought to apply the same principle to some ecologically sensitive areas onshore.

I am neither a blind environmentalist nor a free-market purist, which may be one reason why I was honored in March 2005 by the National Environmental Trust on the one hand and by the Cato Institute, a conservative/libertarian think tank, on the other. There often is a middle ground on these growth-versus-preservation issues. But what the BLM sanctioned for the Otero Mesa wasn't close to a compromise. It was an abdication of responsibility.

The honor from Cato, incidentally, was for being the nation's most fiscally responsible Democratic governor. We also got high marks from the outfits that rate our general obligation bonds, and I took a team to New York to try to make sure our excellent bond rating—it was AA+ at Standard &Poors—was maintained or even improved. In the end, S&P kept us at AA+, but I still thought it had been worth the effort. We got their attention; they wouldn't forget New Mexico anytime soon.

There were elements in our financial management that required more attention. One of the first things I did after taking office was order a performance review of every program in state government to see whether we could improve the efficiency of our operations and the delivery of services to New Mexicans. This will be a long-term exercise, but an annual-reporting requirement already has begun to yield results, generating significant savings.

I worked to revamp the state's inefficient capital planning. Each year there is money available from oil and gas revenue for capital projects—buildings, roads, water systems, and so on. Traditionally, the governor, the House, and the Senate each took a third of the pot to spend as they saw fit. Carving the pork three ways managed to feed a lot of special interests and other favored constituents, but it was a dumb way to allocate precious dollars in a state with pressing capital needs in areas such as education and water infrastructure. I believed we needed a more strategic approach that invested in building critical statewide projects to help fuel New Mexico's economic growth and reserved a much smaller portion for the House and the Senate.

In 2005, for instance, my capital budget called for spending $511 million, more than 20 percent of it devoted to construction of public schools and physical improvements at existing school buildings. I left $144 million for the legislature, about 28 percent of the total, rather than the two-thirds the lawmakers usually got. It was messy politics, because lawmakers like their pork and don't want anyone messing with it. We compromised, getting some substantial improvements in the whole process by designating statewide projects and priorities such as water-use planning, schools, and higher education.

So we've begun to modernize government in New Mexico and we've started to reinvent our state economy. These are not unrelated: In my judgment, a relatively poor state like New Mexico cannot cling to traditions that have outlived their usefulness and tarnish the image we want to present to the rest of the world. Per capita income in New Mexico ranks forty-seventh among the states, but we have begun to move the needle, I think, because of our tax cuts and my administration's efforts to attract new quality businesses. For once, we're finally making some of the good lists—we're consistently among the top ten states in job creation, for instance. Our art market, which brings in hundreds of millions of dollars in sales and tourism, is second only to New York's.

Neighboring Arizona ranks thirty-eighth in per capita income, and my aim is to close the gap between us. If we could do that, it would represent a 5 percent increase in our per capita income, or about $1,300 per person in New Mexico. Today, our economic policies have conservatively produced a projected $1.1 billion surplus over the next five years and 52,000 jobs since we took office. We have cut taxes for every New Mexican.

I am an unapologetic cheerleader for my state, but we're not selling snake oil when we talk about our virtues as a place to visit, live, and do business. "Hey, we've been telling you it's different in New Mexico." That was the tagline on the ads we ran after my first tax cuts were enacted in 2003. It's still different, only now it's even better.

Twenty-one

IN MY FIRST State of the State address on January 21, 2003, the first day of the legislative session, I returned to a theme I had struck during the campaign—that I considered the education of our state's children my most sacred obligation. There was no denying that New Mexico's public schools required attention. We ranked near the bottom in every measure: high school graduate rates; test scores; school attendance; teachers' salaries. We couldn't scrap the system and start over, but we could change it radically. I asked the state's lawmakers and the citizens of New Mexico to give me the tools to act decisively. I would accept responsibility for the results. Right away I wanted a dramatic 6 percent raise for all teachers and a formula for schools to shift funds from administration and bureaucracy to the classroom. In exchange for providing more resources, we'd demand accountability.

In New Mexico, the governor and the legislature played an important role in the financing of education, which accounted for nearly half of the state budget, but governance of the schools lay largely outside their purview. Policies were set by a state board of education, made up of ten elected members and five political appointees of the governor, and a superintendent of public instruction appointed by and answerable to the board. This structure wasn't working.

Dave Contarino, my chief of staff, has terrific strategic instincts. He designed a plan to go to the voters with two constitutional amendments—in effect, a fall referendum that gave New Mexicans the opportunity to overhaul the educational order. Amendment One would eliminate the position of school superintendent and replace the board of education with an elected advisory commission. A new Education Department in the executive branch of government would be created, headed by a cabinet secretary—an "experienced educator," in the proposal's language—appointed by the governor.

Amendment Two would allow the governor to increase the percentage drawn each year from the state's Land Grant Permanent Fund, commonly known as the Permanent School Fund, from 4.7 percent under existing law to as much as 5.8 percent for eight years, at which point the draw would fall in increments and settle at 5 percent.

The fund got its money from two sources: land-office revenue, mainly income from taxes and royalties on oil and natural gas leases, which amounted to $200 million or so the previous fiscal year; and more significantly, return on investment. The fund's value was around $6.8 billion, and investment income had been growing at an annual rate of 10 percent over the previous fifteen years. Even with a higher distribution of money for the schools, we argued, the fund almost certainly would continue to grow in size. We included a trigger mechanism: If the fund ever fell to $5.8 billion, the withdrawal rate would automatically revert to the original 4.7 percent.

The extra funds, calculated at $68 million in the first year, would help to pay for extra tutoring for children in need of it, summer programs, and classroom activities. Crucially, the money also would underwrite higher salaries for teachers, who in turn would be held to higher standards—a pay-for-performance program built around a new, three-tier system of licensing. A teacher with at least six years' experience who met the highest standard would earn $50,000 for the nine-month school year. Overall, salaries would rise 6 percent in year one, notching up New Mexico's teachers from forty-sixth to twenty-ninth in pay among the states. We had to do everything we could to keep talented teachers in *our* classrooms, not in the classrooms of Colorado or California.

Together with Rick Miera, chairman of the House Education Committee in the state legislature, Contarino convinced me to put my political capital on the line to get the two amendments approved by the voters. I had managed to get my tax program and other key priorities through the legislature during the winter session, but my standing as a strong governor who got his way would suffer a real body blow if either of these amendments was defeated. I needed to be in full campaign mode and I needed someone to coordinate our efforts and drive them forward.

Contarino had another inspiration: He hired Amanda Cooper Udall, a talented political operative, to head our campaign. Cooper has a hell of a political pedigree as a member of the Udall clan and is the daughter of Tom Udall, who ran for and won my old seat in Congress. She managed his campaign, has run a few dozen others over the years, and is now my political director. She's smart, works almost as hard as I do, and wakes up every morning thinking about doing great things. Some people have nicknamed her Demanda because of her drive; I call her "The Machine."

The Machine went into gear to raise money, creating a political action committee as the main vehicle. NM CARES (New

Mexico Citizens for Accountability and Reform in Education) brought in nearly $2 million for advertising, direct mail, and other efforts to "brand" our campaign. We wanted everyone in New Mexico to know what was intended when they saw billboards and flyers with the words "YES on 1&2."

Cooper researched the capital of direct democracy, California, and discovered that referendums weren't as simple to get approved as it seemed from afar. The easiest thing for voters to do was to just say no. A California consultant also told us it would be nearly impossible to pass two related referendums at the same time. Then there was the problem of the piggyback effect: once the date for a statewide ballot was established, other initiatives were bound to surface. A couple of dozen did. In Albuquerque, for instance, Martin Chavez, the city's ambitious and aggressive mayor, wanted to put a tax-increase proposal for public safety before local voters. Any other issues on the ballot could hurt us, we felt, especially a proposed tax hike at a time we were asking voters to approve a bigger take from the state's Permanent School Fund. I persuaded Chavez to hold off, and in the end, we managed to clear the ballot statewide except for a couple of items in Santa Fe.

Early polling suggested that Amendment Two would pass easily—people always wanted more money in the schools—but Amendment One might be difficult to pull off. People didn't see a new official in Santa Fe—education secretary—as a solution for making their local schools better. Some opponents, including people in my party, portrayed it as a personal power grab. They were right: it was a demonstration of political muscle. But I wasn't doing it just for the exercise. I believed our proposals would benefit the children, parents, and teachers of the state, and we needed the authority to implement them. If you can't use political power to get good results for your constituents, what's the point of seeking public office?

During what was my second campaign in less than a year, we tried to recruit everyone we could—the unions, the educators, the Association of Commerce & Industry of New Mexico, the state's congressional delegation, the PTA, and any other group with a constituency willing to hear us out. I gave 150 speeches at seventy-five or eighty schools statewide over a couple of months, and Cooper and her people were working seven days a week, twelve and fourteen hours a day. They marshaled a small army of volunteers who went door-to-door throughout the state. The press wondered why I would speak at elementary and middle schools to kids who couldn't vote. It was simple: Our targets were their parents and teachers and the school staffs. We knew it would be a low-turnout election, and that made every vote especially important.

Officially, Republicans were split. The state Republican Party supported Amendment One because a lot of its members loved the idea of deflating the old education bureaucracy. But the party balked at Amendment Two, calling it a "raid" on the Permanent School Fund. After objecting at first, Senator Pete Domenici announced his support—in part, he said, because of the education given him by his own children and grandchildren. The state's other U.S. senator, Democrat Jeff Bingaman, was on board, and we were grateful to have him. But given the GOP's opposition to Amendment Two, Domenici's support was crucial.

On Monday, September 22, the day before the referendum, teachers gave kids stickers for their clothes, complete with smiley face, that read, "Mom & Dad, Please don't forget Tuesday is Election Day!!!" That same day, I campaigned from sunrise to past sunset with speeches in Socorro, Belen, Las Lunas, and Albuquerque—the last an appearance before a conference of two thousand educators. I went straight at them: This is our last chance to improve our schools. Trust me to try and make constructive changes.

Our polling was lousy. We thought Amendment Two would have to carry a problematical Amendment One across the finish line. Exactly the opposite happened. With no effective opposition, administrative reform passed easily, but the School Fund reform, under constant attack from the right, turned into a cliffhanger. It took days of recounts in every county in the state, but Amendment Two finally prevailed by less than 300 votes. We would get our fundamental school reforms—more accountability and more money in the classroom—but we would be held to our promise for real results.

I READ AT LEAST three newspapers a day—the *Albuquerque Journal,* the *Santa Fe New Mexican,* and the *New York Times*—plus a packet of clippings assembled by my staff gleaned from a couple of dozen other publications. I'm in constant touch with key members of my team, especially Dave Contarino, my chief of staff, and I push people hard to make sure I get the information I need to make intelligent decisions. It may take a day or two, but I eventually read everything that crosses my desk. I believe in working day-to-day while keeping the bigger picture in mind. It pays to be flexible. If you spot something that looks right, you have to be prepared to move quickly, not spend a year studying it to death.

I'll take good ideas where I find them. In early March 2003, for example, I read in the *Times* about how Angus King, who'd been governor of Maine for eight years, until early that year, had started a program that gave every seventh- and eighth-grader in the state a free laptop computer. This was a nationally acclaimed program that had impressed other states and that other governors were considering.

When I talked about trying it in New Mexico, some of my staff said people here didn't care about computers. They're more worried that their kids can't read. I thought that was baloney. Why should reading skills and computer skills be mutually exclusive? I decided we should do some research and see where this could go. It turned out that Dell was interested in targeting a couple of states for computers in the classroom. We convinced them that we should be one of them, and in January 2004, we unveiled our program to provide computers for every seventh-grader in New Mexico. We allocated $4 million to support the program, and it's off and running. In the summer of 2003, while we were working on the program and before Dell was fully committed, King, who had ended his eight years as Maine's governor, came through Santa Fe on an RV trip he was taking with his family. I'd never met him before, and was a bit surprised by the postgubernatorial look: He had a big, long beard and looked like Jesus Christ. I said, Angus, you're kind of weird, but that computer program was one hell of an idea and I stole it from you. Today, it is one of the signature programs in our schools.

Veronica Garcia, my new education secretary, is a career educator with experience as both a teacher and an administrator. Our new licensing program is in place, we're putting more money into classrooms, and there are even some anecdotal signs of improvement in student test scores. I'm not fooling myself. It will take many years to turn New Mexico's public schools around and provide a quality education for every child, especially kids from troubled backgrounds. But at least we're moving in the right direction. We've made a start.

BARELY A MONTH after the September 23 referendum, I called a special session of the legislature. In July, a sixteen-year-old girl, Marissa Mathy-Zvaifler, had been killed at a concert in Albuquerque; the man charged with the crime, a janitor, had previously raped a four-year-old girl and, upon conviction, was given probation instead of prison. There would be no serious disagreement here, given the public outrage, and there wasn't: Marissa's Law, as I insisted it be called, which included much tougher penalties for sexual predators, passed overwhelmingly.

The special session also included legislation for a multi-billion-dollar transportation package that included commuter rail in the Albuquerque metropolitan area and other job-creating initiatives. We'd pay for it, I said, with a modest increase in some taxes and fees, mostly on out-of-state trucking companies that cause the greatest amount of the wear and tear on the roads. But neither Marissa's Law nor the transportation bill was the main reason I called the legislature into session. I wanted to see if we could build on the tax changes enacted in February, make better sense of the state tax code, and provide tax relief to those who needed it most—senior citizens and low- and middle-income working families. I endorsed a proposal to pay for the tax cuts with a modest increase in liquor taxes—what amounted to an extra dime a drink. Our polling suggested that four out of five New Mexicans would support it. But only five days into the session, the wheels came off.

I was in Roswell, New Mexico, on Friday, October 31, announcing that a bus manufacturing plant would be reopening with the help of the state government and that it would add about four hundred new jobs to the state economy, when I heard that the State Senate had adjourned after members got nowhere on my tax proposals. No one was sure when they would be back. In America, you can send messages through the press, which was the first thing I did. This special session is costing New Mexicans $68,000 a day, I told reporters. The House is working and I'm working, but your state senators just walked out on eight thousand highway jobs. That got their attention.

Richardson's Rules

> · Use the media if you need to, but keep your negotiations private.
> · Give up the little things. The other guy wants to hold a press conference? Fine.

The law required the Senate to return within five days so long as the state House of Representatives remained in session, and I figured the members would be in the Roundhouse early the next week—in time, I hoped, to hear Mexican President Vicente Fox, who was visiting Santa Fe at my invitation. Even so, this was a major embarrassment. I'd been blindsided, and some of my closest allies in the Senate were a party to it. The motion to adjourn had been supported by Senate President Pro Tem Richard Romero, an Albuquerque Democrat who was planning to run for the U.S. House in the First Congressional District against incumbent Republican Heather Wilson, who'd beaten him in 2002. Romero didn't want to look like a tax-and-spend liberal for the campaign.

One of my political axioms is that when you're hit, you always need to hit back—harder, if possible. It's one way you earn an opponent's or even a wayward supporter's respect. I called Jamie Koch, state chairman of the Democratic Party, and told him to tell the senator he was in deep shit. I didn't take it public—Romero would have lost face—but I had Koch advise Romero that my enthusiasm for his congressional candidacy was in jeopardy. Jamie also needed to tell Romero that I would expect something in return for my making this right again. The Senate came back the following Tuesday, a day earlier than the deadline, and Romero wound up backing the big transportation bill, including the higher taxes and fees. But the tax plan, with or without Romero, was a lost cause. Liquor companies had effectively killed the bill. My friends in the liquor business and I just disagree. I remain convinced that a modest increase in liquor prices would not have hurt their businesses, and would have paid for needed tax cuts, but it was not to be.

Richardson's Rules

· **Have others deliver bad news; it keeps you viable as a future negotiator.**

Romero later became one of my closest allies and is a good friend. I happily supported him against Wilson, but he lost when New Mexico voters returned all three congressional incumbents to office. My postmortem on the special session wasn't as tough on him as my reaction in the heat of the moment. There never was a vote on personal taxes; if there had been, I would not have won. It wasn't because the plan was deeply flawed or that the numbers failed to add up. The truth was that I had committed all my energy through September to the education amendments, and I hadn't devoted the time to talking through with members of the legislature what I wanted to do. As a result, state lawmakers were unprepared to deal with my proposal. There was someone to blame for this debacle, and I looked at him every morning when I shaved. In the aftermath, I vowed never to make that mistake again.

WHEN I TOOK OFFICE, drunken driving in New Mexico had reached epidemic proportions. Our rate of DWI arrests was running 50 percent above the national average, and the death toll on highways was consistently the highest or among the highest in the nation on a per capita basis. DWI was the leading cause of death and injury among New Mexicans forty-four years old and younger, and the estimated cost in medical bills, higher insurance rates, and other expenses topped $1 billion a year.

In New Mexico, on nearly every major road or highway, you cannot travel more than a few miles without spotting a shrine—marked with crosses, pictures of the Virgin of Guadalupe, and flowers—where someone lost his life in a car accident. These shrines are kept up by mourning family members, and the vast majority of these deaths involve drunk drivers. These are a constant and side reminder of the terrible toll this epidemic takes on society.

The reasons for the crisis weren't mysterious. As the *Albuquerque Journal* documented in a fine special report in May 2002, kids started drinking when they were teenagers or younger, and parents weren't doing enough to stop them. Law enforcement wasn't as vigorous as it should have been in cracking down on drunken drivers and on bars that served underage drinkers. The *Journal* investigative staff also revealed what was an intolerable dismissal rate of DWI cases in Albuquerque's Metro Court.

Over nearly three years of work, we have come up with one of the best drunken-driving programs in the country. We started with stiffer laws for repeat offenders—an additional four years added to a drunken driver's sentence for each prior conviction. Before, jail time wasn't mandatory for DWI offenders who violated the terms of their probation; it is now. We also cracked down on repeat offenders in other ways, lowering the DWI blood-alcohol limit from 0.8 to 0.6 and making participation in a treatment program mandatory. Ignition interlocks—which require a driver to blow into a device that measures blood alcohol

and prevent the car from starting if the driver is over the limit—
are required in my state after the first DWI conviction. The greater
the number of convictions, the longer drivers must keep ignition
interlocks in their cars after they serve their time. We may have the
best ignition interlock program anywhere. We set up a "Drunk-
busters" hotline to report suspicious driving and created a radio
and television advertising campaign that featured me hammering
home the anti-DWI point in a concluding six words: "You drink,
you drive, you lose." No exceptions. One of my policy guys was
charged with DWI late one Friday night and he wasn't working
for me three days later. During the 2004 political campaign, I
bagged a fundraising appearance for a Democrat running against
a Republican incumbent in the State House because it turned
out our candidate had a DWI conviction the previous year.

The war on DWI will take time. But there is some evidence
that drivers in our state are getting the message. In 2004, there
was a 15 percent decline in drunken-driving incidents, according
to police statistics, and we have seen continuing improvement in
2005. It's not a trend yet. Still, like the upward tick in our public
schools, it's a beginning.

THERE IS A LOT of wisdom out there, among people most politicians don't rub up against on a regular basis, and I always thought
it was especially important to tap into it as often as I could. That
was one reason I was so addicted to town hall meetings when I
served in Congress. It wasn't just constituent service, it also was
about the ideas constituents brought to me. I'm trying to do the
same thing as governor, with meetings twice a month around the
state with people who have contacted my office or sometimes
just walked in off the street. We schedule these sessions for three
hours or so, and I manage to see maybe fifty people over that

period of time. I'm direct: "What do you want?" I ask them. People want streets or even state government buildings named after New Mexicans who have made a difference, or otherwise deserve to be honored, and why not? Sometimes they want pictures or simply to be thanked for some act. We can really help some people, but the fact that we are willing to listen also reduces the cynicism many people feel toward government.

Richardson's Rules

> · In most meetings, the law of diminishing returns kicks in after five minutes.

When I was a congressman, a lady in Raton said we should get the Santa Fe Trail designated as a historic trail by the federal government. We got it done. My excellent constituent-services staffers, then and now, have done many a good deed. As governor I set up an office in Las Cruces that has two people doing constituent work—such things as getting marriage licenses or social security checks. I still consider solving people's problems a big part of any public official's job.

Even, or especially, at the highest levels of government, one must stay personally connected to the people one represents. Their interests must be your interests, if you are to serve the public good. To this day, I have hundreds of supporters whose loyalty to me and endorsement of my public effort is due to the personal help I provided them or their families, not some policy I pursued in Washington or Santa Fe.

Twenty-two

I SUPPOSE IT WAS inevitable, given what happened in the 2000 presidential election, the attention I was getting as the nation's only Hispanic governor, and the remorseless demands of the presidential campaign calendar. Still, the talk about my appearing on the national ticket as the vice presidential candidate so soon after my inauguration in New Mexico was almost as uncomfortable as it was flattering. Early and often, I said I intended to work hard for the Democratic ticket but that I was not a candidate for the second spot.

The truth was that I was in a tough spot. Republicans, some Democrats, and much of the media had questioned my commitment to New Mexico during the run for governor. They thought I'd abandon the job to seek higher office even before a first term ended. I pledged during the gubernatorial campaign that I would serve a full four-year term, because it would take that long, or perhaps longer, to accomplish what we had set out to do. I had no intention of reneging on that promise. But if the candidate of my party came to me and asked me straightaway to be his running

mate—that my presence on the ticket could be key to victory—
could I really say no?

The chatter persisted for several reasons. One was that I continued to be highly visible—a popular choice for political shows on national television when they were looking for an experienced talking head to discuss foreign policy, Iraq, national security, and energy-related issues. Another was Hispanic America's growing population and potential influence on the presidential election of 2004. And finally, I hadn't made the classic disavowal of the office under any and all circumstances, retired general William Tecumseh Sherman's promise to Democrats in 1884 not to run if nominated and not to serve if elected. In the minds of party activists and political pundits, I was leaving the door ajar, if not wide open. It was a position that didn't bother me much. I wanted to stay on the national political stage, because it was important to me and my state. The nondenial denial suited those objectives even as it reflected my own ambivalence.

In the summer of 2003, as the talk about a possible Richardson vice presidential nomination continued, two targets of opportunity appeared in the crosshairs that figured to help New Mexico and do me some good, too. Key to both was Terry McAuliffe, chairman of the Democratic National Committee. There remained some bad blood between us, because he felt I had wanted the DNC job after the 2000 election. I may have flirted with the idea, but I didn't really want to head the DNC. Even so, Terry was paranoid about any speculation that he wasn't an effective chairman.

Much had happened since those days in late 2000. For one thing, we got creamed in the 2002 elections. Terry had predicted that we'd gain seats in the House and Senate, and we lost seats in both chambers. But I predicted we'd get more Democratic governors, and we did, so I was making the case in party circles that

the governors should get more seats on the DNC and more official responses to President Bush's remarks. We were the only bright
light in the party, I said publicly. McAuliffe, I said privately, wasn't
that strong as chairman, although he was a prodigious fundraiser.
Maybe he should go. Naturally, it got back to him. Naturally, I
didn't mind that it did.

I read that McAuliffe wanted to hold a series of debates for the
Democratic presidential candidates before the primaries, because
there had been so much public bickering among the declared and
even undeclared candidates. He was talking about six or seven debates, and I was going to make damn sure one of them was going
to be in my state. So I called Terry and he said, No way, we've got
to do these in big cities and in early-primary states. I reminded
him that we had moved up our presidential caucus to the first
Tuesday in February, along with Arizona, and said I was going to
push on this if that's what it took. Remember, pal, I'm around.
Terry was a good guy and I liked him, even though I may have
yanked his chain here and there. He also was smart enough to
know that I had some juice. I'd won big. I was Hispanic. I still had
a strong connection to his mentor, Bill Clinton. The next thing I
knew, McAuliffe was in Santa Fe to have dinner and, frankly, to
make peace.

My people decided we had two objectives. We wanted to get
a debate, preferably the first one. That would frame us as an important battleground state even though we only had five electoral
votes. We also wanted the chairman of the 2004 Democratic convention in Boston to be the governor of New Mexico. At first, I
said, No, let's do one thing at a time. Then I switched and agreed
to go for both, figuring McAuliffe would cave immediately on
one of them. It worked out more or less as planned. McAuliffe
said he couldn't make me the convention chairman because that
would be the choice of the nominee. I said, Well, I'm going to

start a campaign. He said that if I got an okay from all the candidates in the field, he'd do it. Terry wouldn't commit to the debate on the spot; he'd take it under advisement. Fine.

After McAuliffe left, we got Hispanic groups and other prominent Latino pols to turn up the pressure on the debate issue. McAuliffe either saw the light or folded, depending on your interpretation, but we got what we wanted. On August 8, I got to announce that the first presidential debate would be held on Thursday, September 4, on the University of New Mexico campus in Albuquerque, hosted by yours truly and the congressional Hispanic Caucus. It would be the nation's first bilingual debate, broadcast by PBS and Univision, the Spanish-language network.

This was a great opportunity for New Mexico, and we had to get the logistics just right. I told our staff to make sure the national press got whatever they wanted—access to the candidates and to anyone in state government, good work spaces, events with our state party. We wanted a visually interesting debate, with an audience that included ordinary citizens and young people, not just pols and activists, and the chance for the audience members to cheer for their candidates. I wanted time to visit with each of the candidates, although I would preserve my neutrality. The entire point was to show McAuliffe and anyone else watching that New Mexico played in the big leagues.

The debate was a huge success. For a couple of twenty-four-hour news cycles, New Mexico was the center of national and even international attention. New Mexicans felt proud, no small thing in a small state with a chronic and unjustified inferiority complex. The press and some campaign aides called it "the Richardson Debate" because I had put it together and tried to be everywhere at once just before and just after the event itself. That got me into trouble after I left one postdebate reception. I wanted to drop by a fundraiser for Joe Lieberman, the Connecticut senator who has been Al Gore's vice presidential choice in 2000 and who was now trying for the top spot on the ticket. We were running late, and I told the driver of our vehicle to step on it. This is a demand not unknown to members of my staff, who have become familiar with my love of speed and motion. But there happened to be a gifted *Washington Post* reporter along for the ride, and he dutifully told his readers how we topped 100 miles per hour on Interstate 40 and how, with "strategic use of sirens," my driver managed to slash a trip that normally takes twenty-five minutes to sixteen. The story was picked up by New Mexico's newspapers, of course, with the *Albuquerque Journal,* the state's largest, displaying it big on the front page. The state police were not amused. We also noticed that some local TV cameramen in fast vehicles took to following me to see how quickly I was going.

I LOBBIED HARD for the convention chairmanship. I knew most of the candidates reasonably well, having served in Congress with Lieberman, John Kerry, Carol Moseley Braun, Dennis Kucinich, Bob Graham, and Dick Gephardt. I was always inviting Al Sharpton to United Nations events when I was in New York. I knew John Edwards the least, so I spent the most time with him during the weekend of the New Mexico debate. I really respected him when he was asked by George Stephanopoulos on television to talk about the death of his son. Edwards said no, that's private, I won't talk about that. I liked that.

I had defended then-senator Moseley Braun when she made a trip to Nigeria to visit its then-leader, Sani Abacha. She never forgot that and said she was with me. Kerry wanted my endorsement of his nomination bid in exchange for *his* endorsement of me for convention chairman. I told him I had to remain neutral, although my lieutenant governor, Diane Denish, did endorse him.

He finally relented and called Terry to convey his approval. In early 2004, McAuliffe made it official.

Being named convention chairman didn't quiet the talk about me and the vice presidential nomination. I kept saying I wasn't interested, and pundits and politicians kept including me on the short lists anyway. After Kerry quickly wiped out the competition in the primaries, he named Jim Johnson, an investment banker and a former aide to Walter Mondale, to run his vice presidential search operation. Johnson interviewed me for a couple of hours at a hotel near Dulles Airport, and I told him what I said to everyone else: I'd committed to a full term in New Mexico. But I still hadn't formally withdrawn my name from consideration. I hadn't done the full Sherman.

On Tuesday, June 29, I was summoned to a meeting with the presumptive nominee. Kerry was in Phoenix for the annual conference of the National Council of La Raza, the country's largest Hispanic organization, and he clearly wanted our talk to be well off anyone's radar screen. As I was ushered into a room in a downtown convention center, there was elaborate security to keep the press away. I had no indication from his people what Kerry wanted to talk about, although it seemed hard to believe the subject of the vice presidential nomination wouldn't come up.

Kerry didn't seem to be in a hurry to get to the point, asking first about my travel logistics—how I got there. Through some awful thunderstorms flying over from Santa Fe, I told him. He said he had been wanting to talk to me for quite some time, then moved to his Topic A. "How do you envision the vice presidency?" he asked. The Gore model? Like Cheney? I told him a partnership worked best—in effect, the Gore model—although the vice president obviously must be the second banana. There had been talk that he wanted a copresident, like a McCain. I said, You don't want to do that.

I knew I was on the list, but I was puzzled about why he wanted to talk to me. It was three or four days before he was going to announce his decision, and I hadn't been given the full financial background check. I asked him about that. He said if I got on the final list, they'd get on it, it would only take three full days. Kerry told me I had a lot of assets. A lot of people think highly of you, he said. He told me he wanted to raise two negatives. The first was my tenure as energy secretary and the security problems at Los Alamos. "It's not a plus," I conceded, "but it's explainable." In fact, there had been security problems that very summer under the current administration. The second was the potential problem of two Catholics on the ticket.

Then I said, "John, I may not want this. I made a pledge to serve a full term in New Mexico." After a brief discussion of the vetting process, I sensed our meeting was coming to an end. But he wasn't done. "What would you want to accomplish as vice president?" he asked. To help Hispanics, to work on education, I said, wanting to nudge the conversation away from Topic A. "John, you should choose someone you are very comfortable with, where there's a personal chemistry between the two of you," I told him, "someone who will be loyal." He left the uncomfortable ground of the vice presidency, but wasn't in full retreat. "Is there another position you'd be interested in?" he asked.

"Yes," I said. "Maybe secretary of state."

"I figured that," he said. "I really want you in the administration." He insisted he'd have a relatively small cabinet, with fewer positions outside the departments accorded cabinet rank. I remembered that Clinton's cabinet was so big it could hardly fit into the Cabinet Room. We moved into territory we both enjoyed—foreign policy—and the conversation began to wind down. Kerry said he'd get back to me in thirty-six hours; I reiterated my concern about breaking my promise.

We talked again by phone on Thursday, and Kerry said how much he had enjoyed our Tuesday-night chat. After the pleasantries, I told him that I needed to withdraw my name from consideration for vice president. Kerry said, Well, gosh, I probably need to move in a different direction, too. It was done, and he accepted the decision graciously and asked me to talk to Jim Johnson directly. Later, we released a letter I wrote to Kerry, formalizing the decision.

Near the end of our conversation, Kerry threw me an unexpected curve: "Do you want to be president?"

"Maybe someday," I said.

IN THEORY, the presidential nominee's people work with the convention chairman's people and the national committee staff to plan the convention, stage events, and schedule speakers. But in practice, the nominee has the bigger vote. Jack Corrigan, a Boston lawyer who had been Massachusetts governor Michael Dukakis's deputy campaign manager during the 1988 presidential campaign, and Sue Casey, Kerry's senior adviser, were handling convention management. They were tough, but so was Amanda Cooper, my political director.

Amanda got into it with them on a bunch of issues, including diversity. The Kerry people were thinking that Monday evening of convention week would be Hispanic night and Tuesday would be African-American night. Wednesday and Thursday, I suppose because Edwards and Kerry would be speaking, would be Anglo nights. Barack Obama, then an Illinois state lawmaker and now the nation's only African-American in the U.S. Senate, was scheduled to give the keynote address on Tuesday. Corrigan had in mind my opening the convention on Monday—Hispanic night—and giving no other speech. That was nuts, and Cooper told him so. She insisted that as chairman I had to be involved all four days, and I was. She also said we required certain perquisites attending the convention chair: plenty of credentials, for instance, and a skybox in a great location.

This wasn't only about me and my visibility. The convention over the last week in July was another opportunity to showcase New Mexico, and we intended to do so shamelessly. Our state tourism bus, dubbed "Santa Fe East," was parked just outside Boston's Fleet Center, where the delegates gathered, and Tourism Department officials provided brochures and complimentary jars of salsa with my grinning face on them. My guys broke the rules by getting several hundred jars of salsa into the convention center, where they became prizes for delegates and reporters alike. I made sure our delegation had a featured position on the convention floor and that our folks got invited to key parties and events. My skybox was strategically located at the top of an escalator, making it easy for guests to arrive and depart without having to squeeze down a corridor too narrow for the borderline chaos and constant motion of a national political convention.

My dance card was just the way I liked it—oversubscribed. I had three hundred media requests. I was on the move from early morning to late at night or early morning the next day. On July 27, the convention's second full day, I had an early breakfast meeting, a second appointment, then a brunch in my honor— one of ten such events that week. This one, at the Algonquin Club in Boston's tony Back Bay, was sponsored by Akin Gump Strauss Hauer & Feld, the huge Dallas-based law firm cofounded by Democratic Party stalwart Robert Strauss in 1945.

The two-hour affair was set to begin at 10:15, and for once I was on time, more or less. I spoke about something dear to my heart—Moving America Forward, an organization I started earlier in 2004 to register Hispanic voters in five battleground states:

Florida and the western quartet of New Mexico, Arizona, Colorado, and Nevada. Bush had received 35 percent of the Hispanic vote in 2000. If we could cut that to 30 or less, we could win. I was warmly received.

We were off well before the event ended, because we already were behind schedule. "What's next?" I asked from my customary spot riding shotgun in the Suburban. The Democratic Governors' Association, said Dave Contarino, my chief of staff.

"Can't we skip this?"

"The last time I looked, you were vice chair of this group," Contarino said.

"Okay, okay, but let's do it quick, in and out in twenty minutes."

The session, at the Boston Campus of the University of Massachusetts, had begun by the time I arrived and went on for another forty minutes before we could leave. Back in the Suburban, we headed for lunch, playing convention-pass poker, trying to decide who got the more coveted passes we had at our disposal.

"Who can I cut out?" I asked my guys.

Michael Stratton, a political consultant from Colorado and an old friend, was handling my daily schedule. He mentioned a few names; so did Contarino.

"Okay, fine, but who else can I cut out?" It was becoming a game, but Stratton was taking it way too seriously, talking about how we could tell people with low-grade passes to accumulate several and then use them to trade up.

"Mike, you're fired," I barked at him. It was at least the tenth time I'd fired Stratton in five days. I fire people all the time, especially the people closest to me; it's a term of endearment, another way to break the tension. Stratton lightened up.

I'm always more likely to say, "You're fired" than "Good job." I could probably use a better technique of praising staff. I've always expected everyone to work as hard as I do. If something isn't done right or is half-assed, I'll tell 'em and push and get it done. Everyone has to be thorough. Get me the answers before you come see me. If I'm stingy with compliments, it's not that I'm heartless, but I like to save them for when I think they're really deserved.

Isabelle Watkins was one of my best people over the years. She would get on my case about this aspect of my management style among other things. She didn't hesitate to tell me I was wrong when she thought I was making a mistake. She was a prize, prompting me to say to her once, "You actually do a good job and I hate saying that."

Quite recently a young woman who was leaving my staff to go to graduate school came to see me before she left. She was only twenty-six but she'd worked for me three years. She came into the office and started crying. I asked her what was the matter. She said she wanted to thank me for being rough on her and pushing her. I do let my staff grow. I'm good at promoting people, at paying them well. Also I'm often prepared to take a gamble on someone I like who may not be quite ready for a job. Or on people who demonstrate to me through their persistence that they really want a position. When they come to work for me, I feel loyal to my people, and they've stayed loyal to me.

This day at the convention, Mike Stratton played along when I fired him. "You've got my letter of resignation," he said. "I go when Dave goes."

"When we go," Contarino chimed in, "we all go together."

"Oh, yeah? When's that?" I wanted to know.

Contarino was pitch perfect. "With all due respect, sir," he said in a voice laced with sarcasm and resignation, "it can't happen soon enough." I doubled over with laughter.

·   ·   ·

MY SPEECH at the convention was in prime time Wednesday night, a featured spot before John Edwards accepted the party nomination for vice president. I kept it short: the Kerry people were stage-managing and they wanted speeches of less than ten minutes with few exceptions. Al Sharpton decided to go his own way. Instead of keeping it tight and positive, he trashed his prepared text and delivered an unscripted, twenty-two-minute stemwinder that battered Bush and brought delegates to their feet with his invocation of the bloody struggle for civil rights in the South of the 1960s.

Unfortunately for me, they were still talking about Sharpton when I followed him to the podium to speak about foreign policy and national security. My call to arms—"it's time for John Kerry"—somehow didn't resonate in the hall when juxtaposed against Sharpton's echo of an earlier Bush: "Mr. President, read my lips," he said. "Our vote is not for sale!"

It wasn't a bad convention, but in retrospect, I think the Kerry people made an enormous mistake with their insistence that everyone stay upbeat, that an emphasis on patriotism and Kerry's heroism in Vietnam alone could launch us into the general-election season. Frankly, I had agreed with this strategy. We generally failed to criticize Bush even though the president's record on public policy, foreign and domestic, provided multiple opportunities to do so. John Edwards's "hope is on the way" and John Kerry "reporting for duty" were hardly substitutes for tough-minded rhetoric we might have used to send the party faithful to the barricades. I left the convention believing we could win in November, but also with a feeling that we'd need to outwork Bush-Cheney, hoping that the Kerry-Edwards ticket caught fire, and counting on some mistakes by the opposition.

We certainly worked plenty hard. My focus was in the West, concentrating on the same states we had targeted for Moving America Forward. Arizona would break for Bush, I figured, but New Mexico, Colorado, and Nevada were all in play; if Kerry could sweep them, with their total of 18 electoral votes, it just might be enough to put him over the top even without Florida, the other state where Moving America Forward was active. We ended up registering nearly a quarter-million Hispanics, but it wasn't enough. The Hispanic vote in America is not homogeneous. Cuban-Americans have tended to vote Republican; Mexican-Americans have leaned toward the Democrats, but not with the kind of allegiance African-Americans have shown.

Bush, whose spoken Spanish isn't as effective as his body language, went after the Hispanic vote and did better than anyone expected, with somewhere between 39 and 44 percent of the total, an increase from his 35 percent in 2000. That was huge in his popular-vote triumph by more than 3.5 million votes and enough for him to carry Florida, Colorado, Nevada—and New Mexico.

Kerry's failure to win New Mexico wasn't because I was sitting on my hands. I had worked my butt off in dozens of rallies and speeches. I taped radio and television commercials for Kerry, in English and Spanish. Moving America Forward registered 35,000 new voters and got most of them to the polls. We got President Clinton to come out and campaign for Kerry less than two months after his heart bypass surgery. Clinton was terrific.

On election night, New Mexico stayed white in a sea of red and blue states; we had an embarrassing period of late ballot counting, but by the time it was done, Bush had prevailed in New Mexico by fewer than 6,000 votes. After the election, there was talk of stolen ballots and bad machine counts in New Mexico, but the evidence was not there. Brian Sanderoff, the state's best pollster, conducted a last-minute poll for the *Albuquerque Journal*. A huge sample of nearly 1,200 voters showed a 3-point Bush lead. We had a superior ground organization—even Karl Rove acknowledged that—but we could make up only three-quarters of the edge on election day. As in many states, there were some problems with provisional ballots, and massive new-voter registration had resulted in difficulties processing new voters at the polls. But the bottom line was that while Native Americans went big for Kerry, too many Anglos and Hispanics who might otherwise have supported him felt uncomfortable with the Democratic candidate. Kerry ran a good race. Bush ran a better one; people just liked the guy and trusted him more on national security and the War on Terror.

Twenty-three

IDIDN'T HAVE TIME to dwell on the results of the presidential
election. It was no sooner over than I had to turn my attention
to the future back home. The New Mexico legislature was due to
convene in January, and beyond that, I would have a reelection
campaign to run. I knew that the legislative session and the gubernatorial race for '06 would turn on the priorities I had established at the outset of my term as the state's chief executive:
economic development and job creation, education reform at every
level, health care, and an assault on the destructive scourges that
infect our culture—drugs, drunken driving, and domestic violence among them.

In our first two years, we had taken some huge steps to secure
New Mexico's long-term future. We had cut taxes that were in-
hibiting economic growth and putting us at a competitive dis-
advantage with surrounding states. We controlled spending and
balanced the budget. We invested heavily in our transportation
and economic infrastructure, and we initiated tough new accountability measures in public education, introduced charter schools,

and enacted other reforms. We also toughened penalties for drunk driving and for domestic abuse, thanks in part to the active work of my wife Barbara, and we increased the counseling of perpetrators to break the cycle of violence.

We built on that record in 2005, when the legislature finally embraced and approved the tax relief that I proposed for low- and middle-income families, redressing my poor management of this issue two years earlier. We introduced a voluntary pre-K pilot program for 13,000 four-year-olds not served by the current system—a response to studies that showed how critical Head Start and other early childhood programs can be to child development.

On July 14, 2005, I declared that 2006 would be New Mexico's "Year of the Child." State revenues were projected to be more than $200 million for each of the next five years, higher than previously forecast. I proposed we invest much of this money in our children. We would give every kid under five health insurance and expand our immunization programs, one of the areas in which Barbara has done great work for New Mexico's kids. (Thanks to her leadership, we've moved from forty-ninth- to fifteenth-best in child-immunization rates.) Child care would be improved, and we proposed offering breakfast to all our public school kids. We'd offer more reading and math programs and physical education—and improve teachers' salaries again. It was further proof of our long-standing commitment to children and education. The state's lieutenant governor, Diane Denish, chaired the children's cabinet and took the lead on a lot of these children's issues. She has been an invaluable partner.

Along with our kids, we had to stand up for our vets. During the 2005 session, we set a standard for the rest of the nation when I proposed and the legislature passed a bill that provides a premium-paid life insurance policy of $250,000 for every active-duty member of the New Mexico National Guard. We are a country at war, and New Mexico is playing its part. We have the highest number of cadets at our national service academies as a percentage of our high school population. Our legislation was a concrete commitment to provide financial help for the families of our troops killed in action. Dozens of states followed New Mexico's lead, and the Congress and the White House ultimately acted as well. When I first proposed our law in January 2005, the federal death benefit to families of fallen soldiers was $12,420, which was utterly disgraceful. Since then, Congress and President Bush approved an increase to $100,000 and dramatically boosted life insurance for military personnel.

All of these successes will serve as the foundation for our re-election campaign in 2006. That campaign will and should focus on our success in expanding opportunities for our citizens. It will and should focus on our ability to work with the legislature and with those who disagree with us to govern effectively and move the state forward. It will and should focus on whether we upheld our basic covenant with the people to manage their funds responsibly and invest them effectively. It will and should focus on the quality of leadership that I had provided to the people of the state in helping to create an environment in which they and their children could realize a brighter future. But most of all, it will serve as a referendum on what was promised and what was delivered.

OF ALL THE JOBS I've had, I believe you can make the most difference as a governor. As a congressman, you're one vote out of 435, although you can help constituents and, if you pick the right issue, you can make a difference nationally. The UN ambassador job was the most fun I ever had. You have leverage because you represent the United States, and if you maneuver well you can get U.S. interests protected. This and energy secretary were important jobs focusing on particular areas of national interest. But in terms of assisting the most people in all aspects of their daily lives, nothing beats governor.

I remembered the strange feeling I had every year when the congressional delegation used to come to speak to the legislature in Santa Fe. I used to give my speech and the place wasn't full. Those who were in attendance didn't seem particularly interested. For my first State of the State address, the place was packed and everyone was riveted.

When I have thoughts like that, Barbara keeps me grounded and keeps my head from swelling. I have too many people telling me how great things are and how well I'm doing. Sometimes what I need is someone to say, Hey, that's not the right thing. This is something Contarino does very well, though I hate to tell him. He'll say, "Boss, you're wrong on this," and I'll say, "Who asked you?"

I take advantage of the wonders New Mexico has to offer when I get to relax. I have a horse (not the one Niyazov gave me), and I try to ride every weekend. Barbara is an accomplished horsewoman. I hunt a little—turkey and elk—and I shoot clay pigeons. I work out in the gym in the governor's mansion and I swim. For my culture, I go to art museums—modern art. As for music, I like country: Toby Keith and George Strait, and also the Eagles and Rod Stewart. Remember, I'm the guy who still liked Elvis when all my contemporaries thought he was past it.

I became a huge boxing fan when I was growing up in Mexico. The kids I played baseball with idolized the local fighters, and I got into it that way. I still love boxing. I think boxing represents the ultimate contest between two individuals, the skill and heart of two people pitted against each other. Muhammad Ali is my all-time favorite fighter. I loved his style and his braggadocio. I went to the Boston Garden to watch the first of the three great fights between Ali and Joe Frazier—this was the "Fight of the Century" from Madison Square Garden in 1971—on closed-circuit TV. More recently, I've enjoyed watching Oscar de la Hoya very much.

New Mexico is a fantastic place to live and work. Barbara and I are lucky to live in the governor's mansion in Santa Fe. It's an attractive building in itself, but the true splendor is the beautiful view it affords of the Sangre de Cristo Mountains. When I get the chance, I like nothing better than to have a cigar out back of the mansion after dinner, watch the ever-stunning New Mexico sunset, and contemplate the challenges still before us.

THERE ARE A NUMBER of issues facing America's governors. I believe we have an *obligation* to provide leadership. We live in an era when too many players in Washington have become consumed by political warfare and apparently lost sight of their role in serving the people of this country. Democrat and Republican alike, we governors depend heavily on our states' relationship with Washington. Our constituents pay federal taxes, and those tax dollars are recycled back to the states under hundreds of federal programs. The relationship with Washington ought to be a partnership based on consultation and a shared interest in the common good.

But there are two problems with the relationship: The first is the tendency of Congress and bureaucrats in Washington to dictate the terms of public policies and programs, even though policies developed in Washington may be ineffective thousands of miles away in New Mexico. The second is the inability of the president and Congress to manage the financial affairs of our nation in a fiscally prudent fashion. Most states must balance their budgets by law. Not the federal government. It has run budget deficits consistently since the late 1960s, except for the last years of the Clinton administration. Washington views the states cynically as a safety valve for its own chronic inability to manage our affairs. It's the worst of all possible worlds: Washington sets the terms of what must be done in certain public programs, then shifts the financial burden to the states, leaving them with unfunded mandates that threaten their fiscal well-being and force them to spend money sorely needed elsewhere.

The worst case in point is Medicaid. Costs are rising, yet the federal government keeps reducing its share of the funding for the program. In my new budget, despite federal cuts, we increased Medicaid spending by 16 percent. Faced with rising costs, we remained committed to providing health care to our most vulnerable citizens. We implemented cost-containment and accountability measures, and these are a viable solution in the short term, but they won't work in the long term if the feds continue to increase the states' share of the costs. I have proposed that we cap state spending at a fixed amount, above which the federal government steps in. If costs rose sharply, the feds could make adjustments in the mandated level of Medicaid services. The point is that Washington, not the Roundhouse in Santa Fe, or the Statehouse in Albany, Austin, Columbus, or Helena, would be the responsible party for what is, after all, a program enacted into law by the U.S. Congress.

BEYOND THE ISSUES facing the fifty governors there are the concerns of every American, the almost 300 million of us in our great nation. It is almost impossible to overstate the significance of the financial challenges that we face. Our national accounts are a mess. We are running huge federal budget and international trade deficits. The budget deficit, the most convenient measure of our fiscal distress, is nothing more than the gap between what Congress and the president decide to spend and what they are prepared to ask you and your neighbors and your employers to pay in federal taxes. At a time of economic growth, it also reflects an absence of fiscal responsibility and political will. Tough decisions about spending and taxes need to be made if the budget is to be brought back into balance, but the president and Congress seem incapable of making them. So we continue to finance the deficit with debt that threatens our economic future and will be repaid by our children, or by their children. Spending now and passing the bill on to our children is simply immoral. To be a legislator, to be a governor, to be president, is to make choices, difficult choices, not to saddle future generations with debts that we ourselves lack the will to pay.

We need to address this profligacy in a bipartisan manner. There is no shortage of strategies—hard spending caps in Congress, an end to certain tax cuts enacted when the fiscal outlook was brighter, a larger overhaul of the federal tax code to build simplicity and equity into the system. I would advocate some combination of these three approaches. But I also doubt that Washington can get from here to there without some political cover. This was the job done by Alan Greenspan's Social Security Reform Commission in 1983. I'd set up a commission on taxes and spending, headed by two wise men with differing political viewpoints—Pete Peterson, the investment banker and former U.S. commerce secretary, and Warren Buffett, the so-called Oracle of Omaha, who is widely regarded as the premier long-term investor of the past four decades. We simply cannot continue to avert our eyes from this gathering crisis.

On international affairs, I tend to get pigeonholed as a multilateralist, a true believer in the United Nations, other international organizations, and our nation's traditional alliances. Guilty as charged, up to a point. I supported President Bush's decision to go to war in Iraq, without a new resolution from the UN, because I was persuaded that Saddam Hussein's weapons of mass destruction posed a threat to the United States and our interests in the world. No weapons were found, and now we know that our intelligence was deeply flawed. Had I known then what I know now, I would not have supported the president's decision to go to war.

Our intelligence fell prey to Saddam's own disinformation efforts, which made the world believe that he was more powerful than he was. There also was an apparent determination of the prowar faction in the Bush administration to shape the intelligence that was available to support a decision to topple Saddam. Those weren't the only blunders. The visions of neoconservatives of a quick war followed by a jubilant reception clouded planning for the demands of occupation in the wake of the collapse of Saddam's regime. The military campaign to take down the regime was brilliant; the Pentagon's managing of the aftermath was not, and we went in with no reconstruction plan and no exit plan. At this point, however, we must see this mission through. We mustn't stay in Iraq past the point where the new government asks us to leave, but neither can we unilaterally pull out before the Iraqis have achieved control over their own internal security. We owe them the opportunity to make their democracy work. We must not undermine their efforts now.

The Iraq experience strengthens the argument for broader coalitions to share responsibility and the financial burdens of our necessary involvement in the world. But we must never give up our freedom of movement or military flexibility, or the right to preemptive action when we are absolutely convinced it is necessary. There are places in the world where the United Nations has played and can continue to play a useful role, but there are clearly situations where we and our allies will have to lead the way. It's difficult to imagine how the "ethnic cleansing" in Bosnia could have been stopped without the intervention of the United States and NATO. Today, it may require some force from the West to augment an African Union contingent if we are to bring an end to the mass killings in Sudan's Darfur region. Multilateralism is not a solution to all problems, but it is also not a dirty word, as the current administration sometimes seems to think.

Neither, I should add, is bilateralism. Nuclear proliferation remains one of the great challenges in the post–Cold War world, and I believe we need to be very active in our diplomatic efforts to curb it. For years the United States insisted on six-party talks with North Korea on its nuclear weapons program and refused to deal directly with the North Koreans. With Iran we have let the Europeans take the lead in negotiations. Neither approach has worked very well. We need to be more flexible. It may be that our negotiating directly with North Korea or Iran would prove to be a mistake, but we shouldn't reject the possibility out of hand. The consequences of failure are too dire. In the summer of 2005, the Bush team shifted policy and began talking directly with the North Koreans within the six-party talks. That's a welcome change, and our North Korean policy seems to be more realistic.

Our national security priorities are wrong. We need to focus on a number of pressing challenges. The first is this threat of nuclear proliferation. The second is international terrorism. One of the weapons we need to combat terrorism is an international entity to share intelligence better than we do at present. We have to be prepared at home, which we are not; we need a real plan. Environmental degradation is also a national security issue. Drought

and the erosion and eradication of viable agricultural land coupled with spiraling world population will create tremendous forces
of instability.

We can't compartmentalize policy anymore. Every part of the
puzzle is interconnected. Of course national security means fighting terrorism, protecting our borders, furthering democracy,
maintaining a modernized and strong military, and more. But
what about energy? Energy clearly cuts across all the artificial divisions of the past. It is a national security issue. It is an economic
issue. It is an issue of foreign trade. It affects our current accounts
and the value of the dollar. And it is an environmental issue. Energy is one of the key strategic issues that will affect our nation's
future. On August 8, 2005, Bush signed a new Energy Bill to end
a yearlong standoff in Congress over national energy policy.

We need a new energy policy in America—now, on a crash
basis—that begins to sever our dependence on a handful of un-
stable oil-producing countries. Of course we're going to be
heavily reliant on oil for many years, as will the rapidly growing
economies in China and India, where there are 2.2 billion con-
sumers aspiring to the middle class and the energy-devouring
gadgetry that comes with it. Inflationary pressure on oil production will only get worse with time. We must pay more than lip
service to renewable energy sources, energy efficiency, and new
conservation technologies. We must respond with the same dedication President John F. Kennedy demonstrated in getting a man
on the moon in less than a decade. We need this level of commitment, not just the minor fixes that come when you tinker
piecemeal with production and conservation.

When you look at the big picture like this, the effective management of our country's financial affairs is also a strategic issue,
as is education. We have to be able to compete globally. Microsoft's Bill Gates and other innovators talk about how our edu-

cation system needs to change and do a better job training kids for the high-technology world of this new century. China, India, and other countries have made enormous advances in turning out "knowledge" workers. Outsourcing used to mean sending old-economy factory jobs overseas to foreign plants paying wages that were a tiny fraction of ours. Today, it means computer chip plants, call centers, and high-tech help desks staffed by workers trained in computer engineering.

When we look ahead, as *New York Times* columnist Tom Friedman describes in his book *The World Is Flat,* the playing field is increasingly level. Microsoft and other technology companies are moving some of their core research facilities to China and India—not to reduce costs but because they cannot find the workers that we need here. This must serve as a clarion call for change.

Twenty-four

BILL CLINTON HAS BEEN somebody I've admired and emulated even though he is a contemporary. Like most relationships worth having, it has been through some ups and downs, but we've been great friends and I love the guy. As I've said, I was angry at him for a while after I didn't get the Interior job, but after I'd worked with him on a number of big initiatives in Congress, we developed a bond.

When he was being hammered on the Lewinsky business, as well as on policies like the health care plan, I stood up and got behind him publicly. I was known as a strong supporter of the president, and as such I'd take enormous hits from constituents. "Stop defending him," people would say. "We like you, we don't like him." But I always believed in what Clinton was trying to do. He would look at you so captivatingly. This was the president and your ego would blow up. He'd always say, "I love you, Billy. I love you, man." I was happy to go to the wall for him.

We talked often during the Lewinsky period. I wasn't one of his closest friends, but I think I was somewhere in his outer circle. He is a great collector of people, and everyone fulfilled a different need. Clinton simply loves people. He finds it difficult to relax with himself, and he'll be the last guy to leave an event. When we held parties for him at the UN, he'd still be there at four o'clock in the morning. His people would say, "We've got to leave, he's got a speech at eight," but they couldn't get him out of the room.

Whatever he and I talked about, I always felt Clinton knew more about the subject than I did, even if I was the specialist in the area: foreign policy, energy, even baseball. I couldn't compete with Clinton on baseball trivia. I had him with boxing, but he could still defend himself. He'd question me closely each time I got back from somewhere. "Tell me about Saddam Hussein. Is he a smart guy?" "Tell me about North Korea. What makes them tick?" He called me after I went to Sudan. In the newspaper, he'd read about the goat meat I ate. "Were you eating that?" And, "What was Kerubino really like?" He has an insatiable curiosity. I knew he wanted to be the one out there in the bush but he was trapped where he was.

The president backed me when I was at the UN and DOE and when I went on my missions, and we've had a good relationship since he left office. I've kept on good terms with Al Gore, too. Clinton and I did have a second strain when I said I wanted to run for Democratic National Committee chair and he supported Terry McAuliffe for the job. I saw Clinton and asked if he would be upset at me if I ran. He said, "No, Billy, I'd never be upset at you, but I want you to know I'd be very strong for McAuliffe." I looked down and pretty soon he was on the other side of the room. I realized there was a little strain there. But we repaired it in December of 2001. Bill and Hillary were vacationing in Mexico, and the four of us had lunch in Acapulco and had a great time.

Then I asked Clinton if he'd come out and help me run for governor, and he said he really wanted to help. I was one of his former aides running and had a good chance to win. But Dave Contarino showed me a poll. Clinton was very unpopular with swing voters, and his association was unhelpful. He said do you want to win by 15 points or do you want to make it close? So Contarino talked me into disinviting him. I knew that would cause a problem. We compromised and held an October fundraiser for my campaign in New York City. Before the 2004 election, Clinton's popularity had rebounded dramatically. He came to New Mexico to campaign for John Kerry, and the two of us drove to Albuquerque together. We were fine again. Just after the election, I went to the opening of his Presidential Library in Little Rock.

I was tapped to speak at the 2005 Gridiron dinner in Washington and told a joke that may just have made him mad at me again. Every year journalists and politicians get dressed up and tell jokes about one another. President Bush did a turn, Senator Chuck Hagel of Nebraska represented the Republicans, and I was the Democrat. I said, "Democratic presidential candidates. We've got a lot of good ones. There's Governor Vilsack of Iowa—he'd bring back the Midwest. There's Joe Biden—he'd bring back the national security voter. And there's Hillary Clinton—she'd bring back the White House furniture." He's probably a little pissed off, but it was meant in fun, of course. I really do love the guy.

I have learned as much from Bill Clinton as I have from anyone in my career. In politics, as in any human endeavor, you must keep learning so you can adapt to the changing realities of the world around you. I have been learning leadership skills since the moment I decided to run at the fraternity house at Tufts. Even then I was assimilating lessons I learned growing up.

I'll freely admit I persisted in student politics not because of any idealism but because I was good at it and found I enjoyed it tremendously. It also filled a place that had been occupied more than half my life by baseball. Politics became my career, and I continue to take pleasure in what I do every day. I like doing TV, for example, appearing on shows like *Meet the Press, Face the Nation,* and *Larry King Live.* I try to shoot straight and be succinct. You've got to be prepared when you go on live TV. We'll go over the murder boards beforehand and I'll ask Dave Contarino or Billy Sparks, "What's the worst thing they can ask me?" It helps, because they usually ask it.

I love campaigning, honing the message and delivering it to the voters. Although it drives my staff nuts, I like to wander off the page when giving a speech. I can read a crowd—I know when they're getting bored or when it's too hot. I can also tell when I'm rambling; when I'm on and when I'm not. I'll then adjust accordingly.

I've taught people how to work a room and how to shake someone's hand. Neither is obvious and each is a necessary skill that has to be perfected. When you need to work a room, you'll have a limited amount of time to do it properly. You can't have a long conversation with one person; you have to move on. At the same time, you can't make someone feel that you're trying to get rid of them. So never look over their shoulder. Always focus on them and look them right in the eye.

When you move around the room, don't head right for the center. If you do, you're liable to become surrounded and trapped. You should move counterclockwise beginning close to the wall. In this way you'll have the best chance of getting to everyone. Start at the wall, move around, and gradually work your way in.

When you're shaking hands, don't give a fish handshake, but

don't crush their fingers either. You should take someone by the hand *and* by the elbow. Then look in their eye and count one, two, three. You can talk to them, sure, but hold on for three beats and look them in the eye for all that time. This way, you'll establish a connection.

WHEN I WAS DECIDING what I was going to do after Fletcher, my liking for politics was overtaken by the vision of public service laid out by Hubert Humphrey and others. Then, after my years as a staffer on the Hill in Washington, these twin strands—public service and politics—came together. After I became a Democrat, I wanted to find out how I could do the most good for the greatest number of people, and I determined that this was in seeking the power offered by elective office. The same aspiration persuaded me to run for governor after I had had the honor of serving in two positions in the Clinton administration and had begun to enjoy the comforts of life in the private sector.

What has driven me to seek public office is helping people. I like people; I feel energized by people. When I'm campaigning, or hosting a town meeting, or traveling on behalf of my state, I relish each interchange with people I meet. I like to shake hands and make that connection I have mentioned more than once. I like the interplay that exists in every human transaction. Ultimately, getting things done for people is what motivates me and what persuades me that for all its foibles, public service is a noble profession. I have always felt that being bicultural has helped me get along with and understand people from different backgrounds and cultures. I have worked hard to promote diversity whenever I have been able. Lea County in eastern New Mexico is two-thirds white and about 5 to 10 percent African-American. In 2004, there was a vacancy for magistrate judge in the county. I could have taken the safe way, followed a lot of advice, and appointed a white person and a Republican (Lea County is overwhelmingly Republican).

Instead, I wanted to do something different and make a statement. I knew there had never been a black judge here, so I called Lemma White, an African-American teacher from the city of Hobbs, which sits right next to the border with Texas. I told Lemma I had some good news and some bad news. Good news: I'm going to make you a judge. Bad news: When election time comes, you're probably going to lose to a Republican, so you're only going to have this about three or four months. I said fight hard, do a good job, be a role model—and she did. Regrettably, she was crushed on Election Day.

The face of our country is changing rapidly. In fifty years' time no one ethnic group will be in the majority. Other demographic changes are taking place: migrations from the East and the West into the Southwest. Rust Belt states are losing people that the South is gaining. I believe New Mexico is what this country is going to look like in twenty or twenty-five years, let alone fifty, with a minority population constantly growing and with quality-of-life issues coming to greater prominence. People will be increasingly concerned with open spaces, ecotourism, sustainability, and healthier lifestyles.

People in the Western states have great respect for the land, respect for individual rights and heritage, and a healthy skepticism of governmental intrusion into their private lives. I am pro-choice and I am also pro-rights—property rights and the right to bear arms. My administration has also fought the federal government and oil and gas interests on developing the Otero Mesa. There is a very broad constituency of hunters, ranchers, environmentalists, people who care about the water and access to the outdoors, all of whom are saying, This is our land, our water, and our heritage.

I believe New Mexico is a microcosm of what the country wants to be in the future. Our ideas for serving the needs of the citizens of New Mexico today are coalescing around what we are calling "New Progressivism." It has its roots in the core values of the Democratic Party that have always stressed *opportunity*. Opportunity has always been a cornerstone of any progressive movement; what is new is the *accountability* that we build into our programs.

What we are proving is that we are pro-people and pro-business and pro-environment at the same time, something that progressives, and Democrats, have traditionally found it difficult to do. Our pro-people initiatives (tax cuts, education, jobs, Medicaid) go hand-in-hand with pro-business programs (high-wage tax credits, tax holidays for start-ups, state infrastructure investment).

The principles of New Progressivism are illustrated as we tackle our toughest challenges on the issues of education, health care, the environment, and job creation. Our objective is to promote opportunity in health care and education and jobs in a fiscally responsible and efficient way to create a stronger community and quality of life.

The key points are these:

We're going to invest in education, and there is nothing more pro-business than investing in education, because businesses cannot function without a well-educated workforce. We will give teachers better salaries, expand pre-K programs, establish charter schools, and run lottery scholarships to the state university. These provide opportunity. But the New Progressive is for accountability. So teachers have to get licenses, and schools have to perform better and conform to tough truancy standards, and students have to have a 2.5 GPA if they are going to get a free ride.

The same applies in jobs and economic development. We'll create opportunity with incentives that encourage quality jobs—the high-wage job credit and investment in technology start-ups. We'll promote tourism, invest in companies and movies by lending them money, work to protect our military bases, but all along there has to be performance and accountability. We expect job creation and we'll get a return on our money and our loans repaid. GRIP (Governor Richardson's Investment Partnership) is a $1.6 billion highway and multimodal transportation program we enacted, but we paid for it by finding $60 million a year in tax revenue. We have tax cuts, but as I always say, we pay for them.

On health care, we invest in a prescription drug program, expand the uninsured programs, and reduce medical taxes, but we couple that with some cost-containment initiatives: tough choices on Medicaid, increased co-pays. We also require those health care professionals we help to practice in rural areas.

In sum, without a strong education system, without strong economic policy, without good health care, it's difficult to argue that you're pro-business. Underscoring these ideas is the message of fiscal responsibility and the goal of a better quality of life for a stronger community. In New Mexico we have had a good run economically, but we have also worked to save money where we could. We undertook a complete performance review of the entire government, something like Al Gore's Reinventing Government. We set high goals—$19 million on IT consolidation, $22 million on reducing Medicaid fraud, $16 million on Save Smart New Mexico, a procurement program that consolidates purchasing through volume buying and at the same time uses more New Mexico firms. We have made good progress toward our targets.

The quality-of-life initiatives are DWI, domestic violence, public safety. Crime issues are also about a culture of accountability.

What we are saying is that if you are going to live in this society, you are going to be held accountable. DWI was a terrible problem. We dramatically increased penalties, mandated interlocks, mandated counseling for repeat offenders, lowered the alcohol threshold, dramatically increased enforcement—and all the numbers we are seeing are positive. And of course you also have to secure the homeland and institute a real energy policy.

Contarino has given speeches on our philosophy to business groups, mostly Republicans, and they have endorsed this approach—funding many of my Republican political adversaries as a holistic approach to improving the business climate. Progressive groups have embraced our approach as a clear path to expanding the economic pie for all groups. We have shown we can move past liberal or conservative agendas of the past to a New Progressivism that works for the entire community.

If this book came with a DVD, I would be able to show you two television commercials that we used when I ran for governor. They demonstrate so many elements of my career to this point. I made an ad in Spanish where I stood by an *acequia*, an irrigation ditch dug off a main channel. People who farm on small plots come together in *acequia* associations, which organize the cleaning of these ditches when they get filled with branches and debris. From there, I spoke of protection of the land, culture, heritage, and traditions of New Mexico. The *acequia* is a wonderful example of a history that we cherish, celebrate, and respect, and of the timeless strengths of community. There is no better symbol for New Mexico than this.

Ten years ago, I stood next to Saddam Hussein in his palace, having negotiated the release of Americans William Barloon and David Daliberti. Saddam called his media into the room, and the two of us were photographed and filmed together. I told Saddam

I wouldn't be using pictures of us together in my next congressional campaign, but I did use them when I ran for governor in 2002.

In the ad, Barloon and Daliberti talked about how this big guy from New Mexico left his wife back home and traveled to a dangerous part of the world to fight for the release of two people he didn't even know. At the end, and it wasn't in the script, Barloon looked directly at the camera and began to tear up. It made a big impression.

The worlds depicted in these ads are so far apart in almost every conceivable way. I'm proud that I was able to stand in both, and that people responded positively to the sincerity of the feeling that inspired the messages. Long ago, I chose a path. I accepted my duty as an American and am gratified by the role I have been privileged to play. In small but perhaps significant ways, I have made a difference in my country. Although our challenges as Americans and as citizens of the world are great, we face them together.

Richardson's Rules

NOTE: These rules are not presented in order of importance. This is the sequence in which they appear in the book.

- Share the credit. Politics and diplomacy are team sports. Acknowledge it.
- Talk about it. It is always better to have a conversation than not to talk.
- Be discreet and don't volunteer too much information.
- Your style can be informal, but you must show proper respect.
- Remember who your friends were when things weren't going so well.
- Aim big. Always try to achieve more than you have to.
- Know where you can settle. Identify eight essential goals and achieve five.
- Take advantage of goals you share. Agree on them and move on from there.

- When you're about to make a major change, cover your bases.
- Don't concede absolutely everything the other side is requesting. Get something in return, even if it's minor.
- Don't be intimidated.
- If you are negotiating an endgame, allow a dignified way out.
- Learn as much as possible about your adversary.
- It helps to be in good shape. You never know when you're going to be called to the negotiating table.
- Find common ground and establish a personal connection.
- You can walk out, but only if you're prepared to walk back in later.
- Deliver a strong message with dignity and without insults.
- Never lie when negotiating, because lies catch up with you. Be direct.
- Find something your adversary likes and use it to your advantage.
- Give up the locale. Don't insist on neutral ground, but go to his or her turf. It's the substance that counts, not the place where you negotiate.
- Carry a bunch of nice pens, but not necessarily of Montblanc quality. When your opponent admires one, give it to him. When your watch is admired, don't give it away. If you do, it's a sign of weakness.
- Use the media if you need to, but keep your negotiations private.

- Give up the little things. The other guy wants to hold a press conference? Fine.
- Have others deliver bad news; it keeps you viable as a future negotiator.
- In most meetings, the law of diminishing returns kicks in after five minutes.